THE VIRGIN GUIDE TO WORKING ABROAD

Also published by Virgin Books:

The Virgin Travellers' Handbook
The Virgin Travel Health Handbook
The Virgin 2003 Alternative Guide to British Universities

THE VIRGIN GUIDE TO WORKING ABROAD

REBECCA HARDY

First published in Great Britain in 2003 by
Virgin Books Ltd
Thames Wharf Studios
Rainville Road
London
W6 9HA

A catalogue record for this book is available from the British Library.

Great care has been taken with this guide to be as accurate and up-to-date as possible, but details such as addresses, telephone numbers, website addresses, email addresses, opening hours, prices and travel information are liable to change. The publishers cannot accept responsibility for any consequences arising from the use of this book. We would be delighted to receive any corrections and suggestions for inclusion in the next edition.

ISBN 0 7535 0744 7

Typeset by Phoenix Photosetting, Chatham, Kent
Printed and bound in Great Britain by CPD Wales

CONTENTS

INTRODUCTION

Forty years ago, foreign travel was a luxury only the most privileged could afford. Since then, the rate of progress has been truly staggering. Now two million people cross international borders every day and the world has opened up economically and culturally in a way that has never been seen before. Some of this has had political effects that are at best dubious, but for the global traveller it is unequivocally good news. The fact is there are relatively few places now that are out of our reach and the chances to broaden your experience by working abroad are truly breathtaking.

The aim of this book was to both inspire and inform people who wanted to work abroad temporarily, providing up-to-date information on visas and different employment situations. The book tries to strike the right balance between sparking ideas and giving the solid information and contacts to make them a reality. Although there is inevitably at times a UK bias (for example, the UK telephone numbers are presented as if dialling from within the UK), the book is aimed at an international audience and includes contacts and advice for non-UK travellers including a section on working in the UK. The book also includes some cautionary tales: according to the Foreign Office, UK travellers are being bailed out more than ever before!

The fact is there has never been a better time to find work abroad, whether working casually or finding work in a more professional capacity. The development of the European Union in particular has assured that Europeans can live and settle abroad almost as easily as settling in another city in their home country – although you will find it considerably easier if you can speak the native language. And with more than ten other European countries set to join the EU within the next three years, the job market should open up further. Whatever your political views on Europe and the single market, it is undeniably good news for the job seeker.

Gap years are booming, and it isn't just for pre-university students. Increasingly, 25–35-year-olds are taking time out from their busy, office-jaded lives to go and see the world, many with the blessings of their employers. And it doesn't stop there. I know one 60-year-old, retired lecturer who now teaches economics in China and loves every minute of it, and a mother of four (and grandmother of four) who spent six months volunteering at an orphanage in India. A recent survey in the UK's *Daily Telegraph* showed that 54 per cent of British people would like to go and settle in another country. Maybe it's because we're working longer and longer hours that the idea of escaping to foreign shores seems the ultimate adventure.

In the course of researching this book, I was amazed at how many resources there are for the prospective working traveller. Many of these organisations have a laudable aim: to promote cultural understanding and global unity, and, given our recent world problems, what could be more important? As you are planning your next travel adventure you could see yourself as this: an ambassador for world peace, doing your bit to create cultural tolerance and understanding.

Whatever your reason for travelling, the message of this book is that working abroad brings huge rewards: increased confidence, resourcefulness and maturity, a new understanding of the world and the ability to get out there and make things happen. I believe that you can do pretty much anything as long as you put your mind to it, and the case studies of other working travellers certainly pays testimony to this idea. If you leaf through the pages and read the stories of people who have been there, done that, you can't help but be inspired. I know they certainly inspired me.

In the words of Louis Armstrong, 'What a wonderful world' – get out there and enjoy it!

Rebecca Hardy

October 2002

PART ONE: PREPARING TO GO

1 GETTING STARTED

How many of us have dreamt about working abroad without ever getting round to doing it? Taking time out to travel can be a life-changing experience and it's no coincidence that those who do it say it's the best thing that's ever happened to them. Year on year, thousands of people decide to take a break from the plodding routine of life, and do something more interesting instead. The fact is that the world is truly there for the taking. Never mind the continual threat of terrorism and all the negative press in the media, there has never been a better time to travel. Low-cost airlines and an increasingly shrinking world are making many destinations more and more accessible. So if you're one of those people who fantasise about trekking through the Himalayas or working on the ranches in Texas, this guide is for you. So close your eyes and think about what you want. Selling ice cream on an Andalucian beach watching the sun slink over the horizon? Working as a film extra in Bollywood? Helping refugees in war-torn parts of Rwanda? Whatever your dream, this book can bring to you everything you need to know about making it happen. But first, it's got to start with you.

WORKING YOUR WAY

Of course experiences like these don't come cheaply. We all know that money is the big obstacle that normally stops us in our tracks, but working your way is the perfect solution. This book will provide you with all you need to know about work opportunities and making the most of them. Not only is working abroad a brilliant way of financing your trip, but it's also a unique way of getting to know a country and its culture. Working can transform your trip from a passive spectator sport into something more compelling – a life-changing experience.

SO WHY GO TRAVELLING?

The fact is there are as many reasons to go travelling as there are wonderful places to visit. Maybe you've got a couple of months to spare before starting university and you want to make the most of the time by doing something completely different. Maybe you fancy taking a gap year and are hankering after adventure before the predictable onslaught of work and studies. Or maybe you're just bored with your life and need a change of direction. Maybe you want to learn a new skill – like scuba diving in Malaysia or learning to talk Portuguese or communicating with dolphins. Whatever you want, the truth is there are millions of opportunities out there waiting for you, and all it will cost is a little research, a lot of planning and a whole lot of motivation.

WHAT WILL I GET OUT OF IT?

Whatever way you look at it, there's much to be gained from travelling – whether it's looking good on your CV, or giving you a whole load of interesting, technicolour memories to wow (and bore) your friends with. It could also improve your chances of getting into university and give you that edge when you get there. Let's face it, it's going to take a lot to faze someone who is used to negotiating their way around the more remote parts of Africa. Then there's employers. Gap years look great on the CV and are often the first thing to be mentioned in interviews. If you've single-handedly run a soup kitchen in Kathmandu or couriered yachts across the Mediterranean, it shows initiative, drive and organisation. Then there are the opportunities – opportunities to meet people, opportunities to try your hand at new skills. Because, as any seasoned wanderer will tell you, things happen when you're travelling. I can't count all the people I've known who have grudgingly sacrificed a career for the joys of a long haul, only to find that exactly the same opportunity came along in a foreign country in a different guise. Maybe it's because you're in a different mindset so you're more likely to attract opportunities to you. Maybe it's being in an alien country, surrounded by fresh people and ways of doing things, which helps you discover different unexplored aspects of yourself. Or maybe you just radiate a certain indefinable spirit that draws good things to you.

NEGATIVE EXPERIENCES

All of this isn't to say that bad things don't happen. Bad things do, and you don't have to read Alex Garland's *The Beach* to realise that. Take the case of my friend Paula. After eight months teaching English in Argentina, she had managed to save up £7,000 in cash, until standing outside a foreign exchange in Rio, Brazil, two muggers swiped the whole lot off her. Or eighteen-year-old Richard – held up by gunpoint in some hick town in America and left penniless and scared out of his wits. I'm sure you've heard of countless stories yourself. The point is the world can be a big, bad dangerous place and you'd do well to remember that. But that's the great thing about travelling. It's a great leveller. You learn to take the rough with the smooth, and see the good and the bad as part of the same great adventure.

THE FIRST THINGS

PREPARATION – DO YOUR RESEARCH

Once you've made the decision to go travelling, your initial euphoria may blind you to the secret of a good trip: preparation. I once landed in Madrid with a friend eager to find a teaching job, only to find that the teaching market was ropey and we'd have been better finding work before we left. Not only that but, as we'd assumed we could find work right away, we only had a few hundred pounds to tide us over – not great in one of the most expensive capitals in Europe. Suffice it to say, our working holiday didn't last long. Three weeks later, our money had run out and we were booking last-minute flights out of there. It was a tough lesson but I learnt a lot from that trip: enthusiasm is not enough. Preparation is vital. So the first thing to do is research. And get organised. Don't sit around and make big dreams, but get out there and make it happen. Choose your country carefully. Do you want to travel around and visit a range of countries, or do you want to stay in one place and really immerse yourself in that culture? Decisions like this affect the kind of experience you have. Is your focus primarily that of the independent traveller, or do you want to further your career? Are you interested in one destination and culture in particular? The important thing is to be clear about your intentions. Vague plans make for muddled experiences, so set your intentions and focus your mind like a laser.

Of course, the possibility is that you may want to land in a foreign country with only £50 in your pocket, and that, for you, is all part of the Big Adventure. Fine. Lindsey arrived in Sydney with only £100 and nowhere to stay, and quickly found work in a telesales company, eventually splashing out on a big apartment. It was the necessity to make money which spurred her on and made her get out there. The point is do your research before you leave, and know, for example, precisely what that £50 can get you, where the cheap hostels are, what kind of work there is and your chances of finding it.

GET SOME MONEY TOGETHER

The second thing is the point at which most people may stumble. Money. Yes, that old chestnut. Unless you've got a small inheritance stashed away, the chances are you need to scrape together a few hundred/ thousand pounds, and, depending on your circumstances, that may not come easy. And yet, rest assured that if the will is there, you can make it happen. Only you may need to make a few sacrifices. Like what? Like working in a crappy job for six months, diligently saving half of everything you earn. Cutting down on big nights out and doing without the latest trainers, CDs, PlayStations, whatever your particular thing is. You also may need to move back in with your parents if you've moved out, or devote yourself to the hard slog of working. The thing to remember is that in travelling terms, a little money can go a long, long way. The price of a CD here can be a few days' living costs in India. A pair of jeans can be a fortnight travelling in Thailand. Never lose sight of this.

HOW MUCH WILL IT COST?

The trick to saving money is to think a little, often. Remember that £1,000 is only 20 installments of £50, which doesn't sound so bad really. It's always good to work with a plan so once you've decided to go travelling, try to work out approximately how much you will need. Ask yourself some searching questions:

How much working/ travelling do I intend to do? For instance, will I be forking out on internal flights there, or do I intend to set myself up in a big city, and work for most of the duration?

How long will it be before I get a job, and how much will I need to tide me over before I find one?

Will I need money to put down on an apartment or are there cheap hostels where I can stay?

EXPENSE SHEET

Tickets, insurance and visa – what kind of ticket are you going to get? Many travellers like the security of an open-return ticket – whatever happens at least they know they can get out of there should things go wrong – whereas others like the exhilaration of leaving things to fate and buying only a single.

Vaccinations – these can be costly but are usually worth it for the peace of mind. Infectious diseases are on the up so travel medicine experts advise erring on the side of caution. Travellers can typically spend £60–£100 for a full set of vaccinations, though some are available on the NHS, and if you intend to do a lot of travelling, the cost can be spread over the cost of many trips.

Living costs – work on approximately £20 a day although it is possible to get by on significantly less. Times this by the amount of days you will be away.

Equipment – clothes, backpack, first aid kit, etc. Again, this will be influenced by what kind of work you intend to do and where you intend to visit. For example, temping in city offices or working in shops will require a smarter wardrobe than fruit picking or conservation work.

Extra transport – internal flights, trains, buses, etc.

Emergency money – depending on where you're going, relying on finding work can be a high risk to take, so it's a good idea to have an ample sum, just in case. This can always be in the form of credit cards – that way it won't cost you extra savings but you can always dip into it, just in case.

All this will be affected by how much you intend to work, the level of pay and whether or not you have work set up before you go. So offset the total with the amount you expect to earn. How much does the job you intend to do typically pay? Make sure this is realistic.

CASE STUDY

Lucia Cockcroft saved up £1,500 before she left for Australia.

I started saving eight months before I left when I was working in a bookshop and living at home with my parents. I managed to save about £180 a month because I wasn't paying any rent. Out of that, I spent £300 on a single ticket to Sydney and about £70 on a working visa – I wanted to work once I was over there and knew I could find a job quite easily. Once there, I had to spend about £300 on staying in a hostel, because it took me three or four weeks to find work. But then I was earning about £9 an hour to work in a bookshop and rented a house with two friends I met there – it overlooked Botany Bay and cost me about £150 a month, which was brilliant. I stayed for eight months and used the rest of the money to take a month off work travelling around Australia.

See? It's easy if you know how. All you need is . . . motivation.

Generally, the recommended amount to allow is £20 per day. But that's for travelling. If you intend to work, then you can subtract that from this total. The amount you will need will be offset by all kinds of different factors such as:

- **Will I have a job before I go?**

- **If I intend to find work, how easy is it to get work? How long will I be supporting myself before I can find work? The chances are it's going to take a whole lot longer to find work in the US than in Australia, say.**

- **What kind of work am I looking for? Temp and secretarial work is going to probably pay better than agricultural work, for example.**

- **How expensive is the city to live?**

- **Do I have any contacts when I get over there? Will I have anywhere else I can stay?**

WHAT KIND OF MONEY SHOULD I TAKE?

As a general rule, traveller's cheques are safer than cash and less likely to get stolen. But they can be hard to use if you're, say, stuck in the middle of a rice field in Thailand. Also bear in mind that banks tend to take upwards of one per cent commission, which can take a sizeable lump out of your savings. Keep the carbon copy separate from the serial numbers on your traveller's cheques in case they get stolen, and leave your parents a copy of the serial numbers in a safe place at home. As a good rule of thumb, I'd make sure I had a credit card with a sizeable limit, just in case, and at least some spare cash in sterling. Also note that some countries, such as China, have currency controls, which restrict the movement of currencies between countries. You can find out which ones operate this system by asking at banks. In these situations you can only change your money into the local currency once you have landed, so take traveller's cheques and change them into cash at the airport.

EMERGENCY MONEY

No matter how much planning you do, there could still be times when you find yourself caught out and in need of some emergency funds. There are several ways to prepare for this:

Keep some emergency funds in a bank account at home. Give a trusted friend permission to draw on the account and notify the bank before you leave. Then, should the occasion arise, your friend can draw out the money and send it to you by transfer.

Arm yourself with credit cards: a couple of credit cards can really come in handy if you find yourself in an emergency. Many cards also come with travel and personal accident insurance cover, 24-hour emergency assistance and, in the case of American Express, even accept faxes for their customers.

Transfer money: most major towns and cities around the world will have Western Union and Money Gram agents where you can have money transferred to you, often instantaneously, provided you show ID. You can also set this up with a local bank although you may have to pay a charge.

TRAVELLING COMPANIONS

So, here you are planning the next big adventure of your life and you're thinking who to share it with. It's a decision that most of us rush into and maybe it's better that way, because the fact is, no matter if this person is the love of your life or your best friend since you were three, the chances are you are probably going to row. It's a fact. So maybe the best question is not whom you are least likely to row with, but how you think you will handle it when you do. If, for example, your prospective travelling companion is the kind of person who bears a grudge and doesn't get over a short, shrift exchange quickly, then you'd be wise to look elsewhere. Why? Travelling is stressful. There's nothing like being stuck in the pouring rain miles from the nearest hostel, with a rucksack that weighs a tonne and only enough money between you to buy a banana, to bring out the awkward bugger in you.

TRAVELLING WITH FRIENDS

That said, there are huge benefits to travelling with your friends and it's not just an issue of companionship. If you're in a tricky situation, there's nothing like the company of someone who knows you well and understands how to soothe, calm and entertain you to keep things running smoothly. Having the same sense of humour also helps enormously, so ask yourself if your future travelling friend finds the same things funny as you do.

Another plus is the convenience. The practicalities of having two of you to share tasks, watch rucksacks as one of you finds accommodation, and so on, can take a huge stress out of travelling. And yet there could be hidden stresses too. The best thing is to take a good hard look at this person and ask yourself the following questions:

- **Could I be with this person every day?**

- **How will this person act if things go wrong?**

- **How well do I really know this person?**

- **Are there things about him/her that really, really bug me?**

- **Or even minor irritations? Things are exaggerated when you're travelling. Remember that you're going to be with this person every day, and that minor irritation could really, really start to annoy you . . .**

TRAVELLING WITH YOUR PARTNER

You're in love and you want to have his/her babies . . . you're soulmates . . . he's your ideal companion . . . what could go wrong . . . don't you know you were meant for each other? Without wishing to be cynical, these can be the last words uttered before the relationship implodes in a flurry of visas, flights and diverging itineraries. In short, think carefully before you go travelling with your partner. You may split up – thousands do – and then you'll be left not only minus your travelling companion but also with a broken relationship in a strange land to deal with. A friend of mine once flew over to Hong Kong to be with his fiancée, only to find once he got there she wanted to finish the relationship. The poor guy was left stranded with nowhere to live and no funds to get home, until his folks back in England had to club together to pay for his flight out of there. Suffice it to say, that was the last time he went travelling.

Of course, you may be one of the lucky ones who make it. Mark and Lynda Whittaker spent a year backpacking and working in Australia and came back home to announce their engagement. Linda says quite seriously that it was the travelling that cemented their relationship, and they're now married with a baby.

TRAVELLING ALONE

Of course, the perfect antidote to all this is to take the plunge and go travelling alone. And why not? Many travellers report it's the best way to get the most out of the experience. Maybe it's the fact that you are forced into the company of strangers that makes it more of an adventure. The open-mindedness you have to adopt can be strangely inducive and spill over into your whole approach to the trip. If you go with someone you already know, you may be less inclined to open your arms to other people and stick to a rigid plan you have both agreed on. Many solo travellers agree that there is something about being alone that makes you more likely to go with the flow and do things you never dreamt of. Will you get lonely? Maybe. But what's so bad about a little loneliness? Solitude can tinge any experience with a dreamy romanticism. I can remember many soulful walks through the French Alps with only my Walkman for company. It was wonderful. Without the inane chatter and semi-hostilities of someone by my side, I could really relax and take in the whole experience. There's nothing like travelling alone to throw you wholeheartedly into the moment, without wishing to get too Zen about it.

ADVERTISING FOR A TRAVELLING COMPANION

The other alternative is to advertise for a travelling companion. This can be done through most magazines and newspapers with a classified section, or target the travelling magazines. The magazine *Wanderlust* runs a section called Connections where you can advertise for a travelling companion.

TRAVELLERS' STORIES

Paul Andrews has travelled around the world on and off for seven years. He has travelled alone, with a friend or with people he has met on the road. 'If you leave the country with someone, you have a responsibility towards them, an obligation to do what they want and make sure they have a good time. But if you hook up with somebody while you're travelling, it's much easier to go your separate ways if one of you wants to go to Morocco, while the other wants to go to Scandinavia. Then, if you want to see them again, you can arrange to meet them in Paris, say, on 1 October. I've done that a few times and it's absolutely brilliant!'

TALK ABOUT IT

Whoever you go with, good communication is key to a good trip. So make sure you talk about the trip before you leave and try to agree on the following things:

Itinerary – where do you want to go, and when? How long do you want to stay for?

Lifestyle – what will you spend your money on? Do you intend to stay in a hostel, rent an apartment, go out clubbing every night or concentrate on soaking up the culture?

Work options – fruit picking? Temp work? Scuba diving? Teaching English? You don't have to do the same thing but make sure you are reading from the same script. Are you heading for the big cities or do you want to explore the less touristy areas?

The point is that the more consensus you have before you leave, the less scope for conflict you'll have when you get there. Talking about the trip in detail now is also a way to foster good relations for when you arrive. A good rule of thumb is that old adage your mother may have told you. Don't let the sun go down on an argument. In short, don't brood and don't nurse resentments. If something annoys you, tell them and deal with it. Work it out together and try to come up with a solution. Otherwise resentments will build, and your exciting working trip will start to resemble an exercise in conflict management.

TRAVELLERS' STORIES

Heidi Wilson came to the UK in 1998 with her long-term boyfriend. For months she had wanted to come to London, but waited instead for her boyfriend to accompany her. Eventually, he agreed, but problems soon set in. While Heidi loved her new life, her boyfriend hated it and soon wanted to leave. Heidi says, 'In the end, after two years, we agreed to go our separate ways. He went back to the States and I stayed here in London. It was a painful split but I don't regret it. Now I'm on my own I go out more and have met more people. My advice to other people is to come on your own and don't waste time waiting for your friends. Travelling alone is great – you meet more people and have more of an adventure. Before I came to the UK, I'd only done minimal travelling because I didn't have anyone to go with. Now I'm on my own, I love it. London is a great place for single girls and next I'm going to Australia – now I've finally done it, there's no stopping me!'

2 PRACTICALITIES

TICKETS, VISAS AND INSURANCE

TICKETS

So you've decided where to go, you've found a way of drumming up the money, now you have to decide what flight ticket is right for you. Open return or single? Round-the-world? Obviously the type of ticket you choose will depend on what kind of work you do, so the first thing to do is make sure you think about it carefully. Ask yourself questions about how flexible you want to be. Do you have one specific destination in mind, say Argentina, and have either fixed up work or feel reasonably confident you can find work there (teaching English, say), or do you fancy taking it as it comes and travelling to other locations? How much money will you take and how sure are you that you can find work?

WHAT TYPE OF FLIGHT SHOULD I BUY?

Obviously, the type of flight you choose will depend on a number of factors such as where you're travelling, your budget and your personality. Many travellers prefer the security of buying an open-ended return. That way, no matter what happens they know they can always leave. Buying a single ticket may be cheaper now, but there's always the risk you might end up stranded with no money left and no easy way out of there.

Other travellers opt for round-the-world tickets which you can pick up now for anything from £700 to £1,500, depending on where and when you want to go, how many stops, and what airline you travel with.

These not only give you the luxury of stopping off at a number of destinations – after all, if you're travelling 10,000 miles, why not use the time to take in some other countries? – but can also serve as proof in obtaining a visa that you are planning to leave the country. Some airlines also operate free loyalty schemes whereby round-the-world trips can earn enough points or air miles to grant you another free ticket. Split tickets, which go via another destination, and often with two airlines, can also be cheaper than a straight direct flight.

SHOP AROUND

Buying a ticket is usually the first real tangible proof that your trip is going to happen so the temptation may be to rush right in and buy the first exotic-sounding ticket you find. Don't. There's a huge choice out there, so take it slowly and make sure you shop around. The trick to getting the best deal is, as always, do your research. Take it slowly, but once you've found a good deal, don't be afraid to pounce. Once you've decided on your budget and destination, do your homework in the guide books, newspaper travel sections and tourist-board websites to find the best way of getting there. Once you've decided what type of ticket you want, start phoning around the travel agencies and tell them your intended route/destination.

Travel agents will have plenty of information they won't necessarily volunteer so it's worth buttering them up and plying them for information. A polite and friendly phone call at the least busy time of the day (such as early morning or late in the day) is more likely to catch them in a relaxed frame of mind, so they are more likely to spend the time talking to you. Make a note of the quotes and then phone round other agencies so you can start to compare what's on offer before making up your mind. If you intend to buy, make sure that the travel agent is registered with the Association of British Travel Agents (**www.abta.com**).

BUYING ON THE INTERNET

As always, the Internet can be your greatest ally and there are plenty of travel newsgroups where you can find out about the best deals. You can also try one of the many fare comparison websites on the Internet such as **www.expedia.co.uk** or **www.travelocity.co.uk** to find out who is flying where and for what price. The travel section of the *Guardian* website also has information on which airlines fly to which destinations – visit **www.guardian.co.uk/travel/cheapflights** – and then contact the airlines directly.

Alternatively, the website **www.priceline.co.uk** allows you to offer your own price for flights to airlines. If you are buying over the web, make sure the flight is covered by Atol (Air Travel Organisers' Licensing, **www.atol.org.uk**) before buying.

TIPS

Read through guide books, newspaper travel sections and tourist-board websites to find the best way of planning your trip.

Cast your net as wide as possible and shop around for the best price – on any one flight, the chances are that the passengers have paid a variety of different prices.

Use one of the fare comparison websites such as Expedia and Travelocity to find out who's flying where and for what price.

If you're travelling a long way, ask about the plane's 'seat pitch' or legroom. According to ergonomists, a 6 feet (1.83 m) person on a long-haul flight should have a minimum of 31 inches (79 cm).

COURIERING

You can save a lot of money by couriering items for business on flights. Check out the International Association of Air Travel (0800 074 6481 www.aircourier.co.uk) and Air Courier Association (00 1 303 279 3600 www.aircourier.org) for more information.

THE OBSERVER TRAVEL AWARDS BEST TRAVEL AGENT

1. **Travelcare**
2. **Trailfinders**
3. **Co-op Travel**
4. **Travel Bug**
5. **Bridge The World**

Best online booking company

1. **eurostar.co.uk**
2. **easyjet.com**
3. **buzzaway.com**
4. **travelcareonline.com**
5. **go-fly.com**

DISCOUNT FLIGHT AGENCIES

Thanks to the rise of the low-cost flight, there's never been a better time to swap your hard-earned pennies for a really good deal. If you're travelling long haul, it's worth going to a specialist. Here is just a small selection:

Cheap Flights (**www.cheapflights.co.uk**) is an online service that lists the day's cheapest flights available from subscribing UK flight agents.

North South Travel, Moulsham Mill, Parkway, Chelmsford, Essex CM2 7PX (Tel: 01245 608 291) is a small travel agency that offers discount fares worldwide and uses all available profit to support projects in the developing world.

Flightbookers/Ebookers, 177–178 Tottenham Court Road, London W1P 9HL (Tel: 020 7757 2444), Gatwick Airport, South Terminal (Tel: 0870 888 8881 **www.ebookers.com**) offers low fares on a good selection of scheduled flights.

STA Travel specialises in low-cost flights for students and under-26s (other customers are welcome) and has branches in London, Leeds, Bristol, Newcastle, Manchester, Liverpool, Oxford, Edinburgh, Glasgow and Aberdeen and on many university campuses. It also has two hundred offices abroad. Check out **www.statravel.co.uk** for more details.

Trailfinders, 194 Kensington High Street, London W8 7RG, Tel: 020 7938 3939; 215 Kensington High Street, London W8 6BD, Tel: 020 7938 3366;

1 Threadneedle Street, London EC2R 8JX, Tel: 020 7628 7628;
58 Deansgate, Manchester M3 2FF, Tel: 0161 839 6969; 254–284 Sauciehall Street, Glasgow G2 3EH, Tel: 0141 353 2224; 22–24 The Priory, Queensway, Birmingham B4 6BS, Tel: 0121 236 1234; 48 Corn Street, Bristol BS1 1HQ, Tel: 0117 929 9000; 4–5 Dawson Street, Dublin 2, Tel: 01 677 7888, Website: **www.trailfinders.co.uk**.

Bridge the World, 47 Chalk Farm Road, London NW1 8AJ, Tel: 020 7911 0900, Website: **www.bridgetheworld.com**.

VISAS

GETTING THE RIGHT INFORMATION

I think that phoning up for visa information could be top of the list of torture techniques. There's nothing quite as frustrating as sitting on the phone, listening to a menu of numbers to be finally put through to a pre-recorded message that doesn't tell you what you needed to know in the first place. And I should know. I've spent hours researching information about visas, to save you lucky people the legwork.

However, the fact is, depending on where you want to go, you are probably going to need some form of visa and/or work permit. If you're an EU citizen, the big exception is working and travelling in the EU, but even here, you will probably require some form of documentation particularly if you are staying longer than three months. (See chapters on separate countries for more specific visa information.) Other countries may demand you apply for a work permit before entering the country, and will only hand them over if you have secured work first. Many will require evidence of sufficient funds (often £2,000) and proof you intend to leave in the form of a return ticket. In short, there are many differing rules and regulations. But there are also loopholes to play around with. If you are required to show proof of funds, ask a friend to deposit a couple of grand in your bank account, photocopy the proof, and pay him back later. If you have contacts in your target country, by all means use them. They can help you fix up work before you leave and find an initial entry into a tightly regulated country. Once you're there, you may be able to drop the work and fix up something else instead. I know someone in Australia who got round the fact she had to leave a job under the conditions of her visa by registering in another name. Other travellers manage to find casual work on a tourist visa, although this can put you in a vulnerable position and mean you are not entitled to state benefits you may otherwise have access to. Also remember that in some countries overstaying your visa or working illegally is a serious offence. In the USA, for example, working illegally may result in deportation.

The good news is that many embassies and consulates now have websites where you can usually download documents and find out all the necessary information. The Embassy World website **www.embassyworld.com** has a database of worldwide embassy contacts. You can also try the country's government's websites, some of which carry some useful information.

The World Travel Guide website (**www.travel-guides.com**) carries country-by-country information including visa requirements.

The website for the UK's Foreign Office (**www.fco.gov.uk/travel**) lists visa requirements for many countries, as does the private visa agency Thames Consular (**www.thamesconsular.com**).

There are also many online agencies that, for a price, offer to arrange your visa for you. These can often be a minefield, however, so going through the consulate might still be the best (and cheapest) option. Try **www.visaservice.co.uk**, a commercial site that can obtain visas for companies or individual travellers. For work permits in the UK, USA and some European countries, try **www.visa-free.com**.

Remember that in some countries (many African ones, for example) the visa situation is constantly changing so make sure your information is up-to-date. Applying for a work permit or tourist visa can often take time, so apply for it well in advance – I once missed out on an all-expenses paid trip to Russia because I couldn't get the visa on time – and as a general rule, don't book your flight before you have your visa definitely approved.

INSURANCE

Yes, I know it's boring but sooner or later we're going to have to talk about it. Insurance. Sensible? Yes. Dull as ditchwater? Definitely, but without wanting to strike too much of a note of caution, you might live to regret it if you don't take some out. The fact is that with all the best intentions in the world, anything can go wrong. Accidents can happen. You may fall ill, you may get mugged, your passport or bags or traveller's cheques may be stolen. According to the government's travel website (**www.fco.gov.uk/knowbeforeyougo**) out of the 53 million overseas trips British nationals make each year, as many as one in seven of them fail to take out adequate travel insurance. Many live to regret it. Make sure you don't.

If you intend to work abroad, some employees and countries will demand that you take out the adequate insurance on condition of taking the job or entering the country. You may also be paying tax which will mean you are automatically entitled to state medical benefits. Make sure you have checked all this before leaving the country.

Leone Edwards worked as an English teacher in Germany and as a condition of working in Germany, had to take out medical insurance. It was a good job because after a skiing accident, she was taken into hospital and given an operation on the knee. She says, 'Taking the right insurance out is not to be underestimated. I was literally not taken into the operation until they'd seen all my paperwork. You don't think it's going to happen to you but it might.'

THE E111 FORM
The E111 form is a certificate which entitles EEA members to urgent medical treatment in the EEA (European Economic Area). It can be obtained from the post office, where it has to be stamped in order to be valid, or from the Department of Health. The free booklet *Health Advice for Travellers* contains an E111 form. Call 0800 555 777 or look on **www.doh.gov.uk**.

Keep it safe, preferably with your passport and carry it with you while travelling in the EEA. Even with the correct E111 form, you still have to pay for the treatments and then claim back the costs later.

Remember too, that Form E111 does not include repatriation.

There are a number of other countries that have reciprocal healthcare arrangements with the UK, which are not dependent on possession of an E111. These are Anguilla, Australia, Barbados, British Virgin Islands, Bulgaria, Channel Islands, Czech Republic, Falkland Islands, Hungary, Isle of Man, Malta, Montserrat, New Zealand, Poland, Romania, Russia, Slovakia, St Helena, Turks and Caicos Islands, NIS (except Latvia, Lithuania and Estonia) and Yugoslavia.

There are one hundred other countries, including popular travel destinations such as the US and Canada, that the UK has no healthcare agreements with. It is therefore vital that you have adequate medical insurance cover.

THE E111 AND WORKING ABROAD
The most important thing to bear in mind is that, unless you are a nanny or au pair, the *E111 form does not cover you if you are living permanently in a foreign country, or taking up work there.* However, if you are working temporarily abroad and it has been confirmed by the Inland Revenue National Insurance Contributions Office that you (and your employer) continue to pay UK national insurance contributions, you are entitled to Form 128.

Au pairs and nannies working in another EEA country for up to 12 months, who are normally resident in the UK, are entitled to Form E111.

Students working abroad as part of their UK studies may be entitled to Form 128 – contact the Inland Revenue for details.

GETTING THE BEST INSURANCE DEAL
Shop around Whatever your circumstances, it's best not to rely on the E111 form, if only because it doesn't include the cost of repatriation. The first thing, then, is to get some comprehensive insurance cover and, always,

shop around. Bear in mind that like most things in life, you get what you pay for and a cheaper policy might not offer the cover you need.

The most comprehensive policies should also include the following things:

- **Personal liability, for injury or damage to others and their property**
- **Cancellation, if you have to cancel or abandon your trip, to start as soon as you book your trip**
- **Twenty-four hour emergency service and assistance**
- **Possessions cover, including money and documents to a specified amount**

It can also cover personal accident (money paid on death or permanent disability) and legal expenses (to help you pursue compensation for damages following personal injury).

Make sure you have good medical cover This should include any medical bills and repatriation, which means an air ambulance service to fly you home. Repatriation cover is important as it can cost thousands of pounds – if you don't believe me, check out the government's travel website **www.fco.gov.uk/knowbeforeyougo** which has some scary figures. If things go wrong you could face a bill ranging from £300 for a scheduled flight from the Mediterranean, to £35,000 for an air ambulance from the USA.

Check you know what your policy covers Make sure you are covered for the whole period you are away and the countries you are visiting. If you are away for a full year, there are certain companies who specialise in annual travel insurance. If you are not sure how long you intend to stay, find a policy that allows you to extend it to cover the additional time you spend away.

Make sure you get a deal that covers everything you want to do. If you have a passion for extreme sports then make sure it's covered in your policy. Some policies exclude 'dangerous activities', for example. So, for all you bungee-jumpers or paragliders out there, it might be wise to pay that little bit extra and take out the most comprehensive policy.

Be honest in your application If your insurance application form asks to be informed of any pre-existing medical conditions, tell them the truth; otherwise, it might invalidate a medical claim.

Read the small print Some policies may guarantee free cover which may not prove adequate if you run into any difficulties. Others may have certain clauses which exclude certain countries and activities. Some policies may exclude manual work and/or refuse to give out money if you were working at the time when the accident happened.

Take the right information Make sure you take with you your policy and the 24-hour emergency phone number. And, if anything does happen, keep as much paperwork as possible, particularly a police report as well as tickets, receipts, medical bills and such, to help prove that what you're claiming for actually happened. Even then, you may not be entitled to as much as you think, as insurers rarely give out full compensation.

Where to buy insurance You can get the numbers for insurance brokers from national newspapers and travel supplements. The government's Insurance & Assistance Partners Page **http://www.fco.gov.uk/servlet/Front** has links to insurers while there are also websites that will search to find you the best deal. Try **www.easycover.com** and **www.1stoptravelinsurance.co.uk.**

Beware travel agents who try to pressurise you into buying insurance with them when you buy a flight ticket. You don't have to take out insurance with them and may well be able to get a better deal elsewhere. There are also certain companies that specialise in offering policies to cover working abroad and many backpacker policies specifically cover casual work. Navigator travel.co.uk specialises in insurance for backpackers and hazardous sports, as do Columbus direct (**www.columbusdirect.co.uk**).

Useful information American Express has launched a Rough Guide to Smooth Travel Finances which has useful advice about obtaining and claiming insurance. Call 0800 619 6248 for a free copy.

PACKING

So, the trip is set and your first day looms. It's time to get packing. Obviously what you will need to take will depend on where you are going and the kind of lifestyle you intend to lead; packing for fruit picking in Greece is going to require a completely different wardrobe than working in the secretarial agencies of Singapore, or building wells in Africa. However, here are some general points to bear in mind.

How long are you going for? What will the climate be like? Will there be a huge variation in climate or will it generally be the same? What kind of work do you intend to do? If you are looking for casual work in bars and restaurants, take some black and whites for waiter or waitressing work. If there's a possibility you might do city work in offices, take smart office clothes. Heading for Muslim countries? Slip in a sarong. The main thing is to think carefully about the kind of work you might end up doing, and pack accordingly. Make sure you have the gear to take the work you find, but do remember to pack lightly, particularly if you're travelling around.

GOOD PACKING TIPS

Pack your rucksack wisely so the weight is evenly distributed and doesn't pull too much on your back.

Think strategically. How can you minimise the amount of luggage you have weighing you down? If you are moving from location to location, you can always send your clothes ahead of you. If, for example, after agriculture work you intend to move on to temping in Sydney, you can send your bulky office clothes on to a poste restante there from your home country before you leave. Likewise, after you've finished with them, mail them back home. You can also rent out special equipment such as camping or diving gear.

Make your rucksack more secure by attaching small padlocks to double zips on the pockets and lid. You can also use a small padlock and chain to secure to luggage racks on overnight trains and buses. Tag your rucksack with a label bearing your name and stick an address label on a side pocket inside.

Make sure your pack is extra waterproofed by buying a special rucksack liner or use a dustbin liner.

Take a day bag and money belt or bum bag. A money belt is one of the most essential things you can buy and will keep all your important documents together. Wear it under clothes and try not to use it to store petty cash or anything that you will have to access every five minutes.

Place toiletries and lotions in waterproof sealable bags to guard against spillages. Do the same for important documents.

CLOTHES

Obviously the type of clothes will depend on where you are going, when you are going and what you intend to do once you get there. I won't patronise you by advising you on what kind of clothes you should or should not wear, but here are a few vital points to bear in mind:

Be aware of extreme climate changes – many countries, including those close to home such as Madrid and farther flung places like China, change drastically from winter to summer. Frank Baker arrived in Beijing unprepared for the cold winter and found he had to buy a whole new wardrobe.

Employ the useful trick of layering, particularly if you're moving from a hot to cold climate. Wearing a few T-shirts on top of each other can provide the equivalent of bulky sweaters or thermal underwear, and unlike thick clothes, won't weigh your rucksack down.

Thick warm socks can be good when hiking in a hot climate as well as keeping you warm in the more remote places of Scandinavia. At the end of a long tiring day they can also be the fashion equivalent of comfort food – snug and warm and very, very soothing.

Fleece jackets are very useful, managing to be both warm and light (they also make comfortable pillows and can be worn with pretty much anything).

Cotton and linen allow your skin to breathe and won't cause the same irritations as artificial fabrics such as nylon and Lycra might – especially in a warm climate.

Don't take expensive designer clothes. Not only are they likely to deteriorate if they're stuffed in a rucksack but there's also a risk that they might be mislaid in transit. It has been known for airline flights to 'lose' luggage, and they and insurance companies rarely fork out full compensation.

Remember the modesty factor – dressing in skimpier than skimpy dresses in Muslim countries is likely to offend. Make sure you have long-sleeved tops, long trousers and skirts to cover the whole body when entering temples and so on. This goes for men too – bare chests won't go down well in certain destinations, and ladies, nor will topless sunbathing. Loose, baggy and fluid clothing in light colours and lightweight fabrics are surprisingly cooling and are also good for protecting yourself from mosquitoes. And remember that perennial essential – the sarong.

Even if you intend to spend your time trekking or working in the harvest fields, it's a good idea to pack one smart outfit, as you never know what opportunities may come along.

Take waterproofs – you can buy transparent macs or ponchos which fold away into a small pack and hardly take up any room.

Make sure your shoes are comfortable and practical. If they're new, make sure they've been well broken in first. As always, think carefully about the type of shoes you take and remember that you could be wearing these shoes for a very long time. Sandals (particularly Tevas) are the favourite shoes for backpacking. Trainers can get very smelly, while flip-flops are ideal for beach living and surviving in a hot climate. Take a few pairs (say, one smart, one pair of sandals, one pair of hiking boots, and one pair of flip-flops if necessary), but bear in mind that shoes can be very heavy and take up vital room.

DOCUMENTS
Keep important documents such as passport, airline tickets, traveller's cheques, credit card and insurance policy in your money belt which, if you are travelling around, should be strapped around your waist and worn under clothes.

Make two photocopies of each document and keep in a separate place away from the originals.

Leave one set of photocopies at home with friends or relatives, who can fax/email them on to you in case of emergency such as loss or theft.

Lonely Planet's ekno service at **www.lonelyplanet.com** allows you to store information such as credit card numbers and passport details online or you can store the details on a message sent to your own email address before you leave, to pick up from a cybercafe anywhere in the world. Some travellers even scan in their important documents and send to their email address.

Other documents to take include international driver's licence, student card and international youth hostel card (if applicable), certificates of relevant qualifications (for example, Tefl certificate), and take eight passport-sized photos for visas, residence permits, travel passes and so on.

Depending on the red tape, different countries may require certain documentation, such as proof of income, for example. Make sure you understand the bureaucracy and rules before you leave so you can take all the necessary documentation.

BUY A GOOD RUCKSACK

A rucksack can be expensive, from £50 to £150, but think of it as an investment. Choose a good brand such as Karrimor, Berghaus, Lowe Alpine, Kathmandu and the New Zealand brand Mac Pac, and try not to buy one that is so bulky it will become a nightmare to carry around. When it comes to size, there are two schools of thought: the first thinks the bigger the better, half-filled as you're bound to fill it up when you're away. The second, more minimalist approach, is to discover the joys of capsule packing. Choosing a small, manageable backpack will force you to pack light and be less of a burden to carry.

WHICH BACKPACK SHOULD YOU CHOOSE?

There are two types of backpacks. One is the hiking pack which loads from the top, sits well on the back and is the standard fare of most backpackers. The second is the travel bag or sack, which is perfect for the working traveller. By zipping the back system away and thus removing all straps and dangly bits, these handy things can transform themselves from the lumpy, unwieldy backpack to the smart, cosmopolitan suitcase – ideal if you are moving from hostel to hotel to camping field!

The most important thing in choosing the perfect rucksack is to make sure it has an adjustable back system so you can change the position of the shoulder straps to suit your frame. The cheaper versions may not be adjustable so it's worth spending more. The waistband should also be hard and stiff, and if you intend to carry heavy loads make sure the hip belt is thickly padded. This will channel most of the weight down to your hips and legs, taking the strain off your shoulders and back.

Make sure the backpack is well made, has strong stitching and is made from heavy-duty waterproof material. Most quality packs are made from ripstop, which appears as a series of squares or checks and contains an extra thread of stitching to stop a tear from developing into a full-blown hole.

ESSENTIALS CHECKLIST

DOCUMENTS
Passport

Air and rail tickets

Visas

Traveller's cheques

Sterling or dollars

Foreign currency

Insurance certificate

ID cards

IYHA membership card

Spare passport photographs

Photocopies of all your important documents

International driver's licence

Details of accommodation and employers' addresses

Maps

Vaccination certificates

TOILETRIES
Shaving oil and razors

Tampons and sanitary towels – make sure you're stocked up so aren't caught out short in remote areas. In developing countries these can be very expensive

Glasses or contact lens gear

Towels

Toothpaste and toothbrush

Sarong

Lip salve

Moisturiser

HEALTH

Anti-diarrhoea medicine and other relevant pills, e.g. anti-malaria and bilharzia pills depending on where you are going (see Health section in Chapter 4)

Rehydration sachets to restore your body after a bout of diarrhoea

Sun cream – protection and after-sun

Calamine lotion

Iodine – to make water safe to drink and sterilise wounds

Sting relief cream

Sterilised needle kit

DEET-based insect repellant

Mosquito net

Existing medication

Small scissors

Painkillers

Bandages

Plasters

Antiseptic cream

E45 cream

Safety pins, gauze and bandage tape

Condoms

Other contraception – if you are on the pill, make sure you have enough pills to last for the period you're away

USEFUL ITEMS

Batteries

Padlock and chain

Knife and fork

Sewing kit

Swiss army knife

Plastic bags – small, big, sealable

Plenty of tissues and wipes – keep in a dry waterproof bag

Travel alarm clock with time zones if you intend to do a lot of travelling around

Travel wash and peg-free washing line

Sunglasses

Phrase books

Torch

OPTIONAL BITS AND BOBS YOU MAY OR MAY NOT NEED

Earplugs – useful in noisy hostels and hotels, or sleeping on trains

Travel plugs – for all your electrical appliances, such as a hairdryer or laptop. The Help for World Travellers website **www.kropla.com** has a list of the different sockets, voltage and phone plugs used around the world

Personal stereo and music, with radio function if you want to take in the local sounds. Having a record function could also prove interesting, say you want to capture the buzz of Bangkok or the roar of Mumbai, or make a audio diary or letters to send back home

Travel iron – bulky, but could be useful if you have to trawl round to interviews and make yourself look reasonably presentable

Sleeping bag – bear in mind that in popular trekking centres in Asia you can rent bags very cheaply

Camping gear

Cigarette lighter – to light campfires, candles, mosquito coils, etc.

Note pad and pen

Camera and film

FOR THE JOB HUNT

Mobile phone and charger – if you're planning on fixing up work once you arrive at your chosen destination, the mobile phone can make the job hunt easier

Business cards – if the work you hope to get depends on creating some kind of professional image you can always print up your name, credentials and contact mobile phone number before you leave and hand around potential employers

Copies of your CV – in a waterproof folder, several copies and a copy on hard disc too

Copies of important certifications – such as a Tefl certificate or driving instructors' course. Again, make photocopies and keep in a waterproof folder

Suitable clothes – if you think you may end up working in catering, take smart black and whites (black skirt/ trousers and white shirt) for waiter/waitress and bar work. For city work, choose comfortable but smart city clothes including one pair of smart shoes. Try to find materials that don't crease easily

3 SKILLS AND OPPORTUNITIES

So here you are, ready and willing to work abroad, you've got the time off and you've worked out a way to save up the money. And now for the big question: what are you going to do? Rest assured, no matter what your skills are, there are literally thousands of opportunities waiting for you. The first step is to begin with the region that most interests you and then narrow down by available opportunities. Once you've found out what they are, you can start to match the opportunities with the skills and jobs you are qualified for.

TIPS ON WORKING ABROAD

Make contacts in your target country

Improve your language skills

Save money

Begin with the region that most interests you and then narrow down by available opportunities

Talk to people and tell them about your plans

Do your research – read the relevant books and use the web and library

Remember personal interests and hobbies can be just as useful in securing work as work experience and qualifications

---

QUALIFICATIONS

One of the fastest ways to find a job is to actively seek a country where there's a shortage of people with your skills. Teachers and nurses are often in demand – New Zealand is currently experiencing a shortage of teachers, while nurses and other medical staff are in short supply in South Africa. Contact the relevant professional organisations or keep an eye on professional journals for overseas opportunities.

Commonwealth teachers may be able to arrange exchange placements in Commonwealth countries. Write to The League for the Exchange of Commonwealth Teachers, Commonwealth House, 7 Lion Road, Tremadoc Road, London SW4 7NQ (Tel: 020 7498 1101, Fax: 020 7720 5403).

AGENCIES

For the rest of us, there are many agencies which can help find work in specific areas (see What to Do for more details). If you are a professional, the *CEPEC Recruitment Guide* may be of some use. It lists recruitment agencies and search consultants in the UK, many of which deal in overseas placements, for professional, manager and executives. You should be able to find this in your local reference library or alternatively contact: CEPEC Ltd, 13 Hanover Square, London W1R 9HD, Tel: 020 7629 2266.

You can also search for specialist agencies on the Recruitment and Employment Confederation's website **www.jobseekers-uk.com**.

Typists and secretaries with shorthand skills and good computer skills could try temping work in big cities. Many temping agencies such as Adecco, Drake Personnel, Manpower, Eagle Recruitment and International Secretaries have a strong international presence and may be able to advise you on the chances of finding temping work before you leave.

SPECIAL SKILLS

Whatever your circumstances, you're bound to have some special skills or experience that you can market abroad and use in an international context. Maybe you've worked as a silver service waitress in an expensive hotel and could impress prospective foreign employers with your ability to juggle four plates, five glasses of wine and still be a dab hand at serving out broccoli.

The other thing to remember is that personal interests and hobbies can be just as useful in securing work. Have you anything you can teach, for example? Teaching English is a hugely popular way of working abroad and with the rise in speaking English touching just about everywhere, there are many places where you still may be able to find work just by virtue of being born a native speaker. That said, equipping yourself with a Tefl certificate is still a wise move (see Teaching English chapter for more details) as the days when being a native speaker was enough are rapidly diminishing.

Sports and outdoor enthusiasts can be sure that there are plenty of companies in need of their skills. Maybe you're a windsurfer/ surfing dude and think you could teach it to other people? Holiday camps such as Camp America will offer you work as an instructor even if you're not qualified to teach, while other big holiday companies such as Mark Warner place watersports instructors in their beach hotels and holiday villages. The same rule applies to divers, skiers, snowboarders, horse riders and entertainers. (See Tourism chapter for more details.)

Extensive travel experience in developing countries can be the ticket to finding work as a tour guide or expedition leader. Much of this work is demanding and requires a commitment of at least eighteen months, but for the right candidates, the rewards can be huge. (For more details see the Working a Passage chapter.)

Many other travellers save up and train abroad. There are many diving courses in diving centres throughout the world, while most countries have schools where you can do a Tefl course. (See Chapter 6 Teaching English for more details.)

WRITING AN INTERNATIONAL CV (OR RÉSUMÉ)

If you're planning to find work abroad, it's important that you have a CV (or résumé) that crosses international borders. Your CV may be the first impression your employer has of you, so it's important that it illustrates not only your skills and work experience, but also that you're culturally aware and know how to adapt to living in another country.

There's no such thing as the perfect CV – what works and doesn't will depend on where you are, the culture of the company and what profession/industry you are applying for. If you have no set idea of what specific work you are likely to do, take a copy of your CV on electronic file that you can update and amend, as you feel necessary. The most important thing is to do your research – find out what the culture of the company is and try to think what particular skills and abilities they will value highly.

- **Try to see a copy of a CV from someone already in your target country. One goal of your CV is to show your familiarity with the culture by using culturally appropriate language; modelling your CV on someone else's will give you a clear idea of style, content and format. Are jobs listed chronologically or reverse-chronologically? Does it include a 'personal interest' section? Does it include details of references? The exact contents and format will vary from country to country, so try to see at least one example or have a look in a library for advice. For example, some European countries require a photo attached with the CV while in the UK or US, this is not necessary.**

- **Try not to make your CV too long. Personally, I think one page is better, but this will depend on your chosen profession and the country. If you are concise you can convey all the relevant information adequately and all the information can be seen clearly. Don't bore them by making grand sweeping statements about your excellent leadership skills and how you managed to single-handedly turn round a sinking company – save that for the interview.**

- **Keep language simple and concise. Bear in mind that the person reading your CV may not speak good English so don't irritate them by over-elaborating or trying to show off your rich and wonderful, varied vocabulary. If they have to keep reaching for the dictionary, it is likely to put them off reading it at all.**

- Although English is widely spoken in many countries, most foreign employers would like to see evidence you can speak the language of their country. So, if possible, have your CV drafted in both languages and state your language skills clearly. Try not to boast you can speak the language more than you can as your employer may easily try to test you and will soon be able to see through you. It could end up putting more stress on you in the end, and lead to some embarrassing, uncomfortable scenarios.

- If you're submitting your CV in English, find out if the recipient uses British English or American English. There are numerous variations between the two versions. Most European companies use British English, and most US companies, use American English. If you use the wrong one, a reader who's unfamiliar with the variations may just presume it's full of mistakes.

- If you submit your CV in a foreign language, try to have a native speaker review your document. This way they can see that any terms used are fully understood and used in their country, and check the translation is accurate too.

- Find out whether a chronological or reverse-chronological format is more appropriate. Chronological order means that your first work experience is listed first; reverse-chronological order means that your current or most recent experience is listed first. If you can't find out, opt for a reverse-chronological format.

- Be aware that the standard paper size is different in different countries. The US standard is $8^1/_2$ inches wide and 11 inches long while the European A4 standard is 210 millimetres wide and 297 millimetres long.

- If you are emailing your CV as an attachment make sure it is in a widely accepted format, such as Microsoft Word. Send a hard copy by snail mail too, to make sure that it's received.

- As with all CVs, make sure you check your spelling and make your copy as presentable as possible. Use the spell check on the computer but also use a dictionary. Spell checks have numerous flaws and are in no way infallible.

- Education terms differ from country to country and merely stating the title of your degree won't necessarily convey all the relevant information. Bear in mind that, in some countries, a university degree can be earned in three years, while in other countries it takes longer. Different professions such as medics or teachers also vary in training length from country to country. If you are hoping to get a job based on your education, be clear and comprehensive about what exactly you studied. Otherwise, highlight the skills and qualifications that are of

particular relevance to the job you are applying for – such as nursing, teaching, computer skills etc.

REFERENCES

Having a couple of names readily at hand of people who can provide character references could give you an edge in a competitive market. However, you don't need to list the names of your referees on your CV, as it only takes up valuable room. As always, see how it's done in your chosen country and follow suit. You could also take with you a printed reference to show on spec. As with all important documents, photocopy the originals and keep them in a separate place. You can also store them on disc and save them electronically so you can download the reference when you need it.

LANGUAGE

How much of the language will you learn before you go? Obviously, the best scenario would be to learn as much as possible so you can mingle with the natives and make the most of any opportunities that come along. That said, you have to go a pretty long way before you meet people who can't string out a few conversational words in English. Despite this, it would be wise not to rest on your laurels. It's all too easy for native English speakers to grow lazy and complacent knowing that the rest of the world is eager to learn the language we were born speaking, and some countries – and often those much closer to home – are ready to give us a nasty prod. France is notoriously difficult for finding work if you can't speak French, even in the summer tourist season. Tracey Smith was sacked from her job in a local auberge in the South of France for not speaking enough French, while Sara Lofthouse and her friend Jane found they couldn't even find work once they'd arrived in Nice, because their French skills were well below par.

Says Sara, 'There was a lot of intolerance in Nice towards people who spoke poor French, particularly English people, and it stopped me from even trying. When I did, they would just laugh or pretend they didn't understand. We'd expected to walk into a job easily and went to the job centre as soon as we arrived. Unfortunately, there was hardly any work and they were very dismissive towards us because we didn't speak enough of the language.'

Some employers will insist you speak at least some of the language and place higher emphasis on language skills. Generally, the more touristy the resort you head for, the less you will need to know. Alex Rayner worked as a windsurfing instructor for Mark Warner holiday company in Sardinia and says, 'The only Italian we were expected to know was an Italian phrase to keep the natives off the hotel's equipment. It was a very sanitised and imported version of Mediterranean life and we were hardly expected to converse with the locals.'

Of course the most polite and respectful thing is to learn as much as you can. This isn't only the most ethical thing to do, but it is also much more likely to open doors and put you in touch with the right people. Speaking at least some of the lingo will mean you have a much wider choice of jobs than if you can only say hello, where are the loos, and then revert quickly back into English.

Luckily, there are hundreds of language courses on cassettes, videos and CDs to save you the expense of forking out on expensive language classes. That said, you can't beat a language course to really polish up your skills. Look in the Yellow Pages or head for the local library or university notice board for details of night schools and language schools. A cheaper option is to offer to exchange one-to-one conversational English classes for private tuition in the language of your chosen destination from a native speaker. This works particularly well if you live in an area where there is a high concentration of tourists or language students; you can advertise in the local paper or put up notices in shop windows, at libraries, or local English schools. You can also do this when you are abroad – it's a great way of meeting locals. Look out for adverts in English-language cafes and bars, or on university and hostel notice boards.

GETTING A JOB BEFORE YOU GO VERSUS FINDING WORK WHEN YOU ARRIVE

Whether you choose to find work before you leave or once you arrive will depend a lot on your temperament and the kind of experience you're looking for. There's no right or wrong way to go about it, and many travellers find that even if things go pear-shaped and don't fall into place easily, it still results in a great adventure, a good laugh and plenty of amusing stories.

GETTING A JOB BEFORE YOU GO

First-time travellers may want to cushion themselves by fixing up work with an international organisation that provides everything for you, from accommodation and flights to travel insurance and red tape. For some countries, like the USA, it can be the easiest way by far to sample the experience of working in that country. The good news is that there are many organisations that can help you find work. Here are some of the big ones. (For addresses of gap-year companies, see the Voluntary Work and Gap Year chapter.)

Bunac (16 Bowling Green Lane, London EC1R 0QH, Tel: 020 7251 3472, Website: **www.bunac.org**) administers a wide range of paid work and travel programmes including Summercamp USA, Work and Travel in Canada, Australia or New Zealand, Summer Vacation Work in the USA and Canada, Work and Travel in Ghana, South Africa and Argentina, and Volunteer Costa Rica.

The Education and Training Group (10 Spring Gardens, London SW1A 2BN, Tel: 020 7389 4431, Fax: 020 7389 4426, Website: **www.britishcouncil.org**) organises a range of internships and placements around the world.

Council on International Educational Exchange (CIEE) (52 Poland Street, London W1F 7AB, Tel: 020 7478 2018, Website: **www.councilexchanges.org.uk**) runs programmes in USA, Canada, Australia, Japan and China.

Council Australia (University Centre, Level 8, 210 Clarence Street, Sydney 2000, Australia) runs programmes across the world for Australian and New Zealand students.

Alliances Abroad (702 West Avenue, Austin, TX 78701 USA, Website: **www.alliancesabroad.com**) organises customised programmes for individuals and groups around the globe who want to learn about other cultures by teaching, interning, volunteering or working abroad.

The International Student Exchange Centre (Isec), (35 Ivor Place, London NW1 6EA, Tel: 020 7724 4493, Website: **www.isecworld.co.uk**) organises a range of placements worldwide including camp counsellors and English teachers for a variety of countries in Eastern Europe and Latin America. It also has a Work and Study Experience Russia programme which arranges work experience in a Moscow company, and other cities, for two to four months combined with a four-week Russian language course at a university.

Au pair work is another popular option. If you go through an agency, it will arrange visas, flights for you (see Au Pair and Childcare chapter), or you can keep an eye open in the magazine *The Lady* for advertisements. Another option is to write to the international chains and see what vacancies they have. If you've worked for a chain such as Virgin Megastore, McDonald's or Borders, there may well be overseas opportunities in other countries. Write to the central offices or keep an eye open in in-house magazines.

WHERE CAN I FIND JOBS?

So where else can you find work? Again, there are hundreds of places. You just have to weed them out with a little careful research. Inspiration can come from anywhere. Maria Hardy spotted an advert in *FourFourTwo* magazine for soccer coaches in the States and found it was the beginning of a whole new career. Here are just some of the resources at your disposal:

The European Employment Services (EURES) website (**www.europa.eu.int/comm/employment**) has details of vacancies throughout the EU and available to all EU/EEA members. It also provides information on living and working conditions, social security, taxation and so on in all EEA member countries. You can also, in theory, speak to one of their Euroadvisers via local Employment Job Centres, although job centres in the UK are notoriously overstretched and you may well be sent in frustrating circles. For job vacancies on the EURES website, go to **www.europa.eu.int/jobs/eures**. Be aware that this network is usually more suited to professionals with sought-after skills, and the jobs advertised often require fluency in the language of the country you are targeting.

To find out about British companies with foreign associates contact the Chambers of Commerce at **www.britishchambers.org.uk**. Most chambers of commerce in other countries will have a list of member companies – some are free, others you will have to pay for.

To find out about opportunities in your profession, read the trade magazines (names and addresses can be found in Benn's *Media Directory* and Benn's *Media Directory International*, both of which are usually available at main libraries) or contact the relevant professional bodies or trade unions.

There are also many specialist agencies for qualified personnel such as teaching, nursing, IT, engineers, architects and so on. Robert Walters (**www.robertwalters.com**) has temporary and permanent vacancies in banking and finance, accountancy, secretarial and call centres and has offices in Australia, Belgium, France, Germany, Hong Kong, Ireland, New Zealand, Singapore, South Africa, Holland, the UK and the USA.

The Internet is a wonderful resource for finding details and inspiration for work abroad. Surfing the web and logging on to a few websites will certainly whet the appetite and provide you with ideas. Gapwork.com (**www.gapwork.com**) allows you to register for a newsletter which lists casual work opportunities in Australia, New Zealand and Europe.

Payaway.com (**www.payaway.com**) is a great website with information on every country including red tape, embassies and list of addresses and useful organisations to find work.

For a list of voluntary work opportunities, try **www.workingabroad.com**, while Americans can use **www.overseasjobs.com**, an online recruitment network that provides career resources including employment opportunities to college and high school students, resort and hospitality staff, expats and international job seekers.

Here are some other good websites for finding work abroad:

www.gapyear.com
www.payaway.co.uk
www.anyworkanywhere.com
www.summerjobseeker.com
www.summerjobs.com
www.hotrecruit.com

You can also keep an eye on the local and national press, which may have overseas work sections. Beware of job adverts that make grand promises, such as those offering cruise work – the reality may be a long way from what they promise. *Loot* has an International Jobs Offered/Wanted section as well as an Au Pair Jobs Offered/Wanted.

Overseas Jobs Express is a fortnightly newspaper with advice, reports and advertised vacancies and is available by subscription or in newsagents: PO BOX 22, Brighton, BN1 6HT, Tel: 01273 699 777.

Home and Away is a monthly expat magazine that runs job vacancies. Write to Expats House, 29 Lacon Road, London SE22 9HE, Tel: 020 8299 4987.

You can also place a Situations Wanted advert in newspapers in the country you are visiting. You can sometimes do this from the UK over the phone or fax, paying by credit card. Alternatively, you can get an advertising agent to do it for you. Look in the Yellow Pages for agents.

Another option is to find work with the big holiday companies where there are innumerable vacancies for all kinds of catering and tourism work. (See Tourism chapter for more details.)

FIND WORKING WHEN YOU ARRIVE
Others prefer the free-fall of landing in a foreign country, and leaving it to fate. Even Sara Lofthouse, who landed in France with only £150, and couldn't find work for three weeks, found the experience exhilarating. Despite not being able to find a 'conventional job', she still managed to stay three months and eventually found work handing out flyers on a beach, busking around the cafes in Nice and working the odd day as a waitress in a local British-owned bar.

'We were living off our wits and the whole experience was brilliant. I changed more in those three months that I did in three years at university. When we went we were quite naïve and had never really been abroad before. By the end we were much more confident and like different people. The most important thing is to talk to people – it's amazing how quickly networks develop.'

However, finding work on spec isn't for the faint-hearted and potential problems shouldn't be underestimated. You may arrive in Rhodes Island on Thursday and find work in a local bar by the next evening, or you may turn up in Magnetic Island, Australia and spend weeks looking for work, while all the time your precious money is dwindling away. So before you opt for this choice, it's good to ask yourself how you really think you'll react in a crisis. Are you the kind of person who thrives off uncertainty? If you're the kind of person who likes steady bets and isn't used to dealing with insecurity, then you may be better off taking the first option and finding work before you leave.

That said, the sense of reward and achievement that comes from surviving off your wits and making it work takes some beating. Most people who take this option say they return home with a new-found confidence and an unshakeable belief that they can handle whatever life throws at them. But no matter how much you relish the exhilaration of landing without any safety net, there are a few sensible steps you can take to make the transition as painless as possible.

Do your research – read about the region and find out what work opportunities exist. Surf the web and try to contact some people who are already there. Make sure you are well prepared so your first few weeks aren't going to be radically different than you expected.

Make sure you speak some of the language – the more you know, the more equipped you will be to adjust to anything and make the most of what opportunities come along, as well as being able to speak to more people.

Make contacts in your target country before you leave – local insider information can be invaluable and put you in touch with useful people.

Tell everyone you know about your plans before you leave – if you're going to Spain, say, you may find out that someone has a friend who lives in Madrid or has an uncle who owns a bar and may need some people.

PERSEVERE

Perhaps perseverance is the most crucial thing in finding work. You may be one of the lucky ones, where job openings just fall in your lap, but the chances are that like most of us, you'll be put through your paces first. What does that mean? That means you may have to leave your CV at 25 bars before being offered to work for one trial evening. You may have to phone fifteen language schools before being invited to one interview. You may have to wait for over three weeks before finding work and in the meantime watch your bundle of emergency cash trickle away, but don't give up. You've just travelled to the other side of the world and tried to find work – did anyone say it was going to be easy?

The other thing to keep in mind is that one thing has a way of leading to another. For example, you may not be able to find work teaching English straight away, but there may be part-time evening work in a bar you could do. Don't turn down opportunities because they're not exactly what you want – take it slowly, don't give up and pretty soon you could be sitting pretty right where you want to be.

HOW TO FIND WORK THERE

Word of mouth – Remember that opportunities come through other people so put on a friendly face and be willing to chat to everyone you meet. That person in the bar might tell you about some work they know in a local hostel. Your neighbour in the next room could put you in touch with someone who is just waiting to hear from you. Sitting in your hotel room every night and watching local TV isn't going to put you in touch with that fastest recruitment network – other people.

Job centres – Most countries have state job centres or private agencies which advertise vacancies. You can usually find the addresses of these by looking in the Yellow Pages under the relevant sections.

Websites – The web is buzzing with online resources and can truly work miracles when you're away. You should be able to find a cybercafe in most locations. Logging onto chat rooms can also put you in touch with fellow travellers who can pass on tips and vital information.

National and local press – Most newspapers will carry some recruitment section and can be a good way of gauging likely opportunities. Many of them will allow you to place your own advert asking for work, which may prove successful.

Legwork – Walking around to potential employers and introducing yourself on the spot can often pay dividends, especially in season in the tourist areas. Whether you're looking for work in language schools, hotels, bars, farms, or on boats, take with you contact details and all the relevant documents. You can print up business cards before you leave, including a poste restante address, the place where you are staying, a mobile telephone number or details of a contact who lives in the country and who can pass on any messages to you. You may also want to take a copy of your CV and/or necessary proof of qualifications and any other work they may be interested to see. Be friendly, enthusiastic, enquiring and brief, and show an interest in their work and their culture.

WHAT YOU WILL NEED:

Mobile phone
Poste restante address
International CV
References
The right clothes
Relevant certificates
International driver's licence
Language skills
Email address

4 HEALTH, SAFETY AND CRIME

HEALTH

More than thirty million journeys are made abroad each year and two million people cross international borders every day. With figures like these, it's easy to be lulled into a false sense of security. However, the fact remains that the world can be a very dangerous place. Of course, you might not be able to make your trip one hundred per cent safe, but you can make sure you take the necessary steps to make it as safe as possible. And the first thing to do is make sure you get the right vaccinations.

USEFUL ADVICE

Dr Richard Dawood is a physician at the Fleet Street Clinic and author of *Travellers' Health: How to Stay Healthy Abroad*, Fourth edition, OUP. He says, 'Have the vaccinations you can, and take malaria pills where appropriate, but beyond that inform yourself as fully as possible. The best protection is knowledge. Make sure you put health top on the menu of research. You might regret it if you don't.'

GETTING THE RIGHT VACCINATIONS

So why is it important to get the right vaccines? Well, for one thing infectious diseases across the world are on the rise, and with world poverty growing, the risks don't look set to go away. Despite this, many travellers don't bother to get adequately protected and return home with some cautionary tales to tell. Luckily these are in the minority, but it's still wise to make sure you're not one of the unlucky ones who gets caught out. Everyone knows someone who travelled to India and spent their whole time chained to a toilet, barely able to move and unable to leave. It's hardly surprising – here in the West we enjoy a level of healthcare that Third World countries can only dream about. Many contagious diseases have been eliminated and our well-sanitised lives keep most of the dangerous bugs at bay. Travelling to countries that are not similarly protected, however, exposes our bodies to conditions they have simply never encountered before and so have never developed any resistance against. But by getting a vaccination, which basically involves being injected with a harmless version of the disease, your body then develops an immunity.

WHICH VACCINES SHOULD YOU HAVE?

Under current law the only vaccine that is compulsory for any country is yellow fever, but there are hundreds of other diseases that it is worth immunising yourself against.

According to Dr Richard Dawood, the most important thing is to do your research. 'The first thing is to familiarise yourself with the risks of your particular destination. Visit your GP or a travel medicine expert, who should be able to tell you about the recommended vaccine requirements for certain countries.'

The following is a general guide to which vaccines are recommended for different global areas. To get more specific information, contact a travel medical expert or visit one of the numerous excellent websites which carry highly detailed information.

- **Typhoid and hepatitis A are both recommended vaccines for most parts of the world, including parts of Europe.**

- **Malaria pills are essential for most places in parts of South America, Asia, Africa and the Caribbean.**

- **Meningitis A and C vaccines are recommended for sub-Saharan Africa, but also Brazil, India and Nepal. (According to the Nomad Travel Clinic over 200 people died from meningococcal menigitis serotype C in Rwanda in June 2002.)**

- **Japanese encephalitis vaccines are recommended for rural and extremely wet parts of Asia.**

- **It's also a good time to update your protection against tetanus, polio and in some cases diptheria, especially if it's more than ten years since you were last vaccinated.**

- **Another to watch out for is rabies, especially in parts of South America, Asia and Africa.**

WHERE CAN I FIND THE RIGHT INFORMATION?

Finding out about tropical diseases may seem like a minefield but there are plenty of good resources out there to help you research the health risks. In the UK the first thing you should do is contact the Department of Health for its free booklet on health risks and vaccines for each country. Call 0800 555 777 or look on **www.doh.gov.uk**. This also includes an E111 form and gives details on medical insurance and getting help in different countries.

The Nomad Pharmacy run an advice line on 09068 633 414 (calls cost 60p per minute) or you can visit their Travellers' Store at 3 Wellington Terrace, Turnpike Lane, London N8 0PX and 40 Bernard Street, London WC1N 1LJ.

The Centres for Disease Control (CDC) (**www.cdc.gov/travel/bluesheet.htm**) and the World Health Organisation (WHO) (**www.who.ch/programes/emc/news.ht**) have set up guidelines and health information for the international traveller.

MASTA Travel Health Centre (52 Margaret Street, London W1W 8SQ, Tel: 020 7291 9333, Website: **www.masta.org**) has up-to-date information on travellers' diseases.

The website **www.tripprep.com** is dedicated to travellers' health and has plenty of up-to-date information about tropical diseases and health risks.

For pre-travel information on any destination, and advice when you are away, visit **e-med.co.uk**. The online support service was created by Dr Jules Eden particularly for travellers who find themselves a long way from a doctor. He also answers queries about travel health in the Travel section of the *Guardian* every Saturday.

HOW MUCH DO THEY COST?

Of course getting these jabs can be expensive and according to a survey done by the Fleet Street Travel Clinic, one of the most common reasons people don't have them is due to the cost. But making sure you have the right jabs can be worth it for the extra peace of mind. Besides, if you are likely to travel often you can spread the cost over many trips. Some injections are available on the NHS – see your GP for more details – or you can see a travel medical expert. Typically people can spend £60–£100 for a full vaccination, although a single vaccination against yellow fever costs around £40. Some anti-malaria tablets are available from pharmacists without a prescription.

TIMING

If you do decide to stick to your GP, make sure you get the most up-to-date information from a travel medical expert or use an online travel clinic website. Travel medicine is constantly changing and your GP probably won't be as up to speed as a travel medical expert. It's also important to make sure you allow plenty of time for the vaccinations to take effect. The World Health Organisation advises that travellers start their arrangements four to six weeks before they leave. The immunisation process may take a few weeks, so it is important to allow your body time to adjust before you travel. Typically, a single vaccine takes two weeks to have the full effect. However, see your doctor even if you are going at short notice – some protection is usually better than none.

TRAVEL CLINICS

British Airways Travel Clinic provides vaccinations, up-to-date advice and travel healthcare products and has 28 regional clinics in the UK. Call 01276 685040 for the one nearest to you.

The Hospital for Tropical Diseases has a travel clinic and recorded message service which lists appropriate immunisations. Tel: 020 7388 9600. Calls cost 50p a minute. There is also a 24-hour malaria helpline running recorded messages. Tel: 0891 600 350. Calls cost 60p a minute.

Trailfinders also run a no-appointment-necessary immunisation clinic at 194 Kensington High Street, London W8 7RG, Tel: 020 7938 3999.

Fleet Street Clinic (29 Fleet Street, London EC4Y 1AA, Tel: 020 7353 5678) provides vaccinations and up-to-the-minute advice.

DISEASES YOU CAN'T IMMUNISE AGAINST

It's also important to be aware that there are plenty of infectious diseases that you can't immunise against. One of the worst risks is dengue fever, an insect-borne disease which has seen a recent massive outbreak in Rio, Brazil, Ecuador and the Galapagos.

Cholera is another disease you can't immunise yourself against. That said, there are oral vaccines for cholera licensed outside the UK, but these are generally not suitable and, according to Dr Dawood, should only be used if you are visiting a country that has a massive active cholera outbreak or working in a refugee camp in a disaster setting. Cholera outbreaks are rare, and spring up only in extremely dirty conditions, but there have been very recent cases in the Ivory Coast, and Burundi, Africa.

ANTI-MALARIA PILLS

Malaria is another example of a disease it is not possible to immunise yourself against. If you are visiting a malaria endemic area, take malaria pills (a prophylactic), which you can buy from a travel medical centre or free on the NHS. Chloroquine is the usual choice of treatment but there are stories of malaria parasites in some regions that are resistant to anti-malaria medicines. Malaria pills also have a history of side effects, particularly the latest high-tech drug mefloquine (Larium) which can cause sleep disturbances, nightmares and anxiety attacks. There was even a story in the newspapers recently where a gap-year traveller committed suicide and her parents blamed it partly on the effects of anti-malaria pills.

Julie Calvert has travelled extensively in Africa and, after suffering the side effects from taking prophylactics, decided to stop. 'I took Larium for eight months whilst in Africa and I would never take it again. It increases heart rate and causes mood swings, and I found it was far better to use repellent, carry Halofen in case I became infected, and cover up in the evenings.'

With bad press like this, the temptation might be to avoid taking the medication, especially if you are going to a big city and staying in expensive hotels. However, any travel experts insist you should. Malaria is a serious disease, potentially a killer, so it's extremely dangerous not to take drugs.

INSECT BITES

Since malaria is an insect-borne disease, the best defence is not to get bitten in the first place. Jason Gibbs of Nomad Travel Clinic in London says protecting yourself against insect bites can significantly reduce the risk of contracting many tropical diseases. He has the following advice:

- **Mosquitoes carry many other diseases such as Japanese B encephalitis so preventing insect bites with repellents and bed nets is a top priority.**

- **Use a fifty per cent Deet (diethyltoluamide)-based product to spray on exposed skin, or if you have sensitive skin, are a young child or pregnant use a citriodiol-based product instead. The best bed nets should be boxed-shaped as they allow you room to move around underneath and get changed, and should be impregnated with permethrin.**

- **You can also spray clothes with permethrin – it's not an insect repellent but the mosquitoes will get glued and burnt by the permethrin crystals.**

- **If you're in high risk areas, canoeing down the Amazon or trekking through the jungle, get the maximum protection by spraying your clothes with permethrin, using a 100% Deet-based solution on the extremities of your clothes (such as collars, cuffs, socks, ankles and hat) and the 50% Deet-based repellent sprayed on the skin. With all that piled on, you should be pretty well protected!**

- **You can also use burning coils, knock-down sprays, plug-ins (where there is a reliable electricity supply) and head nets which are useful for outdoors early evening cooking or fishing.**

- **It is also advisable to cover most of your body by wearing loose, baggy, long-sleeved shirts, trousers and socks.**

The UK Department of Health's free booklet *Health Advice for Travellers* includes a country-by-country checklist showing the medical services available and how they can be obtained. It also has an emergency health checklist on steps to take if you are seeking treatment abroad.

TRAVELLERS' STORIES

Simon Amos contracted malaria while he was in Borneo working as manager for Trekforce's conservation projects in the rainforest. He was travelling around the country, looking for projects to start, when he noticed he was feeling very lethargic. 'I'm normally a very energetic person, and get up about 6 a.m., so was concerned when I couldn't get out of bed in the morning. I also started to get very painful headaches which went on for some time and were accompanied by a mild fever. These symptoms went on for a few months, but I struggled on regardless. At first, the fever was so mild that I wasn't sure what was happening, but over six months the symptoms gradually got worse, until one night I had a fit and was taken into hospital.'

Simon had lost consciousness and gone into convulsions, his temperature reaching 48 degrees. At hospital, the doctors told him he had all the classic symptoms of malaria. 'They did a malaria test at first which came up negative, but then they did ultrasound on my spleen and found it had enlarged, which is a classic sign of malaria.'

Simon stayed in hospital for a week, where he was put on a treatment of antibiotics and quinine. 'The first two nights were very uncomfortable – I lost a stone and a half in a week, and couldn't stop being sick – but after a week, I recovered quickly and was soon back out in the jungle.'

Although Simon didn't take malaria pills ('I live in Borneo so I can't take malaria pills all the time'), he did take all the necessary precautions against being bitten, especially in the highly infected areas. 'I'm very aware of where the malaria pockets are and am usually very careful, using insect repellent and bed nets, but at the end of the day it only takes one little mosquito. The worrying thing is I'm not really cured yet – there's a chance I'll have a repeat attack and will have to seek more treatment.'

FOOD, WATER AND HYGIENE

Many other diseases can be easily avoided by following food and water precautions. The golden rule is 'peel it, boil it, cook it or forget it'.

FOOD PRECAUTIONS FOR TRAVEL TO HOT COUNTRIES

The following information has been compiled by Dr Richard Dawood.

Intestinal infections – especially travellers' diarrhoea – are very common in travellers to hot countries. The chances of being affected range from forty to eighty per cent. The main reasons are:

- **Rapid growth of bacteria and viruses at warm temperatures**
- **A generally increased risk from eating many meals in public hotels and restaurants**

- **Poor hygiene and an increased risk of contamination in poor countries**
- **A contaminated drinking water supply**

Almost all cases can be prevented by careful attention to food hygiene. Here's a quick guide to the kinds of foods that are most likely to be safe, and the foods that are best avoided:

USUALLY SAFE
- **freshly, thoroughly cooked food, served hot (i.e. heat sterilised)**
- **fruit easily peeled or sliced open without contamination (bananas, papayas)**
- **freshly baked bread**
- **packaged or canned food (take emergency supplies)**
- **bottled drinks opened in your presence – safest carbonated**
- **coconuts (usually contain 1pt sweet water)**
- **boiled water, tea**
- **if there's nothing safe on the menu, ask for chips, omelettes, or any dish that must be cooked to order**

USUALLY RISKY
- **shellfish/seafood (need eight minutes' vigorous boiling to be made safe)**
- **salad vegetables, unless thoroughly washed in clean water**
- **rare meat, raw fish**
- **buffets, food left out in warm temperatures**
- **food on which flies have settled**
- **food stored and reheated after cooking**
- **food requiring much handling – canapés**
- **spicy sauces, salsa, mayonnaise, left out on the table**
- **unpeelable fruit (berries, grapes)**
- **fruit peeled by others (fruit buffets)**
- **food handled with dirty fingers**
- **milk products, ice cream**
- **fruit juices from street vendors**
- **ice (in your drinks, but also in your butter dish, etc.)**
- **tap water – even for brushing teeth**
- **utensils are often contaminated: in Asia, disposable bamboo chopsticks are cheap, easily available, and ideal for travel**
- **hospitality: if food is not safe, refuse it**

TREATMENT OF TRAVELLERS' DIARRHOEA
Not all cases need treatment: most cases of travellers' diarrhoea improve on their own within 48 hours.

TREATMENT OPTIONS

The following treatments are available:

Oral rehydration Replacing lost fluid is one of the most important aspects of treatment, especially when fluid losses are made worse by a hot climate or exertion, and especially in children or elderly people. The best approach is to drink plenty of oral rehydration solution (for example, Electrolade, Dioralyte).

Anti-diarrhoeal medication The most effective and fast-acting drug is loperamide (Imodium, Arret); this does not treat the underlying infection, which usually clears up on its own. It should not be used for children; it is otherwise widely considered to be a safe drug; studies have shown that this drug does not prolong infection. The dosage is two capsules initially, followed by one with each loose stool.

Antibiotic treatment The most suitable choice should be discussed with your doctor, and there are advantages and disadvantages that need to be carefully considered, but ciprofloxacin is one possible option. The doctor who prescribes it should give detailed information about side effects and situations in which it should not be taken.

DECIDING WHICH TREATMENT TO USE

The following simple scheme is sometimes helpful:

Mild symptoms Unformed stools, increased frequency: no specific action necessary, consider loperamide (Imodium) if symptoms interfere with your travel plans and daily activities.

Moderate symptoms Watery stool, not causing undue distress: drink plenty, consider taking oral rehydration solution, consider taking loperamide (Imodium) to control symptoms, and consider taking a single dose of ciprofloxacin.

Severe symptoms Copious watery stools, with or without cramps: commence oral rehydration; consider a three-day course of ciprofloxacin.

A more detailed scheme to follow (including treatment of different types of dysentery) can be found in *Travellers' Health: How to Stay Healthy Abroad.*

WHEN TO SEEK MEDICAL ATTENTION

- **high fever (above 40°C)**
- **significant fever lasting longer than 48 hours**
- **diarrhoea lasting longer than four days**

- **severe diarrhoea with or without vomiting, with difficulty keeping up with fluid and salt replacement**
- **diarrhoea with blood**

All of these are symptoms that justify getting skilled advice and follow-up; laboratory tests may also be necessary.

WHAT HAPPENS IF YOU FALL SICK?

The first thing is to make sure you have good medical insurance. As detailed in Chapter Two, this is hugely important; as long as you have comprehensive medical cover, you should be protected. If you are following the advice on packing, you should also have brought a good medical kit, which should well equip you to deal with any emergencies. Don't neglect seeking professional help out of fear or a misplaced sense of pride. Take care of yourself. If you are in a foreign country, you could be exposed to all kinds of risks your body isn't used to.

If you have to see a doctor, be prepared for delays and complications: you are dealing with an unfamiliar health service and you may have to pay a great deal for what may seem, to you, like straightforward, minor treatments. To ease the process, make sure you have all the necessary documentation (such as passport, vaccination certificates, and so forth) and know exactly what your insurers cover you for.

WHAT TO TAKE WITH YOU

If you're outside Western Europe, North America and Australia/ New Zealand carry your own set of sterile equipment, which you can buy from most travel health clinics. This is essential in developing countries or those with a high risk of AIDS. If you already suffer from some medical condition, ensure you take enough of your regular medication with you to cover your whole trip. Make sure you know the brand name and chemical name of the drugs you are using, and check the availability in the country you are visiting. (See Chapter Two for advice on what your medical kit should contain.)

SEXUAL HEALTH

Whether you're clubbing in the Balearic Islands or sunning yourself in St Tropez, it's worth knowing that sexually transmitted diseases are on the rise. Chances are that sexually transmitted diseases (STDs) are more prevalent than you thought: according to figures from the World Health Organisation, there are approximately 333 million cases of STDs (excluding AIDS) worldwide each year, most affecting the fifteen to thirty age group. The highest global prevalences for syphilis, gonorrhoea and chlamydia are in South and South East Asia, and sub-Saharan Africa, but no matter where you are, it's still worth taking precautions. You might not be trekking through the African jungle, but unprotected sex still carries the same dangers.

Symptoms of having an STD are:

Discomfort or pain on passing urine
Unusual penile or vaginal discharge
Slight tingling at the tip of the penis
Genital sores, ulcers or warts
Genital and/or testicular pain
Unusual vaginal bleeding
Swollen lymph glands
Itching and/or rash on the body
Wart-like lumps around the anus
Fever
Pain during sex

SEXUAL HEALTH TIPS

See a doctor if you suspect you have an STD, don't try to treat it yourself

If you are on the pill, take enough to last you for the whole trip

Be careful who you sleep with! Take responsibility for using condoms yourself and don't rely on your partner to bring it up

When buying condoms, check the sell-by-date

If you are travelling in a hot climate, remember that extreme heat may rot the rubber in condoms, so buy them from air-conditioned shops and keep them in the fridge or the coolest part of your backpack

If you are a woman travelling in a traditional Muslim country and don't feel comfortable asking for condoms, take a large stock from home with you

Marie Stopes International (www.mariestopes.org.uk) has plenty of good information on sexual health including the availability of contraception and abortion across the world.

AIDS

AIDS is a global killer and, as there is not yet a vaccination against HIV, taking precautions has never been more important. According to the WHO, in 1999 alone there were an estimated 2.8 million HIV/AIDS-related deaths, and it is estimated to be growing all the time. Obviously the risk of contracting HIV is much more prevalent if you are travelling within the developing world – South Africa, Botswana, Namibia, Zimbabwe, Zambia and Malawi have the highest incidence of HIV in the world, with an estimated minimum of fifteen per cent of 15–49-year-olds being infected. But wherever you are, it is still wise to exercise vigilance and take the following precautions.

Don't
- Don't share a needle or syringe (including dentistry, tattooing, body piercing and acupuncture)
- Don't have unprotected sex with a new partner

Do
- Avoid contact with blood products
- Use condoms
- Carry your own sterile needle set if you are travelling in high-risk areas
- Exercise discrimination in who you choose to have sex with (remember that condoms are still not one hundred per cent protection against contracting HIV)

HOMEOPATHIC ALTERNATIVES

There are certain homeopathic remedies that you can use instead of vaccinations. Homeopathy works on the principle of 'like cures like', which basically means that a substance capable of causing certain symptoms in a person can be used to cure the same symptoms in a sick person. Certain homeopathic treatments, called nosodes, are prepared in great dilution from tissues infected with a particular bacterium or virus. These have been used in some cases to help prevent infection, for example cholera nosode. You can also take a homeopathic prophylactic system for malaria. For more information consult a homeopath. Contact the British Homeopathic Association, 15 Clerkenwell Close, London EC1R OAA, Tel: 020 7566 7800, Fax: 020 7566 7815, Website: **www.trusthomeopathy.org**.

The World Travellers' Manual of Homeopathy (C.W. Daniel Company Ltd) is full of interesting tips not just on homeopathy but other 'natural' remedies from eating garlic to ward off mosquitoes, to removing leeches with a dab of vinegar.

BEFORE YOU LEAVE CHECKLIST – HAVE YOU . . .

- Researched your country by looking at the relevant websites?

- If you're a UK citizen, obtained a copy of the Department of Health's free booklet *Health Advice for Travellers*?

- Found out your blood group? Unfortunately this is not so easy to find out in the UK so it might take some perseverance, or you might have to give blood in order to find out. It's not essential but it could be useful in an emergency.

- Visited your dentist? The last thing you want is to have tooth problems in a foreign country, so book an appointment well in advance and have all fillings, loose teeth or any other problems treated well before you leave.

- Visited your GP for a check-up and told him/her about your travel plans? Do this well in advance – two months, say – remember that you have to allow plenty of time for vaccinations to take effect.

- Got all the necessary medication and equipment (see Packing for what to take with you)?

STEPS FOR SAFE TRAVELLING

- Educate yourself about the health risks in the country you are visiting.

- Immunise yourself against the diseases found in that country.

- Allow plenty of time for the vaccine to take effect. The World Health Organisation advises that travellers start their arrangements four to six weeks before they leave.

- Avoid tap water – boil it or use bottled water from a sealed container for drinking, brushing teeth, or washing food. Don't take ice in drinks.

- Eat mainly cooked food. Check that food has been thoroughly heated through.

- Guard against insect bites. Use a fifty per cent Deet (diethyltoluamide)-based mosquito repellent to spray on exposed skin (or a citriodiol-based product if you have sensitive skin or are pregnant). The best mosquito nets should be box-shaped and impregnated with permethrin. Make sure they are well tucked in and have no tears.

- Even if you intend to stay in the big cities and live in the lap of luxury, don't assume that you are not at risk of contracting a tropical disease in an endemic country.

- Keep it in perspective. Take care, but try not to worry so much you forget to enjoy your trip.

SAFETY

No matter how adventurous you are, there are still certain places in the world which are off limits, no-go areas. Travelling through certain countries in Africa, for example, is ill-advised for even the hardiest and most experienced of travellers. Unless you happen to be Kate Adie, never ever travel in a war zone. No matter how seasoned a traveller you consider yourself, remember that there are certain places which are just not a good idea.

Before you go, research your country and check to see how safe it is. Don't just rely on what you read in the newspapers and books, but go to the best sources of up-to-date information.

The Foreign and Commonwealth Office's website **www.fco.gov.uk** (click on Travel) carries comprehensive advice on which countries to avoid. It also has a travel advice number you can ring on 020 7008 0232.

Americans can contact the US State Department Travel Advisory Service on 202 647 5225 or go to **www.travel.state.gov** for more information.

Most other governments have websites which carry advice on travelling and international trouble spots, and travellers' websites and chat rooms can also be a good source of information. Wherever you go, make sure you have left contacts and details of your itinerary with your relatives and friends.

INTERNATIONAL TROUBLE SPOTS

At the time of writing, the UK's Foreign and Commonwealth Office's website (August 2002) advises not travelling to the following countries. However, bear in mind that these are always changing so make sure your information is up-to-date.

Afghanistan (western and southern districts of Kabul City and the remainder of the country)

Albania (north east border areas between Albania and Kosovo only)

Azerbaijan (western region of Nagorno-Karabakh and the militarily occupied area surrounding it)

Burundi

Central African Republic

Colombia (Choco, Putumayo, Meta and Caqueta provinces and to rural areas of Antioquia, Cauca, Narino and Norte de Santander provinces)

Congo (outside Brazzaville and Pointe Noire)

Ecuador (northern border areas with Colombia, particularly Sucumbios and Orellana provinces)

Eritrea (border areas with Ethiopia)

Ethiopia (border areas of Tigray and Afar only)

Guinea (border region with Liberia and Sierra Leone only)

India (Jammu and Kashmir, apart from travel to Ladakh via Manali or by air to Leh. Along the India/Pakistan border, the areas of Gujarat, Rajasthan and Punjab close to the border, and areas of Ladakh close to the Line of Control)

Indonesia

Iraq

Israel and the Occupied Territories (only West Bank, Gaza, Israel/ Lebanon and Israel/ Gaza border areas)

Kyrgyzstan (south and west of Osh and the Ferghana Valley region only)

Liberia

Namibia (immediate border areas with Angola only)

Nigeria (Bakassi peninsula only)

Philippines (Zamboanga peninsula and islands south west of Mindanao only)

Russian Federation (Chechen Republic and north Caucasus region only)

Somalia (southern Somalia, the north-eastern area (Puntland), Sool and Sanaag regions only)

Sri Lanka (north and east (except Trincomalee and Nilaveli) only)

Sudan (Juba only)

Tajikistan (travel in the mountains and valleys in central Tajikistan, especially the Karategin valley, the roads leading east from Dushanbe to those areas, and all mountainous areas bordering Kyrgyzstan and Uzbekistan)

Uganda (Gulu (including Murchison Falls National Park), Kitgum, Adjumani, Apac and Lira districts, Karamoja (Kotido, Moroto and Nakapiripiri districts), Katakwi district and Bundibugyo district in the west including Semliki National Park – not the Semliki Game Reserve)

Venezuela (border areas, especially with Colombia)

For the following countries, it advises essential business-only travel:

Afghanistan Kabul City (apart from southern and western districts where all travel is advised against)

Algeria

Angola

Azerbaijan (Zagatala area only)

Congo (Brazzaville and Pointe Noire only)

Congo (Democratic Republic)

Democratic Republic of East Timor

Ecuador (San Vicente only)

Towns along the river Elbe in Brandenburg and West Mecklenburg

Germany (Dresden and Grimme (Saxony)

Dessau, Halle and Bitterfeld (Saxony Anhalt)

Haiti

Moldova (Trandniestria (north-east Moldova))

Pakistan

Philippines (areas of Mindanao south or west of Davoa City only)

Rwanda (rural areas in Cyangugu and Gikongoro provinces including the Nyungwe forest only)

Sierra Leone

Solomon Islands (rural Guadalcanal and the island of Malaita)

Sudan (southern Sudan, except for those engaged in essential relief work)

Tajikistan

Yugoslavia (Federal Republic of) (Kosovo only)

CRIME

Travelling to a foreign country is obviously going to put you at an increased risk of falling victim to crime. It's not surprising why – not only are you landing in a foreign country where you may not understand the language or the local culture, but you could also be jetlagged, lost and disorientated. In these conditions, the most street-wise among us might be taken in by the odd dodgy taxi driver or stranger. However, while it's important to take what precautions you can, it's also important not to exaggerate the dangers and hold yourself back from making the most out of your trip. Above all, try not to develop a Johnny Foreigner mentality and see every kind stranger as a threat.

KEEPING SAFE

- **Keep photocopies of important documents in a separate place from the originals.**

- **Carry money and important documents in a money belt under your clothes.**

- **Never fight someone if you are being mugged. Your rucksack, traveller's cheques, wallet etc. may be important to you, but they're definitely not worth sacrificing your life for.**

- **Carry a decoy wallet with a small amount in, say $10, enough to be credible. In the event of being mugged, hand over this wallet instead.**

- **Observe the ways of the natives and try to blend in. The less you look like a tourist, the less your chances of being mugged/harassed/followed etc.**

- **Do what you can to increase your security, but not to the point where it spoils your trip.**

- **Take your own safety locks and lock your hotel door at night. You can also use it on your backpack and secure it to a rack on overnight trains.**

- **Never leave important documents and valuables in hotels or hostels.**

- **Keep a small amount of money separate from your everyday money in case of robbery, so you have cash to use in an emergency.**

- **Avoid wearing or carrying expensive-looking clothes or items such as jewellery, watches or cameras etc.**

- **Be wary of accepting food and drink from strangers, especially on trains. It's not unknown for thieves to drug food and drink and once you are asleep, make off with your things.**

WOMEN TRAVELLING ALONE

Some nationalities confuse the sexually liberated western women with promiscuous, immoral jezebels, so be very aware of the kind of messages you send out. In India, Pakistan and Indonesia, for example, smiling and making eye contact with men can be misinterpreted as a distinct come-on. Two friends of mine were staying in a hostel in Bangalore, India, when they were woken up at 3 a.m. by a porter asking to use their toilet. When they let him, he told them he wanted to go to bed with them both and pulled down his trousers. It turned out he'd mistaken their friendliness for a come-on. Eventually, they managed to get rid of him.

- Carry enough cash on you at all times so you can take a taxi if you feel someone is bothering you.

- If you arrive late at night, either book a pre-paid taxi, or make sure the taxi is licensed by the airport.

- Observe the way local women dress – if it's appropriate, cover yourself up. In Muslim countries, you should cover your shoulders and head. You'll feel less conspicuous and won't draw unwanted attention to yourself.

- Take a sarong – they're easy to pack and you can adapt them for any occasion. They're also pretty handy to have on the beach.

- Some women travellers wear a fake wedding ring to ward off unwanted attention. You can even take a picture of 'hubby' (real or imagined) if you think it might add credibility.

- Plan your routes in advance – that way you don't have to rely on asking directions or drawing unnecessary attention to yourself.

- Hold your head up high and walk confidently. Even if you are lost, try to look as if you know where you are going. That way, you won't appear vulnerable.

- Always lock the hotel/ hostel doors and windows at night. You can make things doubly secure by taking your own padlock.

- If you are travelling on public transport at night, try to sit near the driver.

- Join up with other women travellers, if you want, but don't feel that just because you're on your own, you have to surround yourself with other people.

- Keep your folks back home up to date about your whereabouts. Phone/ email regularly and leave a contact address and details of where you are staying.

- **Be aware at all times but don't let it spoil your trip.**

TRAVELLERS' STORIES

Jilly Coombes caught a taxi from the train station in Mumbai, India, at 11.20 p.m. to take her to the airport for her 6 a.m. flight. Instead of taking her there, however, the taxi driver and his friend insisted on driving her around the streets and demanding more money from her. When she said she didn't have enough, they then said they would take her home to their place and 'show her a good time'. The two men drove her around for five hours, taunting her and demanding sexual favours, until they took all her money and dropped her off at the airport at 4.20 a.m.

Once the taxi drove away, Jilly realised they had taken her suede jacket. 'I couldn't believe it had happened,' she said. 'Most of the Indian people I met were so kind and so giving, it was a shock to leave on such a bad note.'

WHAT HAPPENS IF YOU HAVE TROUBLE?

If you're one of the unlucky ones who has trouble no matter what precautions you take, the first thing to do is contact your relatives and friends at home. You may also want to use the Consul, which is usually a part of the Embassy or High Commission in most countries and is there to help you if you need emergency help overseas. There are also smaller Consulate Offices in cities and towns: before you travel, compile a list of consular addresses in the country you are visiting. If you are British and there is no British consulate where you are, you can use the consulate or embassy of any other EU member state. Remember too, that under UK law, British consulates charge for their services. The Foreign and Commonwealth Office's website has more information on fees.

Here is a list of what a UK consulate can and cannot do for you. Most other consulates will offer the same support, but make sure you check before travelling.

A British consulate can:

- **issue emergency passports**
- **contact relatives and friends and ask them to help with money and tickets**
- **advise on how to transfer funds**
- **at most posts (in an emergency) advance money against a sterling cheque for £50 supported by a bankers card**
- **as a last resort, provided strict criteria are met, make a repayable loan for repatriation to the UK**
- **provide a list of local lawyers, interpretators and doctors**

- **arrange for a next of kin to be informed of a death or accident and advise on procedures**

- **contact British nationals who are arrested or in prison and, in certain circumstances, arrange for messages to be given to relatives or friends**

- **give guidance on organisations experienced in tracing missing persons**

A British consulate cannot:

- **pay your hotel, medical or other bills**

- **pay for your travel tickets except in very special circumstances**

- **undertake work usually done by travel representatives, airlines or motoring organisations**

- **get better treatment for you in hospital or prison than is provided by local nationals**

- **give legal advice, instigate court proceedings on your behalf or interfere in local court procedures to get you out of prison**

- **investigate a crime**

- **formally assist dual nationals in a country of their second nationality**

- **obtain a work permit for you**

DANGEROUS ANIMALS

If you're intending to trek through the jungle or go out on safari, there are some words of advice to heed. Make sure you trek with the guides: most of them have picked up their gems of wisdom through years of experience, such as the warden of a tiger conservation park who advises, 'Never run from a tiger. Instead stand and wave your arms and make lots of noise.' If you are sleeping in the jungle, make sure your tent is zipped up and light fires and lanterns at night. Never walk without your shoes in Asia, Africa and South America where poisonous snakes can bite your bare feet, and if you do meet a snake, don't try to attack it – you'll only succeed in inciting its rage. If you do get bitten, keep your limbs still so the poison will take longer to spread through your body, and immediately send someone to get help.

5 CULTURE SHOCK

YOUR FIRST NIGHT

Finding yourself suddenly in the middle of an alien country can be a strange and bewildering experience. Even if you consider yourself to be Mr or Ms Traveller of the Year, with an effortless knack of wooing the locals and somehow making everything turn out just right, it's still a good idea to pile on the preparation for one of the most crucial times: your first day. Or more importantly, your first night. Because, believe me, there's nothing quite like landing in a foreign country at two o'clock in the morning to find your rucksack's too bulky to carry, the hostel's cancelled your booking for some strange reason you can't understand as you still haven't quite got to grips with the language, your guide book's ten years out of date, and you haven't enough cash to take a taxi to find somewhere else to stay, to cast a cloud over the rest of the proceedings. Of course, bad first days happen and people get over them. Bad first weeks happen, bad first months even, and if things do start like that, it's certainly not the end of the world. But it's far, far better to get off to a good start and do a little planning first.

Of course some people think that too much planning can spoil the adventure of travelling. As one traveller said to me, 'There's a certain amount of randomness that's part of the whole trip. You've just got to go with what happens. I've had some terrible times. I've had to sleep rough, on train platforms, you name it, but I wouldn't change it. You just take it in your stride when things don't go to plan.'

That's all well and good, but remember there are certain places and circumstances where it's just not advisable to leave it to fate. Shastra spent her first night in Delhi being duped by taxi drivers in one of the most common scams in Asia.

I arrived in Delhi airport at 1.30 a.m., and immediately tried to find a taxi to take me to a friend's house where I was supposed to be staying. There was hardly anyone around, but eventually I managed to find a taxi driver waiting outside the airport. I gave him my friend's address and climbed in the car. Then another man got in. We'd been driving for five minutes when suddenly the taxi driver said the roads were blocked because of an election. I thought this was a bit odd because I'd spoken to my friend and she hadn't mentioned any election, so I asked him to take me back to the airport where I could phone my friend and ask her to pick me up instead. But the taxi driver said, 'No, why don't we take you to a tourist office instead and you can phone your friend from there?' I was so tired I just went along with it.

Once they arrived at the tourist office, a man behind the desk insisted on dialling Shastra's friend's number. He then passed her the receiver but she didn't recognise the voice. 'The man said he was my friend's uncle but I'd never heard her mention him. He said that she had gone away for a few days and wouldn't be back that night.'

Shastra was starting to get worried and, when the tourist man offered her a hotel for an outrageous price of US$50 a night, she nearly turned it down. However, she was feeling so tired and disorientated, she reluctantly agreed.

Eventually, they drove me to this seedy-looking hotel on the outskirts of Delhi. I didn't know where I was but I was so tired that when the receptionist took me up to the room I just followed. Once I stepped inside, I heard them bolt the door behind me. I tried the door but I couldn't get out. Then I noticed there was a telephone in the room so I picked it up and tried to dial my friend's number. Just at that moment, someone knocked on the door and asked me for money, 100 rupees. I said no, and eventually the man went away. By this time I was feeling really scared and started to cry. I cried for about half an hour, and then I decided to pull myself together, so had a shower and afterwards, started to pack.

I can't remember falling sleep, but in the morning, I was woken up by the telephone. It was the man from reception. He said, 'Would you like to go somewhere hot? I'll book you a ticket if you want.' I said, 'Yes,' and the next thing, a man came in my room and offered me breakfast for 200 rupees. Just as he came in, I managed to grab my bag and ran out before he could bolt the door again. I went downstairs to reception where there was an Australian couple waiting, and asked to phone my friend. Again, the receptionist insisted on dialling the number and when he handed me the phone, another complete stranger answered. Just at that moment, another man came in and said he'd come to take me to Mumbai, and led me out to a taxi. We'd been driving for a few minutes when I told the man to take me to the airport. He said he'd had strict instructions to drive around in circles and then take me back to the hotel. Just at that moment, the taxi stopped, so I jumped out of the door and ran over to another taxi parked across the street. Luckily, this taxi took me to my friend's house.

Shastra's friends were so horrified to hear of her ordeal, they contacted the *Hindu Times*, who decided to print the story. A couple of days later, Shastra's story and her picture were on the front page. The story was read by a Chief Inspector who sent the police round to interview her, and eventually took her back to the airport. Shastra managed to identify the two taxi drivers, the tourist officer who had made the bogus calls and took them to the hotel. She says, 'It was like being in a film. It turned out the whole thing was an elaborate money-making scam involving twelve taxi drivers, three hotels and one travel agent. Some good did come out of it, however. When I got back to Sydney, I sold my story for A$1,000 to Australian *Woman's Weekly*.'

Compare that with this.

At eight o'clock the aeroplane breezed into San Paolo airport, curled majestically in the slowly darkening night sky, and, with a gentle bump, touched down gracefully on the runway. Before long, we were skipping through customs and climbing into a taxi that was waiting, as if by magic, outside. With the almost perfect Portuguese we had picked up at night school, we gaily laughed and bantered with the taxi driver who not only understood exactly which hostel we wanted to get to, but also told us of well paid work he knew was going in a local bar. As we cruised through the glimmering neon lights of the city, he told us in great detail about all the places we must visit and how to make the most out of our stay. By the time we arrived at the hostel, we had already got the phone number of this bar and several other local bars and restaurants of friends he knew were looking to employ English speakers. And to make things even better, the hostel we had booked our two first nights in and phoned up to check before, was expecting us with keys to our room. And because we had packed our day bags and backpacks so well and efficiently, we had all the necessary documentation at hand. Within moments, we were tumbling into warm pressed sheets, and dreamily looking forward to the next day and following up on the contacts we had made.

PLAN IN ADVANCE

Of course, if things do run as smoothly as this, you'll definitely be in the minority. And with the best will in the world, no matter how much you organise, there are certain things that are totally out of your control. The plane might be delayed, the hostel might forget your booking . . . but you can still do what you can to look after the little things you can control. Like what?

Like, use a little foresight. Airports can be bewildering places, even at home, but especially in a totally alien part of the world where you can't even read the alphabet, let alone decipher the signs. There could also be an awful lot of touts circling you at the airport when you arrive, promising to find you a bed for the night. It's hardly surprising – with that huge rucksack on your back, your Western attire, and your general air of benign confusion, you're probably screaming 'tourist' in big flashing lights to every native within five miles. So the first rule is: book somewhere to stay for your first night, and try to get there at a reasonable time. Otherwise you'll be at the mercy of every dodgy tout in Shanghai, Buenos Aires or Marrakech, or wherever it is you've landed.

If you do book a hostel, try to phone and confirm the booking a few days before you leave. It's amazing how easily bookings can be forgotten or cancelled because of so-called dodgy credit cards. Another good ploy is to make sure you find a hostel in an area where there are plenty of others nearby. That way, if things do go wrong, you should be able to find somewhere else more easily.

What other steps can you take? Make sure you have all the necessary documentation easily at hand. Keep passports, traveller's cheques and airline tickets in your money belt. Get a map of the city before you arrive. Make sure you know at least a little of the language to ask for directions and navigate a taxi to where you want to go. If you know of any local contacts, ask them to put you up for your first few nights, or at least meet up on one of your first days for a basic orientation course. The important thing is to think ahead and try to imagine the things that could possibly go wrong, and do your best to avoid them. Personally, I'd book the first few nights in a hostel close to the station and airport, and take a good pair of earplugs. There's nothing like the roar of a foreign city (traffic, neighbours, late night TV, early morning revellers) to bring on a bout of insomnia, and the last thing I'd want is to start my trip off on zero hours' sleep.

COMFORT FOOD

This might not go down well with all you seasoned travellers out there, in search of the authentic experience, but comfort food can go a long way in easing the transition. I'll never forget seeing an episode of *Floyd on TV* and watching the TV chef Keith Floyd pounce on an English supermarket in Asia, as if he'd discovered the Holy Grail. The look on his face when buying a tin of Heinz spaghetti hoops and Hellmann's sandwich spread was a joy to behold. You may scoff now, but taking the odd jar of Marmite or, for those of you Stateside, a packet of Oreos, could be that much-needed pick-you-up when you're feeling down. What can be nicer than a peanut butter sandwich when you're 6,000 miles from home and lying in a strange hostel in Bangkok suffering from homesickness?

Jo Rea in Madrid says, 'We're all still suffering from the closure of Marks and Spencer which has affected us terribly – we're back to food parcels containing tea bags and other British culinary delights to keep us going!'

Meanwhile, Frank Baker from Beijing says that as much as he loves living in China, there are still times when he craves home foods. 'I wish I'd consulted with people who have been here before. There are so many little things we take for granted in the UK that may not be stocked in Chinese supermarkets: good wine, decent margarine, marmalade, English tea and so on.'

Of course culture shock can kick in even in the most unexpected places. Cathy Merry spent a year in Thousand Oaks, California working in a lab as part of her biochemistry Year in Industry degree course at Manchester University. She says,

Culture shock can be even more intense for Brits precisely because it is English-speaking. This might be because you more fully immerse yourself in the culture so differences seem more striking, or it could just be because you expect it to be the same. Whatever the reason, there were some things that took a bit of getting used to. There is a very strong work ethic in the US and people are used to working very long hours. In the labs, for example, it's very common to work a twelve-hour day. If you weren't the kind of person who working hard comes easily to, you'd find it hard to adjust. I took ten days off for Christmas to go back to the UK and my employers were very disapproving.

Another thing I found difficult was that people weren't very friendly because of the age gap. I was a lot younger than my colleagues who all had families and lived out of the city, and the fact that I was under 21 meant that I couldn't go out to the bars in the evening and socialise with my colleagues. California is particularly strict about enforcing its under-age drinking laws and you have to have a driving licence showing you are over 21 to even get in the door, so I couldn't even drink squash.

SET YOUR INTENTIONS

The best approach to getting your trip off to a good start is to set your intentions with clarity. What kind of trip are you looking for? What steps can you take to make that happen? There's a world of difference between ploughing the rice fields of Japan and sleeping on titami every night in the Japanese-speaking only youth hostel, than kipping en masse on Rhodes beach, as by day you trawl the nightclubs for bar work. In short, the choices you make are ultimately going to reflect what kind of experiences you attract. You may want to drift with circumstances and flow with whatever opportunities arise, but a firm (and not inflexible) agenda can considerably ease any culture shock problems you may initially have.

MEETING PEOPLE

According to Angela Haddow, one of the most important things in her trip to Australia was making the effort to speak to people and build contacts. It was through her network of fellow travellers that she managed to get work, find accommodation, research the local area and generally find her way around. Not only that but she also made some great friends who she is still in touch with now.

If you're the shy, reclusive type, it's good to remember that the more outgoing you are, and the more you make an effort to chat to other people, the more likely you are to pick up the right information. Remember, opportunities come through other people. If you spend every night sitting in on your own, chances are that's where you'll stay. Inside. On your own. Besides, you've just travelled 10,000 miles maybe to the other side of the world, and presumably spent a lot of money getting there: why waste that by talking to the same people you could see down the pub at home?

So why go out of your way to speak to other people? For one thing it will put you in touch with the fastest information superhighway known to human beings. Talk. Chat. Gossip. If you've just landed in the middle of an alien country you've never been to before, perhaps on your own and perhaps looking for work, you're going to need a whole lot of information to help you survive. And the best way to get information? Other people. Fellow travellers and natives alike can tell you about the latest scams, the best way to find work, the cheapest places to stay, the tastiest eateries, the best deals, what bosses to look out for, which harvest fields are looking for workers, how to buy a car, place an ad, the best diving courses, the most remote and beautiful beaches and so on. You get the idea.

However, in order to meet people, you have to seek out the places where like-minded people might gravitate. If you are in a city this shouldn't be too difficult. If you fancy networking with fellow travellers, many cities have thriving expat communities and local districts where non-natives hang out. Remember that even if you don't like the expat scene, they can still be a good source of local information. If you have a particular hobby or interest, see if you can find a local club or group – walking, cycling, running, alternative therapies, yoga, music and so on. Keep an eye on local ads in newspapers and shop windows and take regular trips to the local English language bookshop where the notice board might throw up plenty of ideas. Libraries and universities are also worth checking out. Bear in mind, too, that where you choose to live can have a huge bearing on the ease with which you meet people. Staying in hostels is notoriously good for meeting fellow travellers and staff can be a veritable goldmine of local information.

CHANCE

Never underestimate the value of chance, that mysterious chain of events whereby meeting one person on the street can put you in touch with someone who has a spare room, who lives next door to someone who is looking for someone to work in the kitchens of a local hotel. John Starkie was down to his last ten Francs in Paris when he met Jean Marie, who offered him work on his uncle's apple farm in Tours. He spent three and a half months picking apples. 'That's the thing about travelling, you never know what's going to turn up and you've just got to go with the flow and take what opportunities arise.'

Give things the opportunity to happen by getting out and speaking to people. Remember that the contacts you make aren't just a bunch of new friends you can go out and get drunk with – they're also your support system.

GETTING AROUND

Unless your working abroad stint is part of a career move, the chances are that the whole point of your journey is seeing a bit of the country. Getting around can be an expensive business, so here are a few tips on how to get around as cheaply as possible:

- **Get a discount rail pass. Most national rail companies offer a discount pass for foreign travellers which you can buy from your home country before you leave. These last for a set time – usually a month – and if you intend to do a lot of travelling, can be a good investment. The Inter-Rail ticket offers one month unlimited travel throughout Europe and can be a convenient way to get around if you intend to do casual work such as fruit picking throughout Europe. Rail passes can be expensive, however, so make sure you are going to make the most of them.**

- **Travel by rail at off-peak times – peak commuter times can be sometimes double the price so enquire about the range of prices and times. Also, watch out for fast express trains – you may be able to save yourself a lot of expense by taking a local train scheduled for more stops. Always ask if there are other alternatives.**

- **Buy your own car – this is particularly common in Australia, where many travellers shell out on a cheap, second-hand car to take them on their travels and then sell it when they arrive at the destination. This can work out cheaper than paying for long flights or rail trips, particularly if you are travelling with another person. Make sure the car you buy is in good working order: Ian Maidens and his friend spent £2,500 on a VW Camper van but, when they were travelling through the desert, the engine seized up and they were left stranded 150 miles from the nearest garage.**

- **Couriering: one way of getting low-cost travel is by arranging to deliver a package for a company. One drawback, however, is that you may not be able to take much in the way of luggage, in addition to what you are couriering. Always go through an established, reputable company and make sure you have a follow-up address. It goes without saying, never accept to courier for an individual or you might be arrested for smuggling. You can find air courier work by looking in the Yellow Pages. Contact them at least fourteen days before you hope to travel. (See Working a Passage section.)**

- **Car delivery: this is quite common in the USA and is known as 'drive-away'. Make sure you take your International Driver's Licence. (See the USA section for more information.)**

- **Yacht delivery: experienced sailors may be able to find work delivering yachts, which can be fixed up through yacht delivery** companies. Look in the Yellow Pages for addresses, or else try Reliant Yachts. (See Working A Passage chapter for more information.)

- **Advertise for lifts in the local newspapers' classified sections, under 'Lifts Wanted'. You can hook up with someone who is travelling the same way, although you may be expected to make a contribution towards petrol costs.**

- **Buy return tickets instead of singles.**

HITCHHIKING

By far the cheapest way to travel, however, is hitchhiking and not only that, it can be a great way to see a country. It also comes with some brilliant stories to tell, and can put you in touch with some helpful and friendly locals. Bear in mind that in some countries it is illegal to hitch a lift standing on a public road so head for the service stations. Stand in a visible place and write your destination on a card so your driver can see it.

Of course, most of the time, hitchhiking is enjoyable and safe, but there are some countries, such as the US, where hitchhiking is not really understood, and can be downright dangerous. It's not really advisable for solo women travellers, and bear in mind that by hitching a free ride, you are at the mercy of the whims and timetable of somebody else. This, of course, is part of its charm, but it can also throw up a few surprises, and not all of them welcome. In the course of one week's hitchhiking through Europe, my friend and I: spent one night trying to get to sleep (unsuccessfully) in a lorry driver's bunk, as he snored on the passenger seat beside us; spent three hours waiting for another French lorry driver to finish his five-course meal complete with copious wine and aperitif, and, evidently inebriated, then climb into the lorry and carry on driving; were flashed at and forced to look at pornographic magazines by another driver (scary stuff); and, by someone else, were left stranded in a service station at three o'clock in the morning. Of course, we also met plenty of nice, friendly people, and even the bad times were part of the whole experience. But oh, how we laughed.

John Starkie has this story to tell about his experiences hitchhiking in America:

We were crossing the border between the USA and Canada and were stopped by customs. Unbeknown to us, the driver had drugs in the car, and soon the custom officials were taking the car to pieces in front of our eyes, trying to find more drugs. We were also under suspicion, and everything in our bags was tested, including paracetamols and antiseptics. We were questioned, strip-searched with no gloves and kept there for seventeen hours. Luckily, the driver insisted we knew nothing about it and eventually they released us.

WHERE TO STAY

Choosing the right kind of accommodation can have a huge influence on the type of people you meet. Sometimes the decision will have already been made for you – if you fixed up work before you arrived, accommodation may also be thrown in. Depending on what you do, this can cover a multitude of sins and can vary hugely in quality, so if you're losing some of your wage to pay for the accommodation, make sure it's worth what your employer charges. You may strike lucky and end up like Jen Beckett, shacked up in a luxurious Sydney apartment thrown in for free with her job of managing an ice cream store. On the opposite end of the scale, you may find yourself sharing a cold, grey, cramped room with a total stranger. Voluntary work in developing countries can introduce you to some testing conditions where you may find yourself without electricity or running water.

For the rest of you, you'll be thrown into the fray and have to set about organising this yourself. As the beginning of this chapter emphasises, one of the biggest favours you can do for yourself is to book accommodation for your first few nights. As previously explained, this can relieve the pressure considerably. From thereon, it's a case of finding the best you can afford. Obviously, the cost of accommodation varies from country to country, but depending on your budget you could be looking at:

- **Hostels**
- **Camping**
- **Private apartments**
- **Hotels/ guest houses**

As always, you're encouraged to do your research before you leave and get an approximate idea of how much a week's accommodation will cost in your target destination. If you intend to travel around and pick up casual harvest work, it's worth taking camping equipment. Also bear in mind the sometimes complex residence regulations, where in order to rent an apartment you may have to register as a resident and provide certain documentation. Again, make sure you have read up on this before you arrive and have all the necessary documents with you.

Many travellers begin their trip staying in cheap hostels, and from there on, rent out an apartment with people they meet. Always inspect the property before signing anything and ask your landlord about any extra charges such as heating, water and maintenance.

Youth hostels are well known as a good way of meeting people and are usually reasonably priced. These are an excellent place to find your feet and secure a good base, although you will probably only be able to stay for a certain period. Take out membership of the International Youth Hostel Association, which has youth hostels all over the world. Many countries also have private hostels, which vary in quality. Ask at the tourist office or university campus when you arrive – you may have to book a bed in advance, particularly mid-season.

Another option is university and polytechnic accommodation, which can be cheap and cheerful, and is often not just available to students. Contact the local university before you arrive and ask if they have any rooms or flats to rent out.

STAYING IN TOUCH

We've all done it: made grand promises to send X amount of letters a month and make regular phone calls, only to arrive and forget everything we said. When I was sixteen I once sat down and diligently wrote my address on a whole pack of air mail envelopes to my first love so he could write to me from America. Suffice it to say, those envelopes never came back (nor did he, but that's another story). It's the most natural thing in the world: you're 5,000 miles from home, mixing with an international entourage and doing exciting things you'd never even dreamed about before. Write home? Send emails? Stay in touch? You've got one hundred billion better things to do! What do these people expect, for goodness sake?

The short answer is that some people, notably your parents, would really like to know you're safe. They might not be expecting the next Michael Palin travelogue, but the odd word every few weeks just to say, I'm fine, I'm safe, I haven't been killed/maimed/eaten by lions/abducted by aliens would probably set their minds at rest. Just think of that sixteen-year-old girl waiting at home for all those envelopes. Then think of your mum. Enough said.

Besides, in these enlightened days of technology, there's really no excuse. Even if you're trekking through the Ecuadorian jungle or studying biodiversity in Greenland, the chances are you'll stumble upon a cybercafe or a telephone booth. Well, kind of. The point is it has never been easier to stay in touch. Here are some things to think about:

- **Before you leave, try to come to some realistic agreement with your parents and loved ones about how often you'll be in touch. Don't make grand promises to send a letter every two weeks or a phone call every week if you don't intend to stick to it. You'll only worry people if they're expecting to hear from you every week and you leave it three months before contacting them again.**

- **Hand your parents and loved ones a copy of your itinerary before you leave so they have a basic idea of your whereabouts. If possible, include fax numbers for work and hotels, as well as flight details (times, airports as well as carrier and flight numbers).**

- **If there's a national tragedy which your loved ones are likely to hear about back home, make a point of phoning them asap just to let them**

know you're OK. You might know you're 150 miles from the Kashmir border and everything is safe and well, but your parents back in Romford might not realise that.

UNUSUAL WAYS TO STAY IN TOUCH

Many cybercafes now allow you to feed in images from a digital camera and create your own web postcard. Alternatively, if you have a digital camera, just send over your photographs by email.

Find out where one of the thousands of webcams nearest to you is and arrange with a friend a time when they can see you on the webcam.

Make your own audio diary or letter to send back home, by taking a small dictaphone. Sounds can be an evocative and sensory way to describe your journeys – a street market in Morocco, the roar of the Niagara Falls, or a classroom of Chinese children sending a greeting in Mandarin.

Ask your family or friends to send you the odd parcel of comfort food or treats from back home. I never forget seeing the faces of two American men who had been on the road for six months when they received a parcel from home containing some Oreo cookies and other goodies. Sheer bliss.

WAYS TO STAY IN TOUCH

EMAIL

Email is one of the easiest and cheapest ways of staying in touch. Most cities and towns have cybercafes (to find out the addresses of cybercafes around the world go to **www.cybercafes.com**) and at the click of a mouse your great missive is winging its way through virtual space ready for your loved one to read. The wonders of modern technology! It's simply never been easier – you can set up free email accounts through Hotmail and Yahoo, which you can access anywhere. Even if I was sitting in a cybercafe in Hong Kong I could still check my Yahoo mail which I access every day in London. This doesn't work for all email accounts, however, so make sure it can be accessed from any computer system first. You should be able to access it through the web page of your internet service provider, but it's still a good idea to set up a Hotmail account just in case.

TELEPHONE

There's nothing like hearing a well-loved familiar voice when you are thousands of miles from home and feeling a little frayed round the edges. Some public telephones accept credit cards although the instructions may not be in English which can mean precious time and even money wasted fumbling around. You can also phone from post offices or telephone offices: these tend to have less background noise and can be easier to use. Many telephone offices allow you to make reverse-charge calls or have a Home Country Direct Facility, where you call the operator in your home country and then use a credit card or reverse-charge call.

Telephone charge cards are very convenient when travelling as they are much more convenient than stuffing coins into the phone or worrying about local currency. Basically, they enable you to bill the cost of a call to a pre-existing telephone number (your home number or parents') and are available through most telephone companies. BT does a chargecard but it is inevitably quite expensive. A cheaper option is the international pre-paid phonecard: these are generally cheaper than making a normal international call. Generally, you apply for a card (try One-Tel, Planet Talk, Alpha Telecom) and by paying up-front credit (say £20), you're given a PIN or access number to use when you make a call. Be aware that the rates can vary depending on which country you make the call from, and make sure the system works in the countries you intend to visit.

FAX

Faxes are another fantastically handy way of staying in touch: cheap, easy and simple to use. Before you leave, supply your folks/partner/loved ones with the fax number of hostels, hotels, work, American Express (they accept faxes for customers), should they want to reach you in an emergency.

VOICEMAIL

Voicemail is an extremely handy service for travellers as it allows you to pick up and leave messages on your own personal answer service, from any telephone in the world. A word of warning: you have to pay to pick up your messages as well as leaving them (the answerphone you call is usually based in your home country) so ask people to only leave messages in an emergency. You may also have to buy a keypad before you leave (around £10) in case you can't find a touch-tone phone.

TAKING YOUR MOBILE

The advantages of having your own phone are numerous: it will not only assist you greatly in your job search if you have a telephone number prospective employers can contact you directly on, but it will certainly make you feel safer. It will also be hugely reassuring to people at home knowing that (connections allowing) they should be able to contact you. The downside is the extra burden of carrying your recharger with you: you may have to bring an adaptor as well to use the local electricity. You should also check the cost of making calls abroad, and how these calls will be billed to you. Check with your mobile company how easy this would be in your target destination.

LETTERS

Yes, that old chestnut. Snail mail. As amazing as the wonders of modern technology may be, there's still nothing like reading a long rambling handwritten letter from home. If you've already fixed up work before you leave, or have sorted out accommodation, you have the advantage of already being relatively easy to get hold of. If you have local contacts with a permanent address, you could ask to give their address for relatives to contact you. Alternatively, you can give them addresses of hotels/ hostels you're staying in, although this can be unreliable: you may move on and forget, and there's no guarantee the hotel staff will pass on the mail to you anyway. The best way to receive mail is use a poste restante address. So, what's that?

Poste Restante This is a very handy system if you have no fixed address and it works like this: basically, anyone wishing to write to you can send a letter to the main General Post Office in the city you are staying, which you can collect by turning up and showing your passport. The mail will be kept for anything from one to six months although different post offices operate according to different systems: some may throw away uncollected mail after only one month. In most cases, uncollected mail will be returned to sender.

If possible, it's best to get the address of your main post office from a phone book or guide book. If not, mail should be addressed to your name, followed by Poste Restante, General Post Office and the name of the city. The mail will normally be filed away alphabetically but there could be confusion about whether it is filed according to your Christian name or title or any 'amusing' pet names. Bear in mind that to the people filing it, your name is a foreign language. To avoid any problems, ask people to address mail to an agreed name (minus Mr, Mrs, Ms) so you know what you are looking for: the last name should be underlined and all words written in capitals.

GETTING PAID

Depending on where you are and how long you intend to stay for, it might be worth setting up a bank account. Make sure you have the necessary documentation such as passport, residence permit, proof of income/ employment contract.

TAX AND NATIONAL INSURANCE

If you are working legally and everything is above board, the chances are you're going to have to deal with taxation. Of course tax varies from country to country, and the whys and wherefores of payment depend on a number of criteria. In most countries your employer will deduct contributions for income tax at source, and if you are working for less than the tax year, you may find you are eligible to claim a tax refund (see later in the chapter).

Sorting out your tax can be a complicated business so make sure you check your tax situation thoroughly and, if necessary, get the right advice by hiring an accountant. UK residents can download all the right leaflets from the Inland Revenue's website **www.inlandrevenue.gov.uk/leaflets/c9.htm** or by calling 020 7438 6420 or the order line 08459 000404. The leaflets to ask for are:

IR20 *Residents and non-residents – liability to tax in the UK*
IR 138 *Living or retiring abroad – a guide to tax on your UK income and pension*
IR140 *Non-resident landlords, their agents and tenants*
NI 38 *Social Security abroad*

The Overseas Placement Unit publishes free leaflets called 'Working in . . .' which offer useful information including taxation and social security. Write to The Overseas Placing Unit, Rockingham House, 123 West Street, Sheffield S1 4ER (Tel: 0114 259 6051, Fax: 0114 259 6040) or check out the website **www.europa.eu.int/jobs.eures.**

WORKING ABROAD AND YOUR UK TAX STATUS

Under UK tax law, everyone has a basic personal allowance of £4,535 (in 2002), which they don't have to pay tax on. Beyond this amount, you will pay a proportion of tax depending on your income. EU students working in the EU for less than six months are not liable for tax.

Generally, your liability to UK tax depends on whether you are classed as 'resident', 'ordinarily resident' or 'not resident'. If you are classed as resident (including ordinarily) in the UK, you will normally be liable to UK tax on any income from overseas. You are classed as resident in the UK if you spend 183 days or more in the UK during the tax year, or your visits to the UK average 91 days or more a tax year over a maximum of four years.

You are classed as 'ordinarily resident' in the UK if, broadly, you are resident in the UK year after year. You can be classed as 'ordinarily resident' in the UK even if you are not resident in the UK during a particular year, which applies to many working travellers.

If you leave the UK to work full-time abroad under a contract of employment, you are treated as not resident and not ordinarily resident *only* if your absence from the UK and your employment abroad both last for at least a whole tax year (6 April to 5 April). Even if you stay longer than one year, if your visits to the UK exceed 183 days in total in any one tax year, you will still be classed as a UK resident and will normally be liable to UK tax.

Assessing your tax status can be complicated, so you are advised to read the Inland Revenue literature in great detail and see an accountant if necessary. For more information read *Working Abroad* by Godfrey Golzen and Jonathan Reuvid (published by Kogan Page).

CLAIMING JOBSEEKER'S ALLOWANCE ABROAD

The good news for many working (or not working) travellers is that under EU law, EU nationals can claim Jobseeker's Allowance (JSA) in other EU countries. On the face of it, this may look like an easy way of tiding you over in your first few weeks without work, but in reality it may not be simple as it sounds. Payment can be a long time arriving and can also involve bureaucratic difficulties and paperwork. Start the process well in advance – if you try to just turn up and claim Jobseeker's Allowance abroad, you could well be in for at best, a frustrating delay and at worst, a big disappointment.

In order to claim Jobseeker's Allowance, you must have paid in the necessary contributions. In the UK, for example, this is usually Class 1 National Insurance contributions. Due to the freedom of labour and movement agreement within the EU, contributions you have made in one country can be taken into account if you are claiming unemployment benefit in another EU member country. If you have not paid the necessary contributions and are not entitled to claim Jobseeker's Allowance, you can claim income support instead. However, it's important to note that this is not as easy to claim across international borders as unemployment benefit, and can be difficult to claim at all.

Also remember that in order to be eligible for JSA, you must have left work through no fault of your own. In short, if you decide to walk out of your job, you will have to wait 26 weeks before receiving benefit, unless you can prove there were special mitigating circumstances which forced you to leave your work.

WHEN AND HOW CAN YOU CLAIM JOBSEEKER'S ALLOWANCE IN EUROPE?

If you are an EU National and have been registered as unemployed for at least four weeks in the UK, you can arrange to continue to receive payments for up to three months, paid at the UK rate, while looking for work elsewhere in the EU. Notify your local Employment Service Jobcentre of your intention to look for work abroad, at least six weeks before departure. Get hold of the form (ref-JSAL 22) which has information for people going or coming from abroad and an application form for transferring benefit and the leaflet SA29, which has information on social security insurance, benefits and health care rights in the European community. Alternatively, call the DSS, Jobseeker's Pensions & Overseas Benefit Directorate (Tyneview Park, Benton, Newcastle upon Tyne NE98 1BA, Tel: 0191 218 7652, Fax: 0191 218 7147) for one and a Fact Sheet No. 1 'UK contribution-based JSA abroad'.

What should happen next is your local Jobcentre should provide you with a bilingual letter confirming that you are eligible to claim benefit. The Jobseeker's Pensions & Overseas Benefit Directorate of the Department of Social Security will then decide whether to issue you with an E303 which authorises the Employment Services in the other country to pay UK contribution-based JSA for up to three months. Once you have arrived abroad, you must take this letter and register with the appropriate authorities (which varies from country to country) within seven days. The JSAL 22 leaflet has information about where to register in different European countries.

CLAIMING UNEMPLOYMENT BENEFIT FROM ANOTHER COUNTRY

If you have worked in another EU country and paid contributions into the unemployment insurance fund, you should be eligible to claim unemployment benefit from that country. The exact regulation and length of time required to work there varies from country to country. Also, the amount you will receive varies from country to country. Make sure you register as soon as you lose your job. The authorities should then contact the Contributions Agency for details of your UK insurance record, who will then send them on form 301.

CLAIMING TAX BACK

If you are working in a foreign country for less than the tax year, you may well find yourself paying too much tax. In most countries, your gross pay is likely to be taxed at source and, at the end of the tax year, you may find that you are eligible to claim a tax refund. You can either pursue this yourself by going to your local tax office in your home country and filling in a tax form, or contact one of the numerous agencies who can organise this for you, for a commission of the refund. Try to get hold of one that operates on a no-win no-fee basis, or at least checks that you are eligible for a tax refund before running up a huge bill. ESS are one of the largest and most popular companies and can help you claim tax back from Australia, the US, the UK, Ireland, Germany, Canada, Holland and Japan. Contact them at **www.ess.ie/work** or call 09845 307 07 07. Another to try is Tax Return on

020 7437 9182 (**www.taxreturn.org**). Keep a copy of payslips so you have a record of how much tax you have had deducted from your earnings.

DOUBLE TAXATION

The UK has tax treaties with around one hundred countries to guard against double taxation. If, however, you work in a country which is not covered by an agreement, you may be able to apply for a special relief called 'unilateral relief', or a foreign tax reduction. Contact your Tax Office for more details.

For a list of countries with which the UK has double taxation agreements, look in the booklet IR20 *Residents and non-residents – liability to tax in the United Kingdom*.

ADVICE

- **Get the necessary documentation from the Inland Revenue**

- **Hire an accountant to check your tax situation**

- **When working abroad, keep a copy of your payslips as a record of how much tax you may be paying**

- **Beware of double taxation**

- **If you are a student take the necessary proof and show it to your employer. Under EU law, students working in the EU for less than six months don't have to pay tax**

- **At the end of the tax year, consider whether you may be eligible to claim a tax refund**

COMING BACK

Of course, as every traveller knows, you always have to return and that for many can be a problem. Cathy Merry found that the culture shock kicked in more when she arrived home to the UK after a year working in a lab in California: 'I'd spent a year in America, living in a fantastic house for minimal rent and being paid a good salary to come back and live in student poverty in a dodgy house in inner city Manchester.'

We all know someone who goes travelling for a year and comes back with an ego of gigantic proportions. You may feel that you've gained more worldly experience than your non-travelling friends or even find them narrow-minded or provincial, but beware of taking yourself too seriously and patronising and alienating your friends. Just because they haven't been travelling, it doesn't mean they've done nothing worthwhile or interesting.

Patrick McGuire, who has travelled and worked in India, Morocco, Germany and France, thinks coming back home is as much a skill as travelling in the first place. 'One of the most difficult things is readjusting when you get back. I often feel a bit disorientated and it may take time, but somehow you manage it.'

You may also return home and find that while you have been working as a general dogsbody, your friends have managed to save up a fortune and get the much-coveted career break of the century. Kate Marshall says that she found returning home particularly difficult. 'My friends were well established and had the job, a car, a nice wardrobe, whereas I had a pair of flip-flops and a £1,000 debt. It was difficult to come back skint and start again from the beginning.'

You might feel a bit down at first, but remember, it will pass. Be patient, and know that you'll adjust in time. Keep in touch with any friends you've made from travelling, and try to integrate them into your life. Above all, know that your life has moved forwards, and all the great experiences you have stocked up have stood you in good stead for creating a wonderful future. Anyway, you can always go travelling again, or get a career in the travel industry!

PART TWO: WHAT TO DO

6 TEACHING ENGLISH

Teaching English is one of the favourite occupations for working travellers. And it's not surprising why – not only is demand for native English speakers intense, but in some parts of the world such as South America and Asia, it is relatively easy to just turn up and find work regardless of whether you have a Tefl certificate. It is also a distinctly easier way of securing work before you arrive and can curtail any laborious red-tape procedures, as well as opening up many destinations that are otherwise off the map for working travellers. Pay can also be good and well above the average salary you can expect from other types of 'travelling' work.

However, prospective teachers should be aware that the days when speaking the language you were born is qualification enough with are somewhat in decline. Yes, there are opportunities, but generally, equipping yourself with a Tefl certificate is the key to opening doors. Not only will this lay the world at your feet, making working in virtually any country a distinct possibility, but it will also give you that much-needed edge in a competitive market. Indeed, most Teflers make a career of it – teaching in Istanbul for one year, followed by two years in Argentina, or maybe stopping off in Italy for some seasonal teaching work. If travelling is your passion, and you were born an English speaker, arming yourself with a Tefl certificate could be the best thing you ever do.

THE TEFL CERTIFICATE

So which certificate to go for? Open the classified pages of any newspaper and you meet with a bewildering array of schools offering Tefl certification. As with most things in life, some are better than others. There are two types of Tefl certificates: one is the Cambridge Certificate in English Language Teaching to Adults (Celta) administered and awarded by the Cambridge University examining body (arguably the most respected course). The other is the Certificate in Tesol (Teaching English to Speakers of Other Languages) awarded by Trinity College London. Both are demanding and expensive (costs typically range from £800 to £950) and involve at least one hundred hours of training including several hours' teaching practice.

CELTA SCHOOLS INCLUDE:

International House, 106 Piccadilly, London W1V 9FL (Tel: 020 7491 2598) which also has a centre in Newcastle.

Pilgrims Language Courses, Pilgrims House, Orchard Street, Canterbury, Kent CT2 2BF (Tel: 01227 762111).

Basil Paterson Edinburgh Language Foundation, Dugdale McAdam House, 22/23 Abercromby Place, Edinburgh EH3 6QE (Tel: 0131 556 7696, Website: **www.basilpaterson.co.uk**).

You can obtain a list of centres offering Celta courses from Ucles: Tefl Unit, 1 Hills Road, Cambridge CB1 2EU (Tel: 01223 553355, Website: **www.cambridge-efl.org.uk**).

TESOL SCHOOLS INCLUDE:

Oxford House College, 28 Market Place, Oxford Circus, London W1W 8AW (Tel: 020 7580 9785, Website: **www.oxford-house-college.ac.uk**).

EF English First Teacher Training, 1–3 Farman Street, Hove, East Sussex BN1 3AL (Tel: 01273 747 308, Website: **www.ef.com**).

Language Link Training, 181 Earl's Court Road, London SW5 9RB (Tel: 020 7370 4755, Website: **www.languagelink.co.uk**).

There are also several centres such as Saxoncourt Teacher Training which offer short Tefl introductory courses. Contact Saxoncourt Recruitment and English Worldwide at 124 New Bond Street, London W1S 1DX, Tel: 020 7491 1911, Fax: 020 7493 3657. Other schools such as Berlitz and Linguarama provide their own in-house training to teach in their schools.

Advertisements for all types of Tefl courses are easily found in the *Guardian*'s EFL section (Tuesdays) and in the classified sections of many local newspapers and regional listings magazines such as London's *Time Out*.

WHAT DOES THE TEFL CERTIFICATE INVOLVE?

Generally, you can opt to study Tefl courses in a variety of programmes – full-time, part-time, evening classes and spread over six months, three months or four weeks. International House, arguably the best and most respected of language training schools, runs a four-week intensive RSA/Cambridge Celta course, which consists of morning theory classes and afternoon teaching practice. I did this course in 1995 and was surprised to find it certainly lived up to its course description, 'intensive' being the operative word. Generally, my Tefl course was a challenging and enjoyable experience. As well as offering teacher training, International House is a language school in its own right, so our teaching practice was spent teaching I.H. students who paid a nominal fee to be the guinea pigs for our novice teaching skills. Teaching practice itself could be daunting at times: by only the second day, I was running a class in front of my fellow trainees who were busy making notes and scrutinising my classroom manner. Initially it was terrifying. I remember being so nervous I could feel my legs shaking, but I quickly got used to it. By the end of the first week, we were all conducting lessons with a steely-eyed efficiency, seemingly unfazed by even the most testing of grammar queries.

That said, the course was far from an easy ride. I even know one teacher who described it as 'the worst four weeks of my life', and I think she was only half joking. In short, it can involve a whole lot of hard work; teaching on your second day can be a tough challenge for even the most confident of people. Four weeks might not sound like a long time, but within that short period, we managed to cram in an awful lot of information. The sessions on language threw my native English language into a completely new light as we were seeing it from the perspective of a non-English speaker. Sessions were lively and interesting, the teaching methods were up-to-date and dynamic (although some experienced teachers complained they were impossible to apply to a 'normal' classroom situation), and the overall experience was fun, rewarding but demanding.

WHAT TO EXPECT FROM TEACHING WORK

So what constitutes a normal classroom situation? The fact is that, as most Tefl teachers soon find out, there's no such thing as a 'normal' job. In short, circumstances and conditions change depending on where you are. English teaching covers a whole range of methods, students, conditions and schools and, if you intend to travel abroad, you have no real way of knowing what to expect until you arrive. You could find yourself teaching business English one-to-one for private companies – turning up in plush surroundings with your tape recorder in hand and a copy of the *Financial Times* (I did this in both Madrid and London teaching Japanese businessmen). On the other extreme, you might end up in a remote school in Romania with no teaching materials except a friend's postcard and some photographs from home on which to base a lesson. In these circumstances, ingenuity rules. But bear in mind that for most students learning English is a serious business, and you'd be wise to give yourself a head start by making sure you're up on your grammar rules, especially if you're finding work without a Tefl. As a native speaker, you may think you know everything there is to know about the English language, but there's nothing like a roomful of zealous English learners firing questions about the different conditional tenses and use of reported speech to really rattle those nerves.

BUSINESS ENGLISH

Many of the major cities, particularly in Europe, have vacancies for teachers of business English. Most companies hire out teachers through agencies or private schools, which you can find in the Yellow Pages – these will usually find work for you and pay you a fixed rate per hour. This often involves one-to-one classes, but again it pays to be adaptable. You may even find yourself running group seminars, instructing the business community on negotiating contracts over the telephone, striking deals or coping with difficult clients. Expect to have to work very early in the morning, very late at night and on occasion in very un-ideal surroundings – such as the middle of an open-plan office where work is going on as normal. Business English tends to involve specialised language and you may have to get to grips with the jargon of a particular industry. However, the benefits can be good – when I was teaching business English to Japanese businessmen in London I was frequently wined and dined in the best City restaurants, just so my hosts could practise their English conversational skills (or at least, that's what they said). One student even had his wife lay on a huge Japanese meal for me, complete with sake and sashimi and several bottles of wine. Money also tends to be better than in private or state schools, with private tuition in business English being especially lucrative.

TRAVELLERS' STORIES

Claire Donaghue has taught in Italy and the Czech Republic. After spending ten months teaching in a private institution in Italy, she returned to the UK and found a teaching post in Prague through Saxoncourt Recruitment and English Worldwide.

Prague is a wonderful city to live and I love my life here. I teach business English around 25 hours a week and go round to different companies in the city, teaching bankers and stockbrokers, either in small groups or one-to-one.

Most of my classes tend to be early in the morning or later in the evening, so I have plenty of time off during the day. Having said that, preparing lessons and marking homework can take a long time so it isn't all pleasure and relaxing. Most teachers supplement their income with private tuition, which can be easy to set up once you've established yourself in a school. It's amazing how much work comes by word of mouth. Some teachers pass on their students when they leave to go home for good, and the longer you are here, the easier it gets to attract students.

My students are generally well-motivated and charming and learning English for both work and personal reasons. English is the international language of business so they're just as likely to be conversing in English with a Swedish businessman as they are with an American. They need to be able to entertain clients and talk English over the phone, and generally communicate well. The material I use varies. We have a lot of the standard course books such as Headway but I also supplement my classes with discussions, games, role-playings and activities where students can practise their fluency. I also use authentic material such as books and newspapers – even letters from home can come in handy. The students are usually willing to try different ways of learning, so my classes are usually very lively, and can even be quite volatile. Some of the managers have even had clashes of ego, so class management can be a very important skill.

PRIVATE LANGUAGE SCHOOLS

Many English teachers tend to find work in private language schools. Setting up an English school is frighteningly easy in most countries, so make sure your employers seem above board, are clear about payment, and try to speak to other employers before you agree to work for them.

PRIVATE TUITION

Many English teachers supplement their income by offering private tuition, for which they charge a fixed fee (depending on where you are) per hour. Setting up private tuition can be a very lucrative source of work, but most teachers move into it gradually once they have found regular teaching work. Not only is teaching in schools a more reliable source of income, but it's also a good way of finding private students and you can also advertise on the school's notice boards. To guard against too many cancellations, establish a same-day cancellation fee, so you won't be left out of pocket if a student decides not to turn up.

WHERE CAN I FIND WORK?

Qualified Tefl teachers should have no trouble finding work before they leave. The *Guardian*'s Education Section (every Tuesday) carries advertisements for Tefl teachers and its website GuardianUnlimited has a Tefl directory in its education section, with links to various Tefl experts based in different countries. Go to **www.education.guardian.co.uk** and look in Tefl News.

Another newspaper to check is *The Times Education Supplement* (published on Fridays but available all week from newsagents) which includes posts abroad (**www.tesjobs.co.uk**).

The Internet has numerous websites that carry vacancies and advice. Tefl Jobs Online (**www.tefl.net**) lists Tefl jobs worldwide, as does **www.englishexpert.com** and Dave Sperling's ESL cafe (**www.eslcafe.com**).

You can also try the international chains although these will generally demand greater experience and qualifications, and are more likely to employ teachers from their in-house training courses. International House (**www.ihworld.com/recruitment/index.htm**) in London has a placement section and, as well as the teacher training courses leading to the RSA Cert TEFL, has 120 affiliate schools based in over 30 countries.

Saxoncourt Recruitment and English Worldwide (124 New Bond Street, London W1S 1DX, Tel: 020 7491 1911, Fax: 020 7493 3657, Website: **www.saxoncourt.com/index.htm**) regularly advertises jobs and offers a placement service for EFL teachers and EFL training.

Berlitz have around 400 centres around the world and can be a good starting point for non-Tefl teachers. Prospective teachers will normally have to attend a training session lasting around a week before starting a classroom post. Teaching style differs widely from Tefl training and involves a more old-school style of rote learning.

FINDING A JOB WITHOUT A TEFL CERTIFICATE

The best tactic for non-qualified English teachers to take is to either turn up and find work once you arrive, or else organise a placement through a gap-year organisation.

The Japan Exchange and Teaching (JET) Programme was set up by the Japanese government and places graduates from over 39 countries in teaching and administrative positions throughout Japan. UK graduates should contact Council on International Educational Exchange, CIEE, 52 Poland Street, London W1V 4JQ, Tel: 020 7478 2010, Fax: 020 7434 7322, Email: JETinfo@councilexchanges.org.uk. Website: **www.councilexchanges.org.uk**. Placements last one year, and participants receive remuneration of 3,600,000 yen (£23,000) per year, a return ticket to Japan, training and help in finding accommodation. Programmes start in mid to late August – application forms are available from October each year and must be returned by 7 Dec.

You can also try to fix up work through international chains such as Berlitz and Linguarama, which run their own in-house training courses. Bear in mind that some countries are more easy to find work in with no Tefl certificate than others. According to Nick Rogerson who taught in Venezuela, many of the schools weren't interested in whether you had a Tefl certificate or not, as they would enrol you on one of their own in-house training courses instead. If you do decide to turn up and find teaching work without a Tefl, make sure you have researched the job situation thoroughly first and know what you can expect.

Alternatively, try the voluntary and gap-year organisations. Many of these run teaching abroad placements and come with other perks such as return flights, assistance in fixing up accommodation and a pre-teaching orientation programme. The following organisations have teaching programmes (see the Voluntary Work and Gap Year chapter for addresses):

Teaching and Projects Abroad
i-to-i
Alliances Abroad
Travellers Worldwide
World Teach
Africa and Asia Venture
International Students Exchange Centre

Gap Activity Projects
Project Trust
Bridges for Education

FINDING A JOB ON THE SPOT

Finding work on spec is entirely feasible in many countries. Indeed, in Latin America it's the normal way to find work, as schools rarely recruit from abroad and rely on the high number of backpackers that simply turn up. Take with you a copy of your CV, your Tefl certificate if you have one, and either phone round language schools (you should be able to find addresses in the country's version of the Yellow Pages) or go round door to door. Be prepared for the possibility of an impromptu gruelling interview: I was once put on the spot to answer a series of complex grammar questions by a Spanish English teacher who seemed to be hell bent on demonstrating the arrogance and ineptitude of English Tefl teachers. Another word of warning: although turning up and finding teaching work is extremely possible in many locations, don't be duped into thinking it's an easy ride. Never mind the popularity of learning English, competition can still be fierce as there are an awful lot of Tefl teachers out there. If you do intend to find work once you arrive, at least make sure you've done your research and know what your chances of success are. As always, it helps to have contacts there first, and plenty of money to fall back on in an emergency. Also, don't be deceived by geographical proximity: France is the UK's nearest neighbour and yet one of the most difficult of countries to find Tefl work. Although there are exceptions, most schools and universities demand fluent French and a Tefl diploma at least.

USEFUL RESOURCES

The British Council (**www.britcouncil.org**) has offices in many international cities and can be a good point of contact both before and after you arrive. The British Council Information Centre (Bridgewater House, 58 Whitworth Street, Manchester M1 6BB, Tel: 0161 957 7755) also publishes a free information leaflet *How to Become a Teacher of English as a Foreign Language*.

EL Gazette is a monthly newspaper covering all aspects of the ELT industry. For subscriptions and stockists, write to Dilke House, 1 Malet Street, Bloomsbury, London WC1E 7JN, Tel: 020 7255 1969, Fax: 020 7255 1972.

BOOKS

EL Gazette Guide to English Language Teachers Around the World (11th edition).

Teaching English Abroad (Fifth edition) published by Vacation Work.

7 TOURISM

Every year thousands of working travellers manage to pay their way by working in the hotspots of the global travel industry. The opportunities here can be immense, and hugely variable; whether you fancy cleaning tables in a cheap city eaterie, washing dishes at a local pizza house, or helping school kids to master the skills of sailing, the tourist industry is crying out for willing workers. Pay can be low and hours can be long, depending on where you are and whom you work for. Employers can also be unscrupulous, and whatever work you do, you'd be well advised to check out your employer first to guard against future problems. However, if you are hoping to work without a permit, tourism can also be one of the easiest places to find unofficial jobs. In these cases, be extra vigilant – without the necessary permission to stay in your chosen country, you are effectively renouncing any employee rights or protection.

So what can you do? Just close your eyes and imagine . . . selling ice creams on a beach, handing out flyers for a local club, baking muffins? The following are just a list of the kind of jobs you may find:

Bar work
Waiter/waitressing
Chalet host
Ski instructor or technician
Diving instructor
Windsurfing instructor
Snowboarding instructor
Kitchen staff
Cleaner
Hotel receptionist
Hostel worker
Hostess
Disc jockey
Entertainer
Campsite courier
Snow shoveller
Dish washer

There are also plenty of opportunities for the entrepreneurially inclined. When Patrick McGuire ran out of money in Montpellier, the first thing he did was head for the supermarket and buy five melons. 'I cut them into slices, and walked up and down the beach selling them for five francs each. The interesting thing was that when I started, no one else was doing it, but after a couple of days there was loads of competition. Everyone had cashed in on the idea.'

FINDING WORK

If you are looking to find work before you arrive, it pays to do your research. There are hundreds of websites out there advertising positions and you may hear of openings in the most unlikely of places. Keep an eye open in the usual sources, such as newspapers, magazines and advertisements in shop windows. If you have a specialist skill you wish to find work in, such as scuba diving or windsurfing, read the specialist magazines. You may need to get extra training: this can be expensive, but given it could fund countless future seasonal jobs, it could be well worth the cost. There are also plenty of opportunities to be had with youth organisations and summer camps such as Camp America and Bunac: see the Voluntary Work and Gap Year chapter for more information.

One of the easiest ways to find work is to target one of the many tour operators or campsite holiday firms that recruit staff for their hotels or camps. Fixing up work with these companies can be a good start for fledgling working travellers, not least because perks are often included such as pre-paid return flights, insurance, food and accommodation, and a ready-made social life with your colleagues. Pay can be low, however, and hours long. Of course, the better your language skills, the higher the position you can apply for. Working behind the bar and reception work are generally considered the higher echelons of the hotel ladder, while cleaning and chalet maid work is the least glamorous.

WORKING AS A TOUR GUIDE

If you speak a European language and don't mind living out of a suitcase, you may enjoy work as a tour guide. Tour companies such as Cosmos, Travelsphere, Newmarket Holidays, Page and Moy, Riviera Travel, Wallace Arnold and Shearing all recruit staff to lead their tour guides around the world, for which you receive a decent salary plus free board and food. Languages are often required, although not essential for trips to English-speaking destinations.

Liz Evans has worked as tour guide for seven years for the companies Cosmos and Travelsphere. She found the job after graduating from her German and French degree, when her friend spotted an advert in the university careers library. Liz applied for the job, and two weeks later was posted out to Austria on a one-week 'observation tour'. 'Basically, I had to shadow the tour manager for a week so they could see what I was like and how suitable I was for the job. After that, I was thrown in at the deep end –

they put me on a coach and said I had to do the tour myself. I was terrified – I had never been to Austria in my life and felt I'd only been given the job because I spoke German. There were fifty people on the coach and I felt it was totally down to me whether they would have a good holiday or not.'

The tour went well, however, and pretty soon Liz was being sent out on contracts to various destinations around the world. 'I started off on short tours in Europe but after a year, I was sent on my first long-haul trip to China for twelve days. To begin with I accepted anything. You can't be too choosy otherwise you wouldn't be given any work.'

Seven years later, she spends nine months out of every year living in hotels in a variety of exotic locations. 'It's a lifestyle more than anything. You have to be quite flexible – usually the company give us three months' work at a time consisting of a whole series of tours. Obviously there's more work in the summer and I have to work days when other people are off like Christmas and New Year and bank holidays. But on the other hand, I have long breaks during the winter when I can really relax and spend time with my friends.'

Liz's work involves looking after the holidaymakers, taking them on tours and making sure all aspects of their holiday are running smoothly. The most important thing, she says, is that you are the 'right kind' of person: personable, cool-headed, and passionate about travel, with the ability to deal with any emergencies that arise. 'Basically, you're on call all the time; the holidaymakers have your mobile and hotel number so it's very important that you enjoy being around people. A lot of my work is performing. I get huge job satisfaction. There are times when you have to bite your tongue and not show your feelings, and you always have to look in control even if you're not. If someone ends up in hospital, it's up to you to deal with it, so it can be quite a responsibility at times. The main thing to remember is that people are on your side. They want a good holiday and are looking to have a good time.'

FINDING WORK

- Write to the big hotels and holiday companies which you can find in holiday brochures or guide books. Don't rely on only a handful but cast your net wide. The more you apply to, the more chance you will have of striking it lucky.

- Try to write an application letter in the language of your target country. Make sure your presentation is good and spelling is correct. If possible, try to find someone who speaks the native language well to read through to look for any corrections. Enclose a copy of your CV (see Skills and Opportunities chapter on how to write an international CV).

- For summer tourist work, start your job search in the autumn before you leave.

- Summer seasons vary depending on where you are but you are broadly looking at from Easter to September. If you leave it later to apply, be prepared to be suddenly shipped out at a moment's notice. Hotels in particular have a high turnover and can need replacement staff at short notice: your letter may arrive in their most desperate hour of need.

The following companies recruit staff for holiday seasonal work:

Mark Warner Ltd (George House, First Floor, 61–65 Kensington Church Street, London W8 4BA, website: **www.markwarner.co.uk**) recruits over 1,500 staff for the Alps and the Med each year including hotel staff, nannies, handymen and night watchmen, club managers, and watersports and sports instructors. Applicants must be over nineteen and hold a EU passport. For details, call 020 7761 7300.

Club Med (Kennedy House, 115 Hammersmith Road, London, W14 0QH Tel: 020 7348 3333 or 08453 676767, Fax: 020 7348 3336) recruits reps, sports instructors, receptionists and childminders for its Club Med villages in Europe and Africa.

Powder Byrne (250 Upper Richmond, London SW15 6TG, Tel: 020 8246 5300, Fax: 020 246 5322, website: **www.powderbyrne.com**) has vacancies for summer and winter work.

Eurocamp recruits 1,500 people every year for its self-drive camping and mobile-home holidays in Europe. Contact Overseas Recruitment Department (Ref SJ/02) Tel: 01606 787522 for more details.

First Choice Holidays (London Road, Crawley, West Sussex RH10 2GX, Tel: 01293 560 777) has vacancies for tour reps and other staff.

FINDING WORK ON THE SPOT

Finding work when you arrive can also be quite easy. The seasonal nature of the tourist industry means that many countries rely on foreign workers to fill the huge demand. Obviously, it pays to head for the more touristy locations. In Europe – particularly the Mediterranean coastal resorts – it is generally easy to find work, although with the right amount of determination and a little bit of luck you should be able to land on your feet virtually anywhere. Other good places to try are the Aegean coastal resorts in Turkey, Greece and the Greek Islands, the Balearic Islands (including Ibiza), Spain (particularly the Costa del Sol) and the Algarve in Portugal.

As usual, the more outgoing you are, the more likely you are to draw opportunities to you. Speaking to people and spreading the word that you are looking for work can make the world of difference. Most regional newspapers will have a weekly classified section with advertisements for job vacancies. Also look out in shop windows, university and hostel notice boards, and English bars, cafes and bookshops. Another good move is to be proactive and go round establishments door-to-door and say you are looking for work. Obviously, it pays to know the language, but the more tourist-orientated the area, the less important this is. Be confident and bold, but not too pushy. Use your initiative. Take with you a copy of your CV and make sure you dress (and pack) appropriately. If you think you may well end up working as a waiter/waitress or behind the bar, take black trousers/skirt and white shirt/blouse. And you never know when a smart pair of shoes may come in handy.

SKI RESORTS

Qualified ski instructors can head for the ski resorts, where there are also plenty of vacancies for hotel and chalet staff, ski operators and bar staff in a huge range of establishments such as nightclubs, lift stations and mountain restaurants. There are also vacancies for chalet cooks, although you will usually be expected to have a good cooking qualification, often cordon bleu. That said, some tour operators such as Crystals and Inghams organise their own cookery courses.

As with other types of tourist work, there are plenty of opportunities in ski resorts: the drop-out rate on all jobs can be high, so according to many sources, you can turn up and easily find work, or apply for a job before you leave.

Julian Sykes worked in Val d'Isere in the French Alps and picked up cash-in-hand work washing up in restaurants and working behind bars. Generally, work was easy to come by and he managed to finance several months' skiing. 'Most ski companies will have already hired staff but there will always be cases of hotels and such, being let down last minute, so work can be easy to find.'

The ski season generally lasts from November to April. As always, it pays to apply early, but mid-season applications can often prove successful due to the high staff turnover. If you want to find work in ski resorts, read *Working in Ski Resorts* (Vacation Work), which is an excellent source of the most comprehensive and up-to-date information. The following ski holiday companies recruit hundreds of employers every year:

First Choice Ski, Lakes and Mountains (Olivier House, 18 Marine Parade, Brighton BN2 1TL, Tel: 0840 900320) recruits staff including hotel managers/ assistant managers, chefs, chalet staff, resort reps and general assistants. As well as being a tour operator, First Choice has a hotel division which leases and runs 25 clubhotels and 55 chalets in European ski lakes and mountain resorts.

Inghams Travel (10–18 Putney Hill, London SW15 6AX, Tel: 020 8780 4400, Fax: 020 8780 8805, Website: **www.inghams.co.uk**) is a large employer of ski personnel and recruits from April to October for winter jobs.

Crystal Holidays (King's Place, 12–42 Wood Street, Kingston-upon-Thames, Surrey KT1 1SH, Tel: 0870 888 0028, Website: **www.crystalholidays.co.uk**) employs chalet hosts and assistants, hotel chefs and assistants and resort reps for Summer Lakes and Mountains and Winter Ski in Europe and North America. The majority of staff are required from the end of November to the middle of April, but some additional staff may be required once the season has started.

Thomson Holidays Ltd (020 7387 9321, Website: **www.thomsonholidays.com/jobs**) and Airtours (0870 241 2642, Website: **www.airtours.co.uk**) also cover many ski resorts, while PGL Ski Europe (**www.pgl.co.uk/personnel**) recruit staff to lead school ski trips.

Another good way to find work is to target the *Daily Mail* Ski Show held at Olympia in London in October and November. Contact DMG World Media Group for more details 020 8515 2000.

Also look out for adverts in *The Lady*, *TNT*, *Overseas Jobs Express* and specialist ski magazines such as *Ski and Board*, the magazine of the British Ski Club of Great Britain (Tel: 020 8410 2000, Website: **www.skiclub.co.uk**).

TRAVELLERS' STORIES

Georgie Dow worked as a chalet girl for five months during the winter season (November to March) in the French ski resort of Meribel in the Alps. She says, 'Before I went out, I had to prove that I could cook and look after up to eighteen people so I did an intensive chalet girl cookery course which I found in *The Lady*. The course lasted one week and I supplemented it with a food hygiene course I did at night school.'

This course was the bare minimum, and when Georgie arrived in Meribel she found most other chalet girls had done the six to twelve month cordon bleu Prue Leith course.

It was very important to be a good cook so in the interview I had to come up with a week's worth of recipes for breakfast, packed lunch, afternoon tea and a three-course evening meal. My job consisted of looking after the chalet guests, feeding them and cleaning the chalet. I started every morning at six when I would make them breakfast. I would spend all morning making their packed lunch and afternoon tea (home-made cakes, or flapjacks) and preparing as much as I could of the evening meal. Then, when the guests had gone out skiing, I would clean the chalet from top to bottom, making sure it was spotless. I had to be out of the chalet at 11 a.m., and would go off skiing until 4 or 5 in the evening. Then I would be back in the chalet preparing the evening meal. In addition to this we also had to budget and order the food. Every Saturday there was a changeover of guests, so we had to give our welcome speech and hand out the skis, lift passes, and so on. I cooked the same meal every week – boeuf Bourguignonne, salade Niçoise and banoffi pie – and I've never made any of them since!

Despite being hard work, Georgie said the job was perfect for ski enthusiasts. 'I could ski every day for five months and had free lessons from the ski instructors. There was also a brilliant nightlife. The resort was full of people my own age so it was easy to make friends. Tips could also be good – a £30 tip was quite common because the chalet guests were wealthy, professional people.'

ENTERTAINMENT

Singers and musicians may also be able to find work entertaining in hotels, holiday camps, or cruise liners (see Working a Passage chapter). There are many agencies which recruit entertainers – keep an eye open in *The Stage*, the music magazines and newspapers such as *NME*, or contact agencies from the Yellow Pages. There are also plenty of openings for DJs, particularly in the clubbing meccas of Spain and Greece. Due to the popularity of American and British music, English-speaking disc jockeys are in huge demand in many discos and clubs in Europe. Keep an eye open for vacancies in the music press or contact the nightclubs direct. The website **www.gapwork.com** has a section on Ibiza with lists of nightclubs. There are also several agencies that place DJs in nightclubs and hotels. Try Juliana's Leisure Services (15–17 Broadway, West Ealing, London W13 9DA, Tel: 020 8567 6765) which places DJs and flair cocktail bartenders in hotels in the Middle and Far East.

HOSTESS WORK

Female travellers may want to target some of the many hostess bars and clubs in Asia. These spring up in most cities, particularly in Japan and Thailand, and operate by enticing in businessmen to mix and flirt with hostesses, who are paid to laugh at their jokes and entertain them. Most of these establishments make their money by selling drinks, so hostesses use their charms while all the while making sure their drinks are topped up. Pay can be good – around £17 an hour – and tips can be even better.

Mary Martala worked as a hostess in a hostess bar in Osaka, Japan, so she could save up money to finance a Masters Degree. She says that the hostess bars vary hugely in quality:

There are so many different types of hostess bars ranging from the blow jobs under the table kind to the more middle-class, classy outfits where businessmen wander in and expect to be treated nicely. There's a very specific way of behaving around them. You have to approach the table when they come in to welcome them, and there's a special way of walking. You also have to dress formally, but sexily, in high heels with a tasteful short skirt, although you shouldn't look tarty. Some of the men try it on and you have to somehow manage to ward them off while, at the same time, being nice to them. If they do get too close, the management won't support you or intervene. As far as they're concerned, these men have paid for you to come to their table and they can do what they like to you. Some of the girls found this quite upsetting, so you have to make sure you can cope with it.

Hostess work is usually easy to find: there are many agencies, which are usually advertised in English-language newspapers and magazines you can find in English bars, cafes and bookshops. Word of mouth can also be important, or you can go round the clubs and ask for work directly. According to Mary, it isn't necessary to speak much of the language, as many businessmen like English-speaking women, as they can practise their English too!

8 AGRICULTURE

Whether it's picking olives in Greece or harvesting grapes in California, agriculture work of all kinds is a mainstay for the working traveller. Casual work can be easy to find, as many farmers would have difficulty bringing in crops without the help of foreign labour. The transient nature of harvest work is also perfect for the traveller who wants to come and go as he pleases, and can be a useful last resort for the cash-strapped backpacker. That said, the work is notoriously hard: long hours bent double in relentless sunshine tests the mettle of even the hardiest of workers. Pay is also low, depending on where you are, but there are good points: many farmers provide free accommodation in campsites where you can meet and mingle with other fellow travellers. Plus, think of the suntan you'll have from all those hours spent outside!

TIPS

- **Make sure your harvest information is up-to-date before travelling to the chosen destination**

- **If you intend to do harvest work, take a tent with you. Many farmers offer free accommodation in campsites**

- **Take a sunhat and plenty of sunscreen and aftersun if you are heading for a hot location**

- **Gloves can protect your hands from scratches and stings, and keep you warm if it's cold**

- **Bring an antiseptic cream for cuts and plenty of insect repellent**

WHERE TO HEAD FOR

France, Germany, Denmark, Holland, Switzerland, Italy, Spain, Portugal, Greece, Norway, the USA, the UK, Canada, Australia and New Zealand tend to employ many foreign workers to bring their crops in.

FINDING WORK

Harvesting work is one area where you should easily find work on the spot so head for the big agriculture areas which you should be able to find from any good guide book, and target the bars, pubs and hostels with connections with farmers. Keep an eye open in the regional newspapers and as always, talking to locals and fellow travellers can be a mine of information. Hostels are a good source of information; many include details of work on the notice boards and have good links with local farmers. Employment agencies can also be of use, while the Internet has some websites advertising agricultural work. Australia seems particularly well served in this respect (see Australia section for more details) but there are also some worldwide websites, such as **www.pickingjobs.com**, which carry details of farms looking for workers. You can also try **www.ruraljobs.com**, **www.anyworkanywhere.com** or the Eures website **www.europa.eu.int** for harvest vacancies and information.

Remember that the exact dates of harvests vary from year to year depending on the crop and weather conditions, so don't rely on the dictates of last year's guide book or the inside knowledge of a friend. Harvesting is the time when most backpack labour is needed but there can also be work packing after the crop has been picked, such as bulb packing in Holland.

AGRICULTURAL AND FARMING SCHEMES

Some countries such as Switzerland, Finland, Norway and the UK have special schemes for harvest workers – see those chapters for more details.

UK voluntary organisation Concordia fixes up work for farmer assistants in Norway and Switzerland. Volunteers are paid a minimum of £58 per week plus free board and lodgings. Send an sae to Concordia, Heversham House, 20/22 Boundary Road, Hove, East Sussex BN3 4ET (Tel: 01273 422218, Fax: 01273 421182, Website: **www.concordia-iye.org.uk**).

Working Holidays (**www.workingholidays.de**) arranges jobs all the year round on German farms or in country hotels, living with the family and looking after children and/or horses and farm animals.

The Seasonal Agricultural Workers Scheme (SAWS) is a British government-sponsored scheme which enables full-time students of Eastern and Central European countries to carry out harvest work on farms throughout Great Britain. The scheme is operated on behalf of the government by organisations such as Concordia and HOPS. If your university does not have an arrangement with one of these organisations, the British Embassy may be able to put you in touch with local agents. Apply in October or November for the following year as places are limited and tend to be filled up quickly.

World Wide Opportunities on Organic Farms (WWOOF) consists of national co-ordinators who have a huge network of organic farmers throughout the world who are willing to exchange free board and accommodation for organic enthusiasts to work on their farms. The rules and requirements vary from country to country, but most volunteers are expected to have experience in organic farming from their home country first. Check out their global website **www.wwoof.org** with links to the national member offices. British nationals should send an sae to the UK branch at WWOOF, PO Box 2675, Lewes, Sussex BN7 1RB for an application form.

AgriVenture/IAEA (YFC Centre, NAC, Stoneleigh Park, Kenilworth, Warwickshire CV8 2LG, Tel: 02476 696578, Fax: 02476 696684, Website: **www.agriventure.com**) is run by the International Agricultural Exchange Association and arranges working farming and horticultural exchanges to Australia, New Zealand, Canada, the USA and Japan.

Australian citizens can apply to: AgriVenture/IAEA, Suite 203, Level 2, 65 York Street, Sydney 2000 (Tel: 02 92995300).

New Zealand citizens can apply to: AgriVenture/IAEA, PO Box 20–113, Christchurch (Tel: 03 359 0407).

Canadian citizens can apply to: AgriVenture/IAEA, 105, 7710 5 Street SE, Calgary, Alberta T2H 2L9 (Tel: 403 255 7799).

Citizens from Austria, Belgium, Czech Republic, Denmark, Finland, France, Germany, Iceland, Luxembourg, Netherlands, Norway, Sweden and Switzerland can apply to: AgriVenture/ IAEA, Lerchenbeorg Gods, 4400 Kalundborg, Denmark (Tel: 45 50 51 15 25, Fax: 45 59 51 05 07).

TRAVELLERS' STORIES

Richard Cox, an ex-farmer, spent four months working on a beef farm in Gunma, Japan, as part of a placement organised by the organisation AgriVenture. Says Richard, 'I'd always wanted to go to Japan so when I saw AgriVenture's advert in *Farmer's Weekly* I jumped at the chance. The placement cost around £2,000 including flights, but the farm paid me 70,000 yen (around £1,000) a month on top of free board and food, so I nearly earned it back. Anyway, it was money well spent. I had a fantastic time. The people were wonderful, really polite and, although I only could speak a little Japanese, they really welcomed and included me.'

Richard stayed in a traditional Japanese farm, complete with titami on the floor, as the only foreigner, apart from one Indonesian man. In his weekends off he declined his hosts' offer to show him around, and went exploring on his own instead. 'I wanted to do it on my own because it's more of a challenge. I went to Tokyo and loved it, although I was there at the time of the World Cup and kept bumping into English fans.'

Richard loved his time in Japan and says he would recommend it to everyone. 'I've always had a thing about Japan so did a lot of reading about it before I arrived. But it totally lived up to my expectations. Japan is a brilliant country – the people are great, the culture is fascinating, the food is fantastic and there's nowhere else quite like it. I'd love to go back again.'

9 AU PAIRING AND CHILDCARE

AU PAIRING

If you're prepared to put up with the ignominy of living in someone else's house, looking after their children and running the risk of being a general unpaid skivvy, au pairing is one of the easiest ways to work abroad. Not only does it come with food and board in usually comfortable (even sumptuous) accommodation, but it also often bypasses the need for complicated red tape: au pairs are frequently exempt from work permits although you should check the rules of the country you are visiting. The work is also relatively easy to find – while nannying tends to require more formal training, au pair work is open to any women aged above seventeen who can provide a good character reference. And as more and more women are choosing to return to work after having children and are in dire need of cheap childcare support at home, there is also plenty of work around. Au pairing isn't just the province of the fairer sex: men can and do apply, although the field tends to be dominated by women.

REGULATIONS

The regulations regarding au pairs vary from country to country, so make sure you check the guidelines for the country you intend to work in, and that your agency (if applicable) is aware of them. Here in the UK, the Immigration Rules include the following guidelines for au pair work, which are typical of many countries: au pairs should be aged 17 to 27 (although this is not set in stone) and live for up to two years as a member of an English-speaking family. In return for working a maximum of five hours per day with at least two full days off per week, they should receive a reasonable allowance of £45 a week and the use of a room of his or her own.

GOOD POINTS

- **Having the security and comfort of living in a proper home and not having to fix up your own accommodation.**

- **There is the good chance that you won't have to sort out a work permit.**

- **Being immersed in the culture of which you want to find out more (or why else would you be there?).**

- **Having the opportunity to learn a foreign language from within a native home.**

- **Having the warmth and support of a family who can take you out, show you the sights, introduce you to friends and family networks and take you on holiday (only if you have a good relationship with the host family, of course).**

- **There is plenty of work around.**

THE DOWNSIDE

All of the above can only happen in an ideal situation – and ideal situations do arise, sometimes. If you're lucky, you may end up like Alessandra Calabrese who came over to the UK as an au pair from Sicily. She combined three hours work every day with morning language classes, and had her own room in a beautiful large house in London. Today, five years later, she is still friends with her host family and she takes time to see them whenever she's in England. However, there's always the risk you'll end up with the other extreme. You've probably heard stories of these already. Lecherous husbands, jealous insane wives who have you scrubbing floors and washing clothes to all hours, in between the demands of their screaming, horrible children. OK, so that's your worst-case scenario, but there are lesser risks of which you need to be aware. After all, you'll be living with a family in their own house abiding by their rules and some of this will probably mean a certain curtailment of freedom. Ask yourself whether you are really the kind of person who could fit in with someone else's house rules. Bear in mind that while there are regulations for au pairs which stipulate maximum working hours of around 25 hours a week, with two full days off a week, some families may pile on duties and expect you to work long unofficial hours. I once worked as a campsite manager/childminder/mother's help/general skivvy in a farmhouse in North Devon in the UK and had my weekly day off taken away so the woman could go out clothes shopping. I ended up working ten consecutive days from 7 a.m. to 10 p.m. and, believe me, by the end of it, I was seriously ready to strangle somebody.

TRAVELLERS' STORIES

Julie Calvert worked as an au pair for three months in Madrid, taking care of two girls aged two and eleven. She says,

The family spoke not one word of English and my Spanish was far from fluent. I flew out to Madrid knowing nothing more than I was being met at the airport by a man with a beard (the father had described himself over the phone to me). Upon arrival at the airport, I had never seen so many beards in my life, but obviously my host family recognised me from the hopelessly lost look on my face in the Arrivals Hall. I arranged this job through a European employment agency in the UK. It turned out the family basically wanted a cleaning lady/babysitter/English teacher for next to nothing and were stricter than my own family. I had to be in by 1 a.m. which, in Madrid, is a ridiculous home time, was not allowed to have a key, and had to share my room with the eleven-year-old daughter when the in-laws arrived for a six-week visit.

DO

- Contact a range of agencies so you can compare their services.

- Find out as much as you can about your host family before accepting the post, although given the speed of recruitment, this may not be possible. If you are finding work through an agency, stress how important this is and ask to find out more before committing yourself to a position.

- Get a feel of the family before you start work. If you're already in their home country, ask to meet them before for an interview.

- Make sure you find a reputable agency – a good agency should explain clearly the au pair's responsibilities, hours of duty, pocket money, and any legal requirements. Make sure you have defined time off and are covered by medical insurance, whether paid by the au pair or the host family. Other things to check are: does the position come with paid return flight? Will the agency sort out any necessary visas? If there are any problems or disputes between the family and au pair, will the agency immediately help to resolve the issue?

- Set out ground rules as soon as you arrive, or even better, before accepting the position. Make sure you have come to some agreement about pay, the hours you work, time off, expected duties (what that will and won't include: cooking, cleaning, washing clothes, teaching English, gardening, cleaning toilets etc.), sleeping arrangements (will you have your own room and will that be provided for the length of your stay?) and your right to privacy. Remember that just because you are living in their house, it doesn't mean you're their slave.

- Make an effort to get away from the house in your free time and meet other people. Many au pairs attend language classes and find that a good way to make friends.

WHERE TO FIND ADVERTISEMENTS

The British magazine *The Lady* is famous for being the first port of call for prospective childcare workers and carries many advertisements for both families and agencies looking for au pairs. The Internet is also a good reference guide and a quick search can put you in touch with scores of agencies.

Another possibility is to register with one of the many childcare agencies that recruit for overseas, which you can find in the Yellow Pages. Some of those in the UK are:

Academy Au Pair & Nanny Agency, 42 Milsted Road, Rainham, Kent ME8 6SU, Tel/fax: 01634 310808, email: academy4aupairs@hotmail.com, Website: **www.academyagency.co.uk**.

Ace Au Pairs, 27 Chickerell Road, Park North, Swindon, Wilts SN3 2RQ, Tel: 01793 430091, Email: info@aceaupairs.co.uk, Website: **www.aceaupairs.com**.

Au Pair and Student Placement Agency, Nation House, The Stable Block, Milwich Road, Stafford ST18 0EG, Tel: 01889 505543, Email: **info@internationalaupair.com**, Website: **www.internationalaupair.com**.

There are also overseas agencies where you can fix up work when you arrive or contact from your home country. The chapters on different countries have addresses of local au pair agencies.

The Au Pair in America Programme sponsored by the Interex Change places au pairs in posts throughout America. Contact The Childcare Solution, Emberton House, 26 Shakespeare Road, Bedford NK40 2ED, Tel: 07002 287247.

NANNIES

Like au pairs, nannies also take care of children and tend to live in, however they are generally professionals and have professional training. They also usually only take care of children, not household chores, and tend to be better paid.

Many holiday operators such as Mark Warner and Club Med have vacancies for nannies to work in their hotels and holiday camps. Apply through the companies and look out for other opportunities in *The Lady* and *Overseas Jobs Express.*

Worldnetuk organise a Nanny and Childcare Programme USA. Applicants must be 18–26 years old with childcare training. It also runs an Au Pair Programme USA for 18–26 year olds and Ski/Summer Resort Nannies (no age limit but must have childcare training). Contact Worldnetuk, Southern Office, Avondale House, Sydney Road, Haywards Heath, West Sussex (Tel: 0845 458 1551, Website: **www.worldnetuk.com**).

GENERAL CHILDCARE

There are also other opportunities in the field of childcare. With the growing necessity of learning English, English lessons for small children is a huge growth area particularly in European countries such as Spain (see Teaching English chapter). Other opportunities include: classroom assistants, nursery assistants and crèche work

You may also be able to fix up voluntary work in orphanages in developing countries such as India, many of which are crying out for unpaid help and financial support. These usually won't require childcare training but the authorities are likely to run police checks to guard against attracting paedophiles and criminals.

10 BUSINESS AND INDUSTRY

RETAIL

Walk the length of any international high street and you're faced with a hundred work opportunities. Retail outlets are big business in most countries in the world, and can be a staple source of work for many travellers. However, unlike some tourist and agricultural jobs, shops operate on a more official basis. If you've not got the necessary work permit, they're probably not the best place to head for. Paperwork of all kinds – namely resident permits/work permits/bank accounts – will be expected as a prerequisite.

That said, there is still plenty of scope for casual work, particularly at Christmas. You may also find work doing stocktakes which most shops have around twice a year. Bookshops are usually particularly hungry for extra staff at this time so it might be worth calling in and dropping off your details.

As always, a door-to-door trawl from shop to shop can prove rewarding. Take with you a copy of your CV, dress smartly and look ready and willing to start work. Experience and good references are also hugely important so try to approach retailers with a degree of professionalism. Remember, shops revolve around customer service so presentation skills and general appearance are one of your most marketable assets. If you intend to find work here, bring with you some smart (ish) clothes and a comfortable pair of shoes – standing on your feet all day serving customers can be hard on the feet, particularly in a hot climate.

Be aware too that retail outlets also tend to favour people with experience so the more you can milk this, the better. Put simply, the less in-house training they have to do, the more cost-effective you are as an employee. If you have a certain amount of experience in one field at home, exploit the same market in another country. Jessica Robbins gained ample experience working in the bookshops in her native London so, on arriving in Sydney, she knew exactly where to head for, and she found work almost immediately. By the same token, if you worked for a company with a strong international presence (McDonald's, Virgin, Borders, Boots, even Marks and Spencer), you could do worse than check with the head office to see if they have any international vacancies, or target the same company once you've arrived.

SECRETARIAL AND OFFICE WORK

Another possibility is office work, especially if you have typing and shorthand skills, or are a qualified secretary. With English as the international business language, native English speakers stand a good chance of finding work, although it will certainly pay to speak the native language of the country you are visiting. Qualified and experienced secretaries can try International Secretaries as a good first port of call. Bilingual secretaries obviously will be ahead of the game, although the importance of English as the international language of business is not to be underestimated.

A word of warning to those intending to exaggerate their prowess in typing and secretarial skills: many employment agencies apply strict spelling and typing tests to weed out such impostors. Blag by all means, but just be aware that they may test your grandiose claims. Also, beware of agencies that ask for fees, although most will take a commission from your pay.

TEMPING AGENCIES

Every country throws up its own selection of employment agencies, with some countries such as the Netherlands better served than others, but the international ones are Adecco, Drake Personnel, Hamilton James & Bruce, Hays Personnel Services, Morgan Consulting Group, Recruitment Solutions, Kelly and Manpower.

Employment agencies can also help you find work in factories, manufacturing, retail and other areas. Robert Walters (www.robertwalters.com) lists temporary and permanent vacancies in banking and finance, accountancy, secretarial and call centres, and has offices in Australia, Belgium, France, Hong Kong, Ireland, New Zealand, Singapore, South Africa, Holland, the UK and the USA.

For a list of agencies that specialise in overseas work contact The Recruitment and Employment Confederation, 36–38 Mortimer Street, London W1N 7RB, Tel: 0800 320588 or go to www.jobseekers-uk.com.

Remember too that EU nationals are by rights entitled to use the state employment services in EU member countries, although there may be a language barrier.

TRAVELLERS' STORIES

Three weeks after landing in Sydney, Lucia Cockcroft put on a 'smart-casual suit' and walked the streets of Sydney, taking her CV and registering with temping agencies such as Kelly Services, Drake and Manpower. She says, 'It's as easy as walking down a street. There are loads of temping agencies in Sydney or you can find ads and addresses at the student travel centres. Like in most temping agencies, I was tested for spelling, typing and data-input and then was given my first assignment that afternoon, filing in a bank.'

In addition to office experience, Lucia had completed a basic Pitman secretarial course, and had typing and basic word processing skills, but says she 'wasn't very polished'. 'People with better secretarial skills would be able to find much better assignments than me.'

Most of the work was for big corporate firms and banks based in skyscrapers round Sydney Harbour. 'The work was quite boring, usually filing or data-input, but the location was amazing. I would often stop and stare out of the windows, just marvelling at the view.'

Work came sporadically. 'I'd be offered a day here, a week there, and the agency took thirty per cent commission from my wage. But pay was a lot better than the equivalent in England, around A$15 an hour, and considering that rents are so low in Sydney, that's good money. It certainly helped me to live comfortably.'

SKILLS SHORTAGES AND PROFESSIONAL QUALIFICATIONS

If you have professional qualifications, for example in engineering, IT, banking and finance, it may be worth contacting the relevant professional organisations to see if your target country has shortages in that area. This can be a good way of finding work in a country that otherwise has tight immigration rules. Canada is currently experiencing a shortage in mathematicians, chemists and sales and advertising specialists. Nurses, teachers and medical staff are often in demand in certain countries such as South Africa and New Zealand.

The international engineering group IMI plc offers overseas and vacation placements to degree students of mechanical, manufacturing, or electronic and electrical engineering. Contact IMI Plc, Box 216, Witton, Birmingham B6 7BA, Tel: 0121 356 4848, Fax: 0121 356 2877, Website: **www.imi.plc.uk.**

Engineering, science and technology students can fix up paid employment opportunities in UK companies through The Year in Industry organisation. Placements are professionally supported and may lead to sponsorship. Apply via **www.yini.org.uk.**

Also keep an eye open for trade magazines, many of which advertise international vacancies. You can find listings of all UK magazines in Benn's *Media Directory*, while international ones can be found in Benn's *Media Directory International*. Both are usually stocked in main libraries.

If you are a professional, the CEPEC *Recruitment Guide* may be of some use. It lists recruitment agencies and search consultants in the UK, many of which deal in overseas placements, for professionals, managers and executives. You should be able to find this in your local reference library or alternatively contact: CEPEC Ltd, 13 Hanover Square, London W1R 9HD, Tel: 020 7629 2266.

The Chambers of Commerce (**www.british chambers.org.uk**) publish lists of British companies with associates in different countries.

The British Foreign and Commonwealth Office offers a limited number of short-term attachments to overseas posts for British undergraduates in their penultimate year. Application forms can be downloaded from the Foreign and Commonwealth Office website **www.fco.gov.uk** or call 020 7008 0639.

OTHER OPPORTUNITIES

Other opportunities lie in the field of telesales and selling, market research, call centres, factories and warehouses, labouring and building work. Factory work can be particularly hard work and mind-numbingly tedious, although it can afford an authentic window into the country you are visiting.

If you have building and labouring experience you could well be able to find work with building contractors. Make sure you are properly covered – tales abound of unscrupulous employers who refuse to pay a decent wage. Safety regulations can also vary widely from country to country. Work can be found just by asking around building sites, or else head for places that are under construction such as new hotels and redevelopment sites between seasons in the tourist resorts. Bear in mind that a working day starts early, especially in warmer climates, so make sure you get there early, between 5 a.m. and 7 a.m. You can also target major ports for labour work such as Rotterdam or else try the major exhibitions such as the Frankfurt Book Fair held in October every year. Look out for overseas vacancies in the *Overseas Jobs Express* or try the Just A Job section in Thursday's edition of the London *Evening Standard*. You can also go to the Recruitment and Employment Confederation's website **www.jobseekers-uk.com** which has links to various specialist agencies.

For all kinds of work, look up the European Employment Services, EURES (**www.europa.eu.int/comm/employment_social/elm/eures/index**) database offering all kinds of jobs all over Europe. However, the jobs are usually more suited to those who have sought-after professional skills including language, and the contracts tend also to be more long term. In theory, you should also be able to find out about vacancies in Europe via the NATVACS system at your local Jobcentre. However, in my experience, the UK's Jobcentres are notoriously difficult places to find correct information so you may find yourself going round in circles, with no one knowing what you're talking about!

11 WORKING A PASSAGE

One of the most expensive aspects of working abroad is the cost of getting there in the first place. So what better way to keep costs down, than working a passage? Working a passage means that you can travel for free in return for offering your services. Many gappers have long funded their trips this way, with some proudly boasting a cheap round-the-world itinerary of all the world's most exotic locations. The downside? Spending most of your time at sea or on the road, and doing without the freedom that most casual working travelling brings. However, with a little careful planning, you can arrange to work your way from one country to another with plenty of stopgaps to take in the sights or indulge in some other casual work. According to the website **www.natives.co.uk**, many ski workers move on from a season in the Alps to working on a private yacht in Monaco and Antibes.

PRIVATE YACHTS

What could be more luxurious than earning your keep as the distant lights of Monaco glimmer on the horizon? Working on a private yacht lies at the more glamorous end of the working traveller's market – think of Tony Curtis on board his luxury yacht in *Some Like It Hot*, drinking champagne and feeding oysters to Marilyn Monroe. Of course the fantasy lies a long way from reality: working on board a private yacht can be hard work with long hours and exacting standards to maintain. You may also be working in dangerous weather conditions and not see land for days.

WHAT KIND OF WORK CAN YOU DO?

You can either find work on private yachts (owned by one person who might only spend two weeks in one whole summer) or charter yachts (rented out to people for a set period). Both types require a range of staff, depending on the size of the boat, including deck and maintenance crew, host/hostess, steward/stewardess, chefs, kitchen staff, engineers and the captain or skipper. Jason Whiting, charter manager of a yacht brokers in Monaco, says that for people who are starting out, the best jobs to target are steward/stewardesses or deckhands. Steward/stewardess' duties include bar work, mixing cocktails, preparing tables, tidying and cleaning cabins, and making sure they are immaculate to fit very high standards. It will also help if you have hotel management or restaurant experience. Deckhands, on the other hand, work on the boat's exterior and duties include cleaning the boat, tying up the boat and helping to prepare the 'toys' such as jet skis.

For crewing work make sure you have the experience before you make any grand claims. If you fancy working in this capacity, equip yourself with a sailing course before venturing out: contact the Royal Yachting Association, Romsey Road, Eastleigh, Hants SO50 9YA (Tel: 023 8062 7400, Website: **www.rya.org.uk**) for details about courses and a free leaflet *Careers in Sailing*.

HOW EASY IS IT TO FIND WORK?

It depends on what qualifications and experience you have or what post you choose to go for. Generally, a well-qualified chef with good experience should be able to find work. Pay can be good, sometimes double the salary of a head chef in London. If you don't have the qualifications, get experience working as a chalet or restaurant chef. Iain Martin of **www.natives.co.uk**, an agency that specialises in ski and yacht seasonal work, says, 'If you're not a qualified chef, your chances of finding work aren't high, but you can improve this by handing out an impressive CV and having good references at hand, already printed out. If you're applying to be a hostess or a cabin stewardess, bring photographs of table plans and flower arrangement designs you've done. Be persistent and professional – most people will end up getting work if they hang around long enough and wait. However, couples can expect to get split up as it will be difficult finding work together.'

Pay can be good – chefs and stewards can expect to earn anything from £15,000 to £80,000 a year, while other jobs get around £250 a week as well as free board and food. Earnings can also be tax free as many boats are registered off shore and tend to evade tax regulations.

HOW CAN I FIND WORK?

The best way to find work is to turn up at any of the popular resort harbours and cold call the boats for work or register with an agency. Good places to head for in Europe include the French Riviera. Many yachts are based in Antibes which has a number of agencies, but you could also try Golfe-Juan, Cannes (old port and new), Monaco, Beaulieu-sur-Mer and Cap Ferrat. Barcelona is another option, as is Palma de Majorca in Spain and the Italian Riviera. Outside Europe, you can try Florida (particularly Fort Lauderdale where there are many agencies), the Caribbean and the Americas. Bear in mind that boats tend to spend the summer in Europe and head for the Caribbean in winter. Many get 'crewed up' from Antibes so it's a good place to head for.

For Europe, get there at the start of April and be prepared to stay for a while – finding work on yachts can be immensely popular so don't expect to find something immediately. Be persistent – it might take a long time to find work, but if you stick it out for long enough, you should strike lucky eventually. Take a copy of your CV with you – keep it short (one page) and, for maximum effect, have a photograph of yourself embedded into the paper. Don't promise more than you can deliver. Standards are extremely high: both service and food is expected to be of the utmost quality and if you don't cut the mustard, you'll either end up being dismissed or else thrown overboard. Work can also be hard – one chef says they worked fourteen-hour days for six weeks solid, cooking eight to ten courses. Skippers and crew members should never exaggerate their experience and qualifications.

You can also fix up work by contacting the agencies before you arrive. **Natives.co.uk** is one website that can put suitably qualified candidates in touch with agencies and captains: email them your CV (between the months of March and May only) to iain@natives.co.uk or call Iain on 08700 463355.

Professional sailors can contact yacht agencies. Blue Sails Yachting (**www.bluesails.com**) and Polco Yachts (**www.polco.net**) both offer crewed charter yachts. You can also try the Cruising Association (CA House, 1 Nothey Street, Limehouse Basin, London E14 8BT, Tel: 020 7537 2828, Fax: 020 7537 2266, Website: **www.cruising.org.uk**) or Crewseekers (Crew Introduction Agency, Hawthorn House, Hawthorn Lane, Sarisbury Green, Southampton, Hants SO31 7BD, Tel/fax: 01489 578319, Website: **www.crewseekers.co.uk**).

Many activity holiday operators recruit sailing staff. Sunsail (**www.sunsail.com**) employ 'team players' in the Med, while Sunworld Sailing, a large water-based leisure firm, part of Thomas Cook, offers summer jobs on land and sea during April to the end of October. Contact **www.sunworld-sailing.co.uk**.

Flying Fish run sailing courses (as well as watersports courses) and then place sailors in their sailing centres around the world. Contact Flying Fish, 25 Union Road, Cowes, Isle of Wight PO31 7TW, Tel: 01983 280641, Fax: 01983 281821.

WATCH OUT FOR ...
Tax complications, red tape and difficult employers. Yes, you are offshore so may be exempt from paying tax and pay can be very lucrative. However, it may not be as straightforward as it seems. Also bear in mind that by working on a private yacht, you will be working for a private employer. Contracts are unusual and you will have virtually no employees' rights or protection. You may also be dropped off at a moment's notice on the other side of the world and have to fund the rest of your journey home.

TRAVELLERS' STORIES

Ian Maidens spent the summer season working as a marine engineer on board a small, chartered yacht based in Antibes. He spent four months sailing around the French, Italian and Spanish coast, round the Greek Islands and to Turkey. In a crew of nine, he says that he was seen as the skivvy, with the skipper and two chefs right at the top of the pecking order.

People think working on a yacht is all about lounging around on the deck sunbathing but at times it was hard work. For one thing, we had to wear a uniform and weren't allowed to be seen sunbathing. That said, there were times between charters when we had the yacht to ourselves for two days and we could go offshore and sit on the beach instead.

The quality of your time there depends on the skipper. Unfortunately our skipper was a nightmare, and there were rumours that he'd lost his job working on the bigger boats because he'd been caught embezzling money! You can lose your job at any time – there's no such thing as a verbal warning. You're working tax-free with no contract so the skipper can finish you at any time, and if he doesn't like you, you're off – it doesn't matter where you are. I got dumped in a little island in Greece and had to pay for flights back to Athens and then the UK. I also missed out on £800 worth of my share of the tips that the skipper had been holding on to until the end of the season.

There were good points, however. 'It was a real eye-opener to see such wealthy people from close quarters, particularly in Monte Carlo and St Tropez. One wealthy businessman used to spend the morning sitting on deck doing business on his laptop, and then spend the afternoon playing on his speedboat. I saw him one day lose a £200 million deal and he couldn't care less. It was all peanuts to him. You also get great perks – not only can they give huge tips (typically £2,000 per charter for the whole crew) but we were also taken out for some expensive meals in St Tropez.'

Smooching with the rich however does have its drawbacks. 'They were paying a fortune to hire out the yacht, so expected a very high level of service. We were on call all the time – if they were awake at three o'clock in the morning then so were we, attending to their every need.'

CRUISE LINERS

If the idea of working a passage appeals to you, but you don't have the experience needed for private yachts, you can always try finding work aboard a luxury cruise liner. Cruise holidays of all kinds are incredibly popular and range from small intimate ships catering for up to 500 passengers to round-the-world cruises complete with all-night casinos. There are also plenty of specialist cruises catering for a particular market such as 'themed cruises' (murder mystery, gay/lesbian or singles, for example) and cruises to view marine wildlife. There is also a huge range of destinations and itineraries, from round-the-world in 180 days to touring the Galapagos Islands to setting sail through the Antarctic. Cruises can last for anything from two days to one year.

WHAT WORK IS AVAILABLE?

Cruise ships are effectively floating hotels and, as such, require all the huge variety of staff a sprawling holiday complex needs. A typical super liner (with one to three thousand passengers) will employ up to one thousand workers, including bartenders, cocktail waiters/waitresses, casino staff, hairdressers, beauticians, hosts/hostesses, manicurists, nurses, nursery assistants, receptionists, cashiers, shop assistants, pool/spa assistants, catering staff, cleaners and laundry assistants, dancers, musicians and entertainers, DJs, stewards and stewardesses, maintenance staff (such as plumbers, electricians and carpenters), computer technicians, photographers, security officers, office/accounts. Work comes with free food and accommodation (of course), which can range from a small, dingy cabin close to the engine, to something in more salubrious surroundings.

Qualifications and pay will vary depending on the post, but if you have your heart set on finding work here, you should be able to find something. Cruise liners are particularly popular with entertainers and singers – epitomised by Jane Macdonald's rise to fame after appearing in the TV programme *The Cruise*.

HOW DO I FIND WORK?

The best way to find work is to contact one of the many agencies or concessionaries that recruit staff for the big cruise lines. Different cruise lines use different companies to do their hiring for them so it may be worth contacting the cruise line first. The American website **www.cruise2com** carries cruise line profiles and links to other useful websites. There are also many specialist books on the market that list this information and a random search on the Internet will bring up some names.

The website *How to get work on a cruise ship* has information about work as well as links to other useful websites and cruise lines. Go to **www.geocities.com/TheTropics/Cabana/1590/index.html**.

Another place to try is the trade magazine *Caterer and Hotel Keeper*, which lists vacancies for catering staff. Entertainers can try *The Stage*.

The online agency **www.openwideinternational.com/services.html** recruits talented performers, singers and dance couples for entertainment programmes on cruise ships and in hotels throughout the Caribbean.

There are also some websites that carry vacancies such as the website for Blue Seas' International Seafarers Exchange (**www.jobxchange.com**) and Ocean Crews Maritime Employment (**www.maritimeemployment.com**) which carries listings for jobs ranging from sea maintenance to stewardesses.

YACHT DELIVERY

If you are an experienced and qualified sailor, you may be able to find work 'delivering' yachts as part of an experienced crew. Look out for adverts in *Yachting Monthly* or hang around the harbours and yacht brokers to see whether anyone is looking for crew members. Most people deliver yachts for the pure love of sailing so, unless you're a skipper, which requires extensive training and years of experience, don't expect to get much in terms of pay. The routes also tend to be straightforward and direct, with stop-offs at a minimum. Most skippers are paid a flat fee and will want to reach the destination as quickly as possible.

Reliance Yacht Management specialises in all aspects of yacht delivery and management. Go to its website **www.reliance-yachts.com** for details of crew vacancies or contact 127 Lynchford Road, Farmborough, Hampshire, GU14 6ET, Tel: 01252 378 239, Fax: 01252 521 736.

Rupert Wainwright delivered yachts for Reliance Yachts after he was made redundant from his IT job last Christmas. He says, 'I've always loved sailing so did a Yachtmaster Qualification with the RYA which consisted of three courses in all, costing about £500 each, and part of which I did in the Canaries. I then looked on the Internet for delivery agencies and found Reliance. I sent my CV and application letter, and got a call the next day asking if I wanted to do a 180-mile delivery from Portsmouth to Plymouth. It was a start so I agreed to it.'

Two weeks later Reliance asked him to do another trip, this time to St Raphael in the South of France sailing round Sardinia, Italy and Sicily across to the Greek islands. The route took ten days and, he says, was a wonderful experience. By far the best trip, however, was his next assignment, sailing from Les Sables d'Ollone in France to Florida in a brand new luxury boat with three other people.

This was absolutely amazing – we were sailing for eight weeks and went from Finistere at the northern end of Spain, past Portugal and out to Madeira. We then went across to St Maarten in the Caribbean, which took four weeks. For thirty days we could see lightning at night – it lit up the whole sea and at times could be quite frightening. I'm a city person so being so far out at sea was incredible, and the longest we went without stopping was 22 days. Every night I could see these fantastically colourful shooting stars, which seemed so bright and close. After St Maarten we went past the Bahamas and on to Fort Lauderdale in Florida.

AIRLINE COURIERING

Some businesses will pay for some of your flight costs in return for transporting a package overseas. Make sure you only go through a reputable company, and never carry items for an individual. Check out the International Association of Air Travel (0800 074 6481, **www.aircourier.co.uk**) and the Air Courier Association (00 1 303 279 3600 **www.aircourier.org**) for more information.

DRIVE-AWAY

'Couriering' cars (known as drive-away) is popular in America, where for an agreed sum you are hired to drive a car from one destination to deliver it to another in a specified period of time. Although not advisable for women, drive-away can be a great way of travelling cheaply through the States – see the US and Canada section.

OVERLAND TOUR GUIDES

Those of you with plenty of good travelling experience may be tempted by the adventure of working as an overland tour guide. However, it has to be stressed this isn't for the fainthearted – or even for the short-term. The top three overland companies, Exodus, Dragoman and Guerba, have high standards in recruiting leaders, and typically demand that you are at least 25 years old and well travelled independently in Third World countries. In addition to this, you should have either a LGV or PCV driver's licence (which cost around £800), leadership experience, good mechanical skills and languages (depending on the country). Most tour leaders stay for around three years, with some tour operators even stipulating in the contract that they must work for at least eighteen months. The work also usually comes with unpaid training: Exodus operate an in-house training course where successful applicants spend up to fifteen weeks training in Africa, on a subsistence allowance which pays for food and drink. Participants are then placed in their first paid position, working for twelve to fifteen months as a co-leader and being paid around £100 a week. After this, they eventually graduate to work as an expedition leader, where pay goes up to £250 a week.

Other smaller overland tour operators such as Kamuka may have vacancies for couriers, who may be able to work for less than a year. However, even these should have experience travelling in Third World countries. Look out for vacancies in *TNT* and occasionally *Wanderlust* and the London newspaper, the *Evening Standard*.

OVERLAND TOUR OPERATORS

Dragoman Overland Expeditions, Camp Green, Kenton Road, Debenham, Suffolk IP14 6LA, Tel: 01728 861133, Website: **www.dragoman.co.uk**

Exodus, 9 Weir Road, London SW12 0LT, Tel: 020 8673 0859, Website: **www.exodus.co.uk**

Guerba Expeditions, Wessex House, 40 Station Road, Westbury, Wilts BA13 3JN, Tel: 01373 826611, Website: **www.guerba.co.uk**

Kumuka Expeditions, 40 Earl's Court Road, London W8 6EJ, Tel: 020 7937 8855

For details of other overland tour operators, go to the Overland Expedition Resources website **www.go-overland.com**

12 VOLUNTARY WORK AND GAP YEAR

For people with the right skills and enthusiasm, there are plenty of voluntary organisations out there that are eager to hear from you. Whether you fancy trekking with elephants, playing games with orphans, editing an English language newspaper in Romania or mediating for peace in war-torn Afghanistan, rest assured the world is overflowing with opportunities for 'unusual working holidays'. Although much of the work has a specific aim to help communities, most volunteers take part for less altruistic reasons. That said, the added bonus of helping people will give you the kind of saintly glow of satisfaction impossible to achieve from lying on a beach all day. It will also introduce you to interesting people, and give you a pretty unique window into a culture you've never seen before quite from this perspective.

WHAT WORK CAN YOU DO?

There are such a variety of voluntary organisations out there, that it's impossible to sum up the entire range of experiences on offer. Work can involve myriad things, including eco work, conservation, renovation, health work, teaching, special needs or archaeology. Many voluntary programmes run on the basis of work camps, where participants live in the same place, often a large tent, and work is focused on completing a specific task – such as renovating a fifteenth-century church or clearing land to make a park for children or planting trees.

TRAVELLERS' STORIES

I spent one month in a tiny village high in the Alps, about 15 km outside St Marcellain sleeping in a tent with twelve volunteers. I was the only English person amongst eight other nationalities – Dutch, French, Polish, Yugoslavian, Turkish, Czech, Algerian and Spanish – although most of the time we spoke English. The work was hard and physical, but working in the Alps was incredibly exhilarating. We worked every day from 8 a.m. to 2 p.m. building paths for climbers and skiers in the mountains. At the weekend, we hiked over the Alps to visit neighbouring camps where we spent the evenings sitting around the campfire, playing the guitar, talking until the early hours and sleeping outside under the stars.

The French village where we lived was extremely relaxed and welcoming. Many of the villagers had moved to the mountains after the 1969 student revolution in Paris, and had been living there ever since, working on their farms and making the local hazelnut wine which we all got so used to drinking. I can remember visiting the nearby farmhouse, and sitting in the stone-flagged kitchen, the cat dozing by my feet, cracking nuts from a large wicker basket and lazily trying to chat in my GCSE French.

HOW LONG CAN YOU GO FOR?

Basically, there are three types of volunteering – short term (lasting three to six weeks), medium term (lasting two to six months) or, for the seriously committed, long term (one or two years). Long-term volunteering usually involves skilled professionals such as doctors or teachers working in a developing country, and is most famously organised by VSO (Voluntary Service Overseas). For the purpose of this book, however, we will concentrate on short-term and medium-term opportunities.

HOW MUCH WILL IT COST?

Again, the variety of programmes makes it impossible to generalise. Some organisations, like Concordia for example, require only a registration fee of £80 and perhaps a small amount of money for a food kitty. Other more elaborate programmes, such as eco programmes in Africa, can cost around £1–£2,000, which might not include flight but will include free board and food, training and equipment. Payment for work is obviously minimal, but some gap-year placements may include a small amount of pocket money per week.

WHAT WILL I GET OUT OF IT?

Quite simply, it will put you in touch with the most fascinating people, in the most unusual of locations. Most people who do voluntary work love it. It will also look pretty good on your CV. The experience will probably change you – it may even be life-transforming. After two Greenforce animal conservation projects in Borneo and Zambia, Maria Jacovides gave up her job in a London magazine publishing company and is now training to be a National Park ranger in South Africa. She says,

I'd already done some conservation work in Australia and loved it so much, I was determined to do more. Eventually I booked two ten-week projects with the voluntary organisation Greenforce, which cost around £2,000 each. The first one was in Borneo, where I was working on marine biology and went diving every day to collect data on bio-diversity. The second was in a National Park in Zambia. For ten weeks I studied elephants, antelopes, lizards and birds, noting their behaviour patterns. Amazingly I didn't need any qualifications, just bags of enthusiasm, as the company gave me in-depth training.

We lived in very basic conditions, camping in a huge army tent and taking turns to do chores. Cooking was a huge ordeal and it took a whole day to prepare the meals. The kitchen was a straw bamboo hut and we cooked on an open fire that had to be built every day. One thing I learnt was that

people can be annoying anywhere. Even in an amazing environment, you still come across the same problems you find in an office, but I still came away with an amazing sense of achievement. I'm now training to be a ranger which involves a month in a National Park in South Africa learning things like four-wheel driving and shooting a rifle.

WORKING IN DEVELOPING COUNTRIES

One of the most important things to consider in committing to any kind of volunteer programme, is whether you can cope with the kind of conditions you may have to live in. Many voluntary organisations run in developing countries, where hygiene and health conditions will obviously not be up to Western standards and basics we take for granted such as running water, electricity and a good level of healthcare might not exist. Some organisations which support sustained development programmes will be operating in countries known to be international trouble spots. Many of these countries rely on aid workers so it can be in the nature of this work that you will be taking on board a certain degree of discomfort. However, that said, you are advised to think very seriously about how well you may adapt to living in difficult circumstances. One woman, who doesn't want to be named, chose to do some work in the Sudan, where there's been a civil war raging for the last twenty years, and was horrified to find she couldn't cope with the conditions to which she was exposed. Others, of course, relish the chance to see the culture from the other side and give whatever help is necessary.

SETTING UP VOLUNTARY WORK YOURSELF

There's also a chance of fixing up voluntary work yourself. There are hundreds of opportunities in South America, for example, where intrepid explorers may be able to find work protecting indigenous tribes, or working in the jungle. The South American Explorers (**www.samexplo.org**) have plenty of information on voluntary opportunities. Other people offer work on the spot to orphanages or communities where they think help is needed. If you do this, check the visa situation with the Embassy or consulate.

TRAVELLERS' STORIES

Anne Seymour worked in an international children's centre in the Ukraine, which she set up through the voluntary work organisation Concordia. She soon found that the work unsettled any assumptions she had had:

My destination was Artek, a children's camp in the Crimea, and I had assumed upon myself the role of intrepid and benevolent young woman, off to right the world's wrongs in two weeks. I packed my headscarves, my floaty long skirts and my wooden-beaded necklace, all ready to fit in with my perceived view of an international volunteer, bohemian and hippyish. I had convinced myself that I was doing the world a favour, going all the way to the isolated peninsula of the Crimea to bring a little ray of Western sunshine to the children's lives. And the reality? I was in for a real wake-up call.

My make-up-less face and floaty outfits looked somewhat out of place on a kids' camp where the children wore Estée Lauder make-up by day and Prada shoes by night. The Ukrainian staff, to whom I thought I would be an indispensable source of help and ideas, turned out to be indispensable to me by their unflagging kindness and assistance. And I learnt far more from the kids than I could have possibly have taught them.

I was forced to reassess all my presumptions about those I'd meet, about the experiences I'd have, and about myself. I could never, for example, have thought that my experience at Artek would lead me to watch Ukraine's 10th Anniversary of Independence in the company of President Putin of Russia, to spend a day on a private yacht, or dance to the Beatles in front of five hundred kids.

VOLUNTARY WORK AND GAP YEAR ORGANISATIONS

WORK ABROAD INTERNSHIPS

Bunac (16 Bowling Green Lane, London EC1R 0QH, Tel: 020 7251 3472, Website: **www.bunac.org**) runs a wide range of paid work and travel programmes and a voluntary project on Volunteer Costa Rica.

The Education and Training Group (10 Spring Gardens, London SW1A 2BN, Tel: 020 7389 4431, Fax: 020 7389 4426) places graduates as language assistants throughout the world.

CIEE (Council on International Educational Exchange) (52 Poland Street, London W1V 4JQ Tel: 020 7478 2018, Website: **www.councilexchanges.org.uk**) runs programmes in the USA, Canada, Australia, Japan and China.

Council Australia (University Centre, Level 8, 210 Clarence Street, Sydney 2000) runs programmes across the world for Australian and New Zealand students.

Alliances Abroad (702 West Avenue, Austin, TX 78701, USA, Website: **www.alliancesabroad.com**) organises customised programmes for individuals and groups around the globe who want to learn about other cultures by teaching, interning, volunteering or working abroad.

CONSERVATION

African Conservation Experience (PO Box 9706, Solihull, West Midlands B91 3FF, Tel: 0870 241 5816, Website: **www.afconservex.com**) organises placements lasting one to three months on game reserves in South Africa and Zimbabwe.

Coral Cay Conservation (The Tower, Thirteenth Floor, 125 High Street, Colliers Wood, London SW19 2JG, Tel: 0870 750 0688, Website: **www.coralcay.org**) sends volunteers to Fiji, Honduras and the Philippines for marine and rainforest conservation expeditions.

Earthwatch (57 Woodstock Road, Oxford OX2 6HJ, Tel: 01865 318838, Website: **www.earthwatch.org/europe**) organises placements with scientists around the world conducting research into rainforests, endangered species, archaeology and restoration. Placements last from two days to three weeks.

Greenforce (11–15 Betterton Street, Covent Garden, London WC2H 9BP, Tel: 020 7470 8888, Website: **www.greenforce.org**) organises Work on the Wild Side conservation projects round the world in the Amazon, Africa, Malaysia and the South Pacific, ranging from monitoring marine life to working with wild animals. Placements last from ten weeks. No experience needed.

Trekforce Expeditions (34 Buckingham Palace Road, London SW1W 0RE, Tel: 020 7828 2275, Website: **www.trekforce.org.uk**) sends people on eight- to twenty-week expeditions in conservation projects in South-east Asia and Central America, concentrating on working in the rainforest and with local communities.

WORKCAMPS

ATD Fourth World (44 Addington Square, London SE5 7LB, Tel: 020 7703 3231, Website: **www.atd-uk.org**) organises workcamps and street workshops in Europe aimed at tackling extreme poverty. Placements last for two weeks and take place during July–September.

Concordia (Heversham House, 20–22 Boundary Road, Hove BN3 4ET, Tel: 01273 422218, Website: **www.concordia-iye.org.uk**) has the International Volunteer Programme which organises workcamps for 16–30-year-olds.

Projects last from two to four weeks and range from renovating old churches to assisting at a French film festival.

UNA Exchange (Temple of Peace, Cathays Park, Cardiff CF10 3AP, Tel: 02920 223088, Website: **www.unaexchange.org**) sends volunteers to camps abroad for two to four weeks working on a range of projects including social, environmental work and play schemes. It also has a 'North–South' Programme in 32 countries in Africa, Latin America and Asia.

VOLUNTARY

Bridges for Education Inc (94 Lamarck Drive, Buffalo, New York, 14226 USA, Tel: 1 716 839 0180, Website: **www.bridges4edu.org**) sends Canadian and American students and graduates to teach English in Eastern Europe.

Council International Volunteer Projects (Council Exchanges, Twentieth Floor, 3rd Avenue, New York, NY10017, USA, Tel: 212 822 2600, Website: **www.councilexchanges.org**) organises two- to four-week voluntary placements for young Americans working in nature conservation, construction and archaeology.

Peace Brigades International (PBI Britain, 1B Waterlow Road, London N19 5NJ, Tel: 020 7281 5370, Website: **www.peacebridges.org**) is a peace-seeking non-governmental organisation providing physical and moral support to peace activists whose lives are threatened by violence. It sends international volunteers to provide an international presence in war-torn areas throughout the world for one year.

Quaker Voluntary Action (Friends' Meeting House, 6 Mount Square, Manchester M2 5NS, Tel: 0161 819 1634) runs short-term two- to three-week volunteer projects in Europe, Japan and the USA from working with the disabled to environmental protection.

Teaching & Projects Abroad (Gerrard House, Rustington, West Sussex BN16 1AW, Tel: 01903 859911, Website: **www.teaching-abroad.co.uk**) runs one thousand voluntary placements in teaching, as well as medicine and journalism, in China, Ghana, India, Mexico, Mongolia, Nepal, Peru, Russia, Romania, South Africa, Thailand, Togo and the Ukraine.

i-to-i (1 Cottage Road, Headingley, Leeds LS6 4DD, Tel: 0870 333 2332, Website: **www.i-to-i.com**) runs working holiday placements teaching English as a foreign language in Latin America, Russia, Africa and Australasia.

Cross-Cultural Solutions (47 Potter Avenue, New Rochelle, NY 10801 USA, Tel: 1 800 380 4777, 1 914 632 0022, Fax: 1 914 632 8494) sends volunteers abroad to provide humanitarian assistance in Brazil, China, Costa Rica, Ghana, India, Peru, Russia and Thailand. Volunteers must be over eighteen. No experience required.

Travellers Worldwide (7 Mulberry Close, Ferring, West Sussex, BN12 5HY, Tel: 01903 700478, Fax: 01903 502595) runs teaching and work experience, conservation voluntary placements worldwide.

Voluntary Service Overseas (317 Putney Bridge Road, London SW15 2PN, Tel: 020 8780 7200, Website: **www.vso.org.uk**) places professional and graduate volunteers in developing countries working in community-based projects. There is also a Youth Programme for 18–25-year-olds with a UK passport.

World Wide Opportunities on Organic Farms (WWOOF) (PO Box 2675, Lewes, Sussex BN7 1RB, Website: **www.wwoof.org**) sends volunteers to organic farms throughout the world.

WorldTeach (c/o Center for International Development, Harvard University, 79 John F. Kennedy Street, Cambridge MA 02138, USA, Email: info@worldteach.org, Tel: 1 800 4 TEACH 0 (483 2240) or 617 495 5527, Fax: 617 495 1599) sends volunteer teachers on placements throughout the world.

GAP YEAR

Africa and Asia Adventure (10 Market Place, Devizes, Wiltshire SN10 1HT, Tel: 01380 729 009, Website: **www.adventure.co.uk**) runs unpaid teaching or conservation projects lasting four to five months throughout Africa and Asia, followed by an exciting safari for school leavers or undergraduates aged between 17 and 24.

Gap Activity Projects Limited (Gap House, 44 Queens Road, Reading, Berkshire RG1 4BB, Tel: 0118 959 4914, Website: **www.gap.org.uk**) organises worldwide voluntary work opportunities for eighteen- to nineteen-year-olds including teaching English, caring for the sick, assisting on community projects, conservation work and outdoor activities.

Project Trust (Hebridean Centre, Ballyhough, Isle of Coll, Argyle PA78 6TE, Tel: 01879 230444) is an educational trust which sends two hundred school leavers overseas every year. Projects range from teaching to development work, outward bound activities, health and childcare. Placements last twelve months.

RESOURCES

For lists of voluntary organisations that operate in developing countries, check out *World Volunteers: the World Guide to Humanitarian and Development Volunteering* (Green Volunteers Publications).

13 TRAVEL WRITING AND PHOTOGRAPHY

If you fancy yourself as a budding writer or photographer, you could try contacting the press and trying to sell your stories or pictures. Travel writing is hugely competitive so unless you're already a professional, the chances of being commissioned to write something before you go are minimal. However, there is always the exception to the rule. You could follow in the footsteps of Shastra, who managed to sell her story about being kidnapped by Indian tax drivers outside Delhi airport, to Australian *Woman's Weekly* for A$1,000.

Generally, your best bet is to submit articles on spec to regional or student newspapers, enclosing a sae. If you're on email, so much the better – take with you a list of contacts before you leave so you can email articles when you arrive.

Most magazines will expect to see articles illustrated with photographs so if you fancy breaking into travel writing, polish up your photography skills by taking a short night school course before you leave. Submit slides instead of photographs and try not to pester the editor as it will only irritate them – if they're interested they'll contact you. Expect that you might not be paid for the first few pieces, but bear in mind that a few cuttings and successfully completed assignments could well lead to more. For more advice read *Travel Writing and Photography: All You Need to Know to Make It Pay* (Traveller's Press) by Guy Markes. Keep your eye open in the national newspapers such as the *Observer* for young travel writers' competitions. You never know, your experiences in Nepal could be the start of a glittering literary career.

JOURNALISM

Fledgling journalists can use their time abroad to garner their skills. The huge advantage of being a native English speaker can open many doors for you and, with a little initiative, you should be able to fix up voluntary work on newspapers and radio stations in Asia and Africa. Patrick McGuire used his travelling experiences as ideas for radio reports, and has since built a career in the BBC World Service, while journalist Lucia Cockcroft managed to find her first paid position writing for *TNT* magazine in Sydney. English teacher Andrew Dobbie says that in Cairo in Egypt there are also many openings on English language newspapers.

Eager to travel and get her first job as a hack, Sarah Roe wrote to 25
English language publications around the world and eventually found work
in Budapest for the *Central European Business Weekly*. Writing in the
Overseas Jobs Express, she says, 'Because Central and Eastern Europe is
in such a transitional phase, there are considerable opportunities for less
experienced Westerners. A bit of initiative and a lot of enthusiasm can land
you a highly responsible position which you would be unlikely to get with
similar qualifications back home.'

PART THREE: WHERE TO GO

EUROPE

14 EASTERN EUROPE AND RUSSIA

EASTERN EUROPE

Without a doubt, the most common and easiest way of working in Eastern Europe is through English teaching and voluntary work. Teaching in particular has huge potential and Eastern Europe has gathered quite a reputation for the fledgling Tefl teacher eager to find their first job. It's not hard to see why. Since changes in the former Soviet Union and the reunification of Germany, English has become the language of choice for the young and ambitious, eager to reach out to the West. As a result, there are hundreds of English schools around and teaching is by far the best way of financing a working holiday. Demand is huge, but prospective teachers are advised not to rest on their laurels. Competition can be heavy, particularly in the big cities like Prague, Bratislava, Budapest, and Warsaw, and you'd be well advised to arm yourself with a Tefl certificate before setting out. Generally, the further you go from the big cities, the less competition there will be. The pay is generally much lower than in Western Europe, but with low living costs and sometimes free board and lodging, teachers can make a comfortable living. Just don't expect to be able to save up your dosh for a holiday in affluent western Europe!

Most of the opportunities lie in the huge number of private schools, which tend to pay better than the state jobs. However, teaching posts in state schools can come with good perks, such as health insurance and a long-term contract. Many teachers also supplement their income with private tuition.

Here are some teacher recruitment agencies:

Language Methodology Centre (JODM), ul Dombatantow 20, Walbrzych 58 302, Poland, Tel/fax: 48 47 8694.

English for Everybody (Czech Republic), Spanielova 1292, Prague 6 16 300, Czech Republic, Tel/fax: (02) 301 9784.

The Hungarian Chamber of Language Schools has a database of qualified English teachers that are consulted by member schools. Write to the Hungarian Chamber of Language Schools, Rath Byorgy u. 24, Budapest 1122, Tel/fax: 01 155 4664.

Americans can try the American and international schools in Eastern Europe. For more information on American schools funded by the Department of State, contact Office of Overseas Schools, C/OS, US Department of State, Room 245, SA-29, Washington, DC 20522-2902, Tel: 703 875 7800.

THE CZECH REPUBLIC AND SLOVAKIA

The English language is hugely popular in the Czech Republic, probably because it seems to represent the freedom of the West after years of enforced Russian-language learning by the Soviets. Opportunities abound, particularly in the larger cities. Once there, it shouldn't be hard to find work. English teaching jobs are advertised regularly in the classified sections of both Czech/Slovak and English-language newspapers. In the larger cities, you can check the notice boards of English-language bookshops and the British Council library in Bratislava for teaching positions.

Most teaching jobs tend to be in the private sector and are particularly in Prague and Bratislava. Most prospective teachers are expected to have a RSA or Tefl certificate and a level of professionalism that they will be keen to see you demonstrate. Jobs may be plentiful but they are also demanding. Teaching in the Czech Republic should certainly not be seen as the soft option.

For vacancies check out the *Prague Post*, an English-language newspaper for the expat community, or try the Czech newspaper *Annonce* which specialises in classified ads. Again, try putting up fliers in the English-language bookshop and libraries, or checking their notice boards for work. The British Council in Prague is based at 14 Vorsilska, Prague 1,Czech Republic.

Contact the British Council either there or in your home country before you leave for a list of schools operating in the Czech Republic. Berlitz have three schools in Prague. The addresses are Na Porici 12, Prague, Czech Republic, Tel: 02 487 2052; Kouritska 18, Prague, Czech Republic, Tel: 02 324 473; Vlakova 12, Prague, Czech Republic, Tel: 02 27 71 01.

VISAS AND REGULATIONS

Getting together the right documentation to enter the Czech Republic can be a complicated and time-consuming business. Since a new Residency Law was passed in 2000, most foreigners must apply for a long-stay visa before entering the country. For this you will have to show your passport, which must be at least 9–15 months valid (depending on length of stay), proof of sufficient funds to cover living expenses, a document proving the purpose of your stay (work permit) and proof of accommodation.

You will also need to apply for a residence permit in advance if you intend to work for over ninety days. This requires proof of a work permit, which can only be issued by your future employer and will only be granted if they can prove they can't find someone Czech suitable for the job. Contact the Czech embassy or consulate for more details.

HUNGARY

Hungary is the most difficult of Eastern European countries in which to find work teaching English. Some of this is down to the fact that they are thought to speak the best English in Eastern Europe. But much of the difficulty is due to the fact that employers place a high emphasis on qualifications in all their various forms. It is also rumoured that you are more likely to face competition from Hungarian English-speakers than you are in other Eastern European countries. Therefore, to find work here you will almost certainly need to have a Tefl certificate and often prior experience.

That said, there is still plenty of work around, with hundreds of private English-language schools scattered throughout the country from cosmopolitan Budapest to small, rural towns. There are also other posts to be found in public schools, universities and business corporations.

The best way to find work is to keep an eye on the English-language newspapers such as *Budapest Week*, *Budapest Sun*, and the *Budapest Business Journal*. All have good classified sections listing teaching positions and other available jobs. There are also two popular Hungarian newspapers that are well known for their free classifieds – the *Expressz* and *Hirdetes*.

Like Poland and the Czech Republic, Hungary is a great place to supplement your income with private tuition. Post your services in all the available notice boards such as in English-language bookshops, libraries and universities. Aim for students and the business community. The British Council English Teaching Centre is based at Benczur utca 26, Budapest, Hungary, Tel: 01 321 4039.

VISAS AND REGULATIONS

To work in Hungary you must fix up a work permit from your country of residence before arriving there. This requires a labour permit, which your future employer must obtain from the Hungarian labour office. Contact the Hungarian embassy or consulate for more details.

POLAND

Poland has the most potential for finding English teaching work, both in the major cities such as Warsaw and Krakow and in the more out-of-the-way places. Private schools tend to pay better, but public schools in Poland come with loads of perks such as free room and board, prearranged visas and residency permits. If you are interested in applying for a position in one of Poland's public schools, contact: Ministry of National Education, Department of International Cooperation, Al. J. Ch. Szucha 25, Warsaw PL-00918, Poland, Tel: 02 628 0461 or 022 29 72 41, Fax: 02 628 8561.

Unlike Prague and Budapest, Warsaw lacks many English-language newspapers which can help you find work. However, the *Warsaw Voice* may carry some useful adverts. Some teaching positions are advertised on the notice board at the British Council, where you can also place an ad for private tuition. The address is: British Council English Teaching Centre, Al Jerozolimskie 59, Warsaw 00-697, Poland, Tel: 02 628 7401, 02 628 7401, 02 628 7403, or 02 621 9955.

OTHER WORK

Poland has a high unemployment rate so, beyond teaching, other opportunities are in short supply. Speaking Polish is a distinct advantage or, if you possess a high level of expertise in an area that Poland is lacking, do a little research before you leave and try to find work before you go. Find out which companies have branches in or links with Poland and send them your CV and covering letter. According to many expats, Poland is a great place for networking, and spreading the word that you are looking for work can open some much-needed doors for you. You should be able to get a list of all the British companies that do business in Poland by contacting the Chamber of Commerce; visit their website at **www.britishchambers.org.uk**.

The United States Department of Commerce in Poland publishes a similar list. For more information, contact: American Cultural Centre, Senatorska 13/15, Warsaw 00-076, Poland, Tel: 022 26 70 15.

VISAS AND REGULATIONS

EEA and US citizens do not need a visa to enter the country but your stay will be limited from 14–90 days depending on your nationality. British people have up to 180 days.

In order to work you will have to get hold of a work visa from your country of origin before you leave. For this you will probably have to show proof of qualifications (particularly your Tefl certificate if you intend to teach English) and proof from your future employer. This will get you a residence permit, which, on arrival in Poland, you should take to the regional employment office to obtain a work permit.

Contact the Polish embassy for details, where you should also be able to get a handout called *Visas For Teachers*.

VOLUNTARY WORK IN EASTERN EUROPE

Many voluntary work organisations arrange work in Eastern Europe such as International Voluntary Service (Old Hall, East Bergholt, Colchester CO7 6TQ, Tel: 01132 304600, Fax: 01206 299043) and Christian Outreach (1 New Street, Leamington Spa CV31 1HP, Tel: 01926 315301).

You can also try Teaching and Projects Abroad, which organises voluntary placements in teaching, medicine and journalism, in Russia, Romania and the Ukraine. Write to Teaching and Projects Abroad, Gerrard House, Rustington, West Sussex BN16 1AW, Tel: 01903 859911, Website: **www.teaching-abroad.co.uk**.

RUSSIA AND THE FORMER SOVIET REPUBLICS

The first thing to say about working in Russia is to state the obvious – don't expect to make fistloads of money. In fact, finding work is well nigh impossible and, like Eastern Europe, if you want to experience authentic Russian life, there are two avenues open to you: voluntary work or teaching English.

Teaching English is a particularly good move and one which most teachers who try it say is a fascinating experience. Hard work, but fascinating. There are ample vacancies about and many posts come with good packages including accommodation in hostels or with host families, and travel costs, with visas sorted out. That's a good job because Russian visas can be a minefield. English is not widely spoken in Russia and so learning some of the Russian language is almost imperative.

ENGLISH TEACHING

Teaching in Russia requires different tactics than in other countries. For one thing there's the labyrinth of the Russian visa system, which makes many Russian employers not in a position to offer you legal work (see Visas and regulations section). Some teachers report that working for the Russian-owned schools rarely leads to 'official' work, and to head for the international chains instead. Some even go so far as to caution teachers to make sure they get a visa which enables them to both enter and leave the country. Rumours persist that one unnamed school was so tired of losing its teachers that it made it very difficult for them to leave by issuing them with a one-way visa instead! The unhappy teachers then had to apply for an exit visa, which could only be done through the school authorities and took three weeks to process.

The crucial thing is to make good contacts and build up an elaborate support system. Read around the subject first and always check the small print.

If you're an affluent westerner, it's also wise to remember that you are an easy target in a country that is still largely in economic tatters. This can make private tuition particularly difficult, so at the very least, make sure you know the people you are teaching well, and build up students gradually.

Remember too that what you may deem a fair price could be out of the reach of many natives.

VISAS AND REGULATIONS

Visas in Russia are a complicated affair and constantly changing, so check with your Russian embassy or consulate first. However, if you've fixed up work through a voluntary organisation or even an international language chain, your visa should be arranged through them.

All foreign nationals are required to have entry visas to travel to Russia. These can be obtained at the local Russian embassy or consulate. Proper authorisation (invitation) from the Ministry of Foreign Affairs (MFA) or specially authorised travel agencies is required. However, to get an invitation for work purposes, your future employer must be able to apply for a work visa. Not all are legally entitled to this, which is why some teachers say the Russian-owned schools are the most problematic ones. Once you have this invitation you will be sent an application for a multiple entry visa, which lasts three months. After this period, this can then be turned into a work permit. Again, not all employers are able to apply for this so make sure you check with them first.

The US-based website **www.visatorussia.com** contains plenty of up-to-date information about the various visas and is well worth having a look at.

FIXING UP WORK BEFORE YOU LEAVE

Teaching work exists but may be a little hard to get as most schools haven't the money to recruit teachers from abroad. However, your best approach is still to fix up work before you leave. Check the usual Tefl lines of enquiry and read the *Guardian*'s Education section on Tuesdays and *The Times Educational Supplement*. If you are qualified and experienced, the best thing to do is contact the main chains for vacancies – EF English First, Language Link and International House all have schools in Moscow.

International House (**www.ihworld.com/recruitment/index.htm**) in London has a placement section and contacts with many schools throughout Eastern Europe. You can visit their Moscow school website at **www.bkc.ru/eng/jobs/index.html** where they give details about applying for a job in Russia.

Saxoncourt Recruitment and English Worldwide (**www.saxoncourt.com/index.htm**) regularly advertises jobs in Russia and offers a placement service for EFL teachers and EFL training.

Most packages will provide your flights and accommodation and at least a local salary (minimum $300 per month).

FINDING WORK WHEN YOU ARRIVE

Turning up to find teaching work is possible but not easy, particularly outside Moscow and St Petersburg. Be careful about pay and conditions of service (see Visas and regulations section) and try to learn a little Russian first.

The English-language press (*Moscow Times*, *Moscow Tribune* and *St. Petersburg Press*) carry job adverts.

The British Council (**www.britcoun.org/russia/index.htm**) has offices in many cities in Russia and can be a good point of contact both before and after you arrive. There may be job adverts posted on their notice boards.

The website **www.russia.org** carries lots of useful information aimed at English teachers in Russia, ranging from finding work to teaching materials, language exercises to travelling around Russia and finding accommodation.

Another useful resource is the *Guardian* newspaper's website GuardianUnlimited. Its education section has a Tefl directory with links to various Tefl experts based in different countries. Go to **www.education.guardian.co.uk** and look in Tefl News.

TEACHING AND VOLUNTARY WORK

If you don't have a Tefl certificate, your next option is to apply for voluntary work. There are several organisations that can place voluntary teachers in schools around Russia, as well as other opportunities such as journalism and conservation work.

Bunac run a programme placing first-time teachers in Russian schools for one-year contracts. The programme costs £1,500 (in 2002) and covers travel, training and accommodation. Teachers receive a monthly salary in the local currency equivalent to $450 a month plus free accommodation with the bills taken care of, usually in a shared furnished flat. To apply you must be a native English speaker, over eighteen, and educated to A-level standard. Visit **www.bunac.org** for more information or write to the address in the Voluntary Work and Gap Year chapter.

The International Student Exchange Centre (Isec) has a number of opportunities. Not only does it recruit camp counsellors to work in children's summer camps in Russia and the Ukraine, but it also recruits qualified English teachers for language schools in Russia, Latvia and the Ukraine for a placement fee of around £100 (teachers should be qualified).

There is also a Work and Study Experience Russia programme which arranges work experience in a Moscow company, and other cities, for two to four months combined with a four-week Russian language course at a university. Wages are low by western standards but include accommodation and the language course. Placement fee is £240. Contact International

Student Exchange Centre, 35 Ivor Place, London NW1 6EA (Tel: 020 7724 4493, Email: outbounder@btconnnect.com, Website: **www.isecworld.co.uk**).

Travellers Worldwide runs teaching, conservation and work experience placements in Russia. Contact them at 7 Mulberry Close, Ferring, West Sussex BN12 5HY Tel: 01903 700478, Fax: 01903 502595, Email: info@travellersworldwide.com. Prices start from £995.

Teaching & Projects Abroad runs medicine, teaching and journalism placements in Russia for suitable candidates. Prices for the Russian teaching and journalism placements are £1,295. The medicine programme is only open to medical students but if you're a fledgling journalist, you could gain valuable experience working on a Russian newspaper with seasoned journalists who have previously had to work in an unfree world. Picture that on your CV! Contact Teaching & Projects Abroad, Gerrard House, Rustington, West Sussex BN16 1AW, Tel: 01903 859911, Email: info@teaching-abroad.co.uk.

Americans can contact Cross-Cultural Solutions, a non-profit organisation that sends volunteers abroad to provide humanitarian assistance to various countries in a range of long-stay and short-stay programmes. Its Russia programme operates in Russian orphanages or adult care homes. Contact Cross-Cultural Solutions, 47 Potter Avenue, New Rochelle, NY 10801 USA, Tel: 1 800 380 4777; 1 914 632 0022, Fax: 1 914 632 8494, Email: info@crossculturalsolutions.org.

EMBASSIES

Bulgarian Embassy, 186–188 Queen's Gate, London SW7 5HL, Tel: 020 7584 9400; 1621 22nd Street, NW, Washington DC 20008, USA, Tel: 202 483 5885

Czech Embassy, 26 Kensington Palace Gardens, London W8 4QY, Tel: 020 7243 1115; 3900 Spring of Freedom Street, NW, Washington DC 20008, USA, Tel: 202 274 9100, Website: **www.czech.cz/washington**

Hungarian Embassy, 35 Eaton Place, London SW1X 8BY, Tel: 020 7235 2664; 3910 Shoemaker Street, NW, Washington DC 20008, USA, Tel: 202 362 6730

Polish Embassy, 73 New Cavendish Street, London W1N 4HQ, Tel: 020 7580 0476; Consular Division of the Polish Embassy, 2224 Wyoming Avenue, NW, Washington DC, USA, Tel: 202 234 2501

Romanian Embassy, Arundel House, 4 Palace Green, London W8 4QD, Tel: 020 7937 9666; 1607 23rd Street, NW, Washington, DC 20008, USA, Tel: 202 332 4848

Russian Embassy, 5 Kensington Palace Gardens, London W8 4QX, Tel: 020 7229 2666; 2650 Wisconsin Avenue, NW, Washington DC 20008, USA, Tel: 202 298 5700, Website: **www.russianembassy.org**

TRAVELLERS' STORIES

Sarah Fisher worked on a local newspaper and taught in a primary school in Brasov, Romania as part of a three-month placement with Teaching and Projects Abroad.

She says, 'It was almost certainly the most fantastic three months of my life. Not only was it an incredible learning experience, but I also got to meet masses of people, from Romanians to fellow volunteers hailing from Britain, America and Belgium. I really enjoyed the experience and gained greatly in confidence and skills, as well as taking advantage of the opportunity to travel to some fascinating parts of the country.'

For the journalism part, Sarah worked on two different newspapers – *Monitorul* and *Objectiv* – shadowing the full-time journalists and cameramen, writing her own articles and covering local news stories. 'The first culture shock was certainly that I couldn't understand the language at all, which was particularly problematic in the workplace of the newspaper offices. The people were extremely friendly, however, generally spoke good English and wanted to talk to you about their country and local issues. The history of Romania is really interesting, from the early Saxon influences to the immense damage inflicted by the Communist era.'

Sarah found the climate a little strange at first: 'While I was there, it was very cold to start with and the whole of the city was covered in ice, which in turn was covered with snow, making it rather difficult to get anywhere fast (and keep your feet warm and dry)! That was quite daunting but in the summer apparently it gets very hot and the climate is quite extreme.'

There was also a strong network with other volunteers: 'When I first got there, there were only four of us but by the time I left we numbered around thirty! We regularly met up in the pub for some neat vodka or a pint (cost about 20p)! We all stayed with host families but you can also rent apartments very cheaply and it is easy to get by, with supermarkets and shops selling everything you'd need. I stayed with two other girls in the apartment of a local family. Being English, we always had a cup of tea together in the afternoons and a weekly tradition of chocolate and red wine. Relations with the family were generally fine, though their difficulty with English led to some entertaining misunderstandings: they once asked us to remove the "misery" – meaning mess – in our room!'

15 FRANCE

Who hasn't dreamt of living in France, mooching down to the local patisserie to indulge in *pain au chocolats* and strong black coffee? Unfortunately, getting a job in France isn't easy. Thanks to high unemployment, most employers are unlikely to offer a non-national a job, when there are so many French natives queuing up for work. It is also important that you speak good French, even for seasonal and short-term work. Sara Lofthouse found that without the necessary language skills, the French jobcentre wouldn't take her seriously. That said, most people who arrive in France looking for work usually find it – it just might take some time and lot of perseverance. One of the good things about working in France is the minimum wage (*salaire minimum interprofessionel de croissance*), which in the beginning of 2002 was set at 43FF 72 ct (just over €6) per hour. You can find out the exact amount by going to the national website for French statistics **www.insee.fr/fr/indicateur/smic.htm**.

VISAS AND REGULATIONS

As France is part of the European Union, EU nationals require no work permit for employment in France and have up to three months to look for work (renewable so long as you can prove that you are purposefully looking for a job). Passports are still needed and if you plan to stay for over three months, you will need to apply for a resident's permit (*une carte de sejour*) from the town hall, (*la mairie*) or local police station (*la prefecture de police*), which entitles you to various state benefits.

This will require: 150FF/€22.8, four passport photos, a birth/marriage certificate, original and translation, proof of residence such as an electricity/gas/phone bill, and proof of employment/financial resources, such as a contract or bank statement.

Opening a bank account can be tricky and can only be done if you intend to stay for over three months. You can fix that up in the UK before you leave by popping along to a French bank such as Credit Lyonnias or BNP, or in France by showing your passport, *carte de sejour*, proof of address and birth certificate. You may also have to show proof of your income such as a contract and tax return.

NON-EU NATIONALS

Work permits are required for non-EU nationals, which must be obtained before they leave their home country. Work must be pre-arranged and their employer must prove that the post cannot be filled by a French or EU national.

AMERICANS

The Council on International Educational Exchange (633 Third Avenue, 20th Floor, New York, NY 10017-6701, Tel: 1 888 COUNCIL) run a scheme by which American students with a working knowledge of French are allowed to look for a job in France at any time of the year and work for up to three months on an *authorisation provisoire de travail*. Contact the Council on International Educational Exchange for more details.

BUREAUCRACY

Dean Pateman taught English to adolescents in a lycée in France. He says, 'France is very bureaucratic and it's a good idea to have a ready supply of photocopies of qualifications, birth certificate and such and also a ready supply of passport photos. It may have changed but when registering for my *carte de séjour* at the police station I had to give four or five. Opening a bank account can be problematic – you need proof of salary and accommodation, despite the fact that in order to get accommodation you need proof of a bank account! Try to enlist the help of a senior colleague – the head teacher of my school was pivotal in bridging the gap. This is particularly true in places where foreigners are not a commodity.'

USEFUL ADVICE

Dean Pateman has the following tips:

- **Learn the language. Something is always better than nothing in France.**

- **Don't expect to live in the lap of luxury.**

- **Expect bureaucracy to be time-consuming, confusing and often inaccessible and you'll feel less let-down and homesick.**

- **Try to integrate in some way with the local community – sport or other clubs or societies. The expat world is actually very limited and isolated on many occasions.**

- **Take tea with you. Liptons is *not* an acceptable alternative. Ever.**

TOURISM

If you want to work in France, the best thing to opt for is tourist and summer/seasonal work. During the summer the country needs many extra staff for their thriving tourist market. Despite the minimum wage, pay can be quite low, but it can give you a useful footing to secure more permanent, better-paying work.

Head for the Alps in winter for the ski season (Nov–April) and Cote d'Azur for summer work (June–September). It's best to fix up work before you leave through one of the numerous holiday companies that operate in France including Club Med, Mark Warner, Inghams, Europcamp, Crystal Holidays, Powder Byrne and PGL Activity Holidays, where you can apply for a wide range of jobs including kitchen staff, chalet maids, bar staff, waitressing, sports instructors and nannies. Bear in mind that many of these companies may require good French. Another option, of course, is Disneyland Paris, recruiting for a massive 12,000 jobs in summer and 8,000 in winter. Go to **www.disneylandparis.com** for more information.

SKI RESORTS

As well as the large ski companies listed above, there are numerous independent ski companies who recruit for a wide range of staff including chalet hosts, chefs, nannies, ski instructors and technicians, and kitchen and bar staff. Look in any specialist ski brochure or guide, or else do an Internet search.

The following ski companies recruit staff for their chalets and hotels – apply well before the start of the season: Simon Butler Skiing (**www.simonbutlerskiing.co.uk**), Simply Ski (**www.simply-travel.com**) and YSE Limited (**www.yseski.co.uk**).

Ski Staff (**www.skistaff.co.uk**) specialises in placing chalet and hotel staff with British ski companies in the French Alps, while Ski France (**www.skifrance.fr/welcome**) has a job search and classifieds section.

Many of the jobs on offer will require specialist skills, such as ski instructors and technicians. Chalet hosts will be expected to cook to a high standard and will often be cordon bleu trained, although some ski companies provide their own training. Plenty of travellers turn up and find work, however, in the numerous bars, restaurants and hotels, washing dishes in restaurants, cleaning and bar work. Try to head for the big ski resorts such as Courchevel, Meribel, La Plagne, Chamonix and Val d'Isere at the beginning of the season and ask around for work. Meribel is a very popular resort with the British and is a particularly good bet for people who don't speak much French. Many of the ski resorts have websites which you can check out first.

CAMPSITES

France also has many luxury campsites where you may be able to find work. Again, you can find a list in specialist holiday brochures or guides. Knowledge of French is usually preferred.

Carisma Holidays (**www.carisma.co.uk**) recruits couriers and site managers for French campsites during the summer, and you can also try Eurocamp (**www.eurocamp.co.uk**) who employ people for two months during the summer to put up tents around France.

WORKING ON YACHTS

There is also work to be found in Antibes and Cannes, and along the Riviera in general (try Golfe-Juan, Cannes, Monaco, Beaulieu-sur-Mer and Cap Ferrat), where many of the world's most luxurious private and charter yachts are moored. Experienced sailors and crewers may be able to find work on yachts, while there is also plenty of work around for experienced steward/ stewardesses and chefs. Again, make sure you get there at the start of the season in April and be prepared for tough competition for jobs: working on yachts is popular. You can cold call for work, taking your CV around the boats, or try one of the many yacht agencies. Beginners with no experience of sailing may be able to find work as deckhands, although even this is becoming more regulated. If you're lucky, you may be able to work your way around the world, as many of these yachts go over to Jamaica and Barbados for winter. Obviously, safety is a huge issue, so never exaggerate your skills and claim to be a skilled sailor if you're not. (See Working a Passage section)

There is also work to be found on the boats on land, cleaning off fluid dropped by the planes flying to and from nearby Nice airport. Richard Jones managed to subsidise a holiday in Antibes working this way, which he found just by going round the boats and asking for work. He says, 'You might get only a day's work cleaning, but one job usually leads to another. Someone will say that a friend needs someone to clean the decks and pass on your name.'

AU PAIR

Demand for au pairs in France is high, and work is relatively easy to find. Non-EU au pairs are legally required to be aged between seventeen and thirty, have a student visa, be registered on a language course before arriving and have some knowledge of French. There are many agencies that place au pairs in France, for year-long positions or for short-term work over the summer such as Anderson Au Pairs & Nannies (**www.childcare-europe.com**) and Atout France International (**www.atout-fr-international.com/us/afius**). Also try Alliance Francaise, 55 rue Paradie, 13006 Marseille (Tel: 04 91 33 28 19, Email: info@alliancefrmarseille.org).

Many of the large holiday companies such as Mark Warner and First Choice Holidays also recruit for nannies with childcare experience.

You may also be able to find a job once you are there by visiting one of the

Centres d'Information Jeunesses (CIJs) or through notice boards, English language press and newsletters.

TEACHING

Despite its close proximity to Britain, English teaching work isn't easy to find: most private language schools and institutions insist on a Tefl certificate at the very least, and usually prefer a diploma. Unlike many other EFL destinations, you are also expected to speak French. That said, some Tefl teachers strike lucky and manage to find work – lucky being the operative word. You can find addresses of language schools by looking in the Yellow Pages.

The Education and Training Group (British Council, 10 Spring Gardens, London SW1A 2BN, Tel: 020 7389 4764, Website: **www.britishcouncil.org**) places undergraduate university language students as language assistants in French schools, as well as in other French-speaking countries such as Belgium, Quebec and Switzerland.

FRUIT PICKING

Fruit picking is a popular way to earn hard cash, particularly apple picking and grape picking. The best way to get work is head for the nearest Agence Nationale Pour l'Emploi or ANPE office, the national employment agency of France. This has offices throughout the country and sets up seasonal offices in regions to deal with seasonal demands. As such, they can help you find work apple picking and grape picking in the harvest periods. If you find out the harvest dates, it's possible to work your way around the country, starting in the south where the crops ripen first. Some pickers meet in one farm, and then when the season ends, head further north together in search of other work.

Harvest Guide For France

Strawberries	Loire Valley	April–May
Cherries	Rhone Valley, Central France, Perigord,Languedoc-Roussillon	May–June
Strawberries	Rhone Valley, Central France, Perigord,Languedoc-Roussillon	May–June
Hay	All over France	June–Aug
Maize	Auvergne and the South West	July–Sept
Pears	The Rhone and Loire Valleys and Paris Basin	July–Sept

Courgettes (Zucchinis)	Provence	July–Sept
Raspberries	Brittany, Central France, the South West, the Auvergne and Aquitaine	July–Sept
Gherkins	Brittany, Central France, the South West, the Auvergne and Aquitaine	July–Sept
Mange-Tout	Provence	July–Sept
Melons	Vienne	July–Oct
Apples	Provence	Aug–Sept
Tomatoes	The South West, the East and the Paris Basin	Aug–Sept
Apricots	Provence	Aug–Sept
Tobacco	The South West, the East and Paris Basin	Aug–Sept
Grapes	Beaujolais, Bordeaux and Languedoc	Sept–Oct
Capsicums (Peppers)	Provence	Sept–Oct
Apples	Brittany, Normandy, The Dordogne, Languedoc and Central France	Sept–Oct
Plums	Brittany, Dordogne and Medoc	Sept–Oct
Grapes	Pays de la Loire, Alsace, Central France, Burgundy, Aquitaine and Champagne	Oct
Olives	Provence	Nov–Dec
Chestnuts	The South, Ardeche and Corsica	Nov–Dec

This is a rough guide and harvest times vary according to weather and conditions. For more details contact The 'ANPE' (Jobcentre) in your chosen region by telephone or in person. This information is taken from the website **anyworkanywhere.com**.

Although fruit picking is good fun, it is notoriously hard work, and you will need to be relatively fit. Pickers can earn around £25 a day on top of free accommodation and food. Many farmers allow free camping on their land. John Starkie found work on an apple farm in Tours when he was down to his last 10FF in Paris:

'I spent three and a half months picking apples with around seventy other people. We had a brilliant time. The people were great and were a really mixed bag of nationalities including French, English, Moroccans, Algerian and Polish. The owner's nephew and I were responsible for the harvesting, and had to get up at 4.30 a.m. every morning. We started the day with a huge cup of coffee and croissants and after that, went off into the fields and got the equipment ready for the other pickers. The best thing was seeing the sunrise coming up over the fields, and we ended up really healthy because we were eating so many apples.'

THE JOB SEARCH

The European Employment Services' (EURES) (**www.europa.eu.int/comm/employment_social/elm/eures/index**) database has a listing of all kinds of jobs all over Europe. Jobs tend to be professional, long term and require foreign language skills.

If you're interested in exploring more long-term business opportunities, you can obtain a list of British companies with associates in France from the British Embassy.

The weekly trade magazine *L'Hotellerie*, published at 5, rue Antoine Bourdelle, 75015 Paris, lists vacancies in the tourist industry.

EU nationals are allowed to use their French national employment service ANPE (*Agence Nationale pour L'Emploi*) which has offices all over the country and can give you details of seasonal vacancies in harvesting summer and ski resorts. However, it also has a reputation for favouring only French speakers so polish up your language first.

People who can speak good French can check out private employment agencies Manpower, Kelly, Bis, Select France and Ecco in large cities for admin and industry temping work.

The *Centres d'Informational Jeunesse* (CIJ) dotted throughout the country can help people find jobs, as well as providing accommodation and advice on temporary work. Not only do they publish advice leaflets on seasonal work (contact CIJ at 101 Quai Branly, 75740 Paris Cedex 15 (Tel: 01 44 49 12 00/ **www.cidj.asso.fr**) but they are also a good source for temporary vacancies.

Check out the French newspapers *Le Monde* and *Le Figaro* for their job advertisements.

The Paris Job Site (**www.parisjobsite.com**) has information on careers fairs and relocating to Paris, as well as a jobs search facility.

FRENCH EMBASSY

French Embassy, 59 Knightsbridge, London SW1X 7JT, Tel: 020 7201 1000; 4101 Reservoir Road, NW, Washington DC 20007, USA Tel: 202 944 6000, Website: **www.info-france-usa.org**.

16 GERMANY

Despite Germany's current economic recession, the country continues to attract foreign workers in droves. Much of this is because of Germany's excellent standard of living. German salaries are the highest in the world, averaging about £21 per hour, and, despite the high unemployment, there are good prospects for foreign workers and travellers. Job opportunities exist in all fields of work although you will need a good standard of German.

VISAS AND REGULATIONS

EU citizens have the right to live and work in Germany without a work permit. However, even if you are looking for work, you may have to prove that you have adequate means to fund both your stay and your return journey out of there. You must also have a resident's permit if you intend to work. You will then have to start a complicated procedure which will involve registering at various places, usually in your town hall. If you are not staying in a hotel, you must register at the *Einwohnermeldeamt/ Meldestelle* (Residents Registration Office) for a registration certificate. This is normally at the town hall, and you will need to take your passport, a copy of the lease or rental agreement and a completed registration form.

If you intend to spend more than three months in Germany, you must then register at the *Auslanderbehorde* (Foreign Nationals Authority) as soon as you have begun work. You will need to take with you proof of employment (a contract or letter of employment), two passport photos, a copy of your resident's registration and your passport.

NON-EU NATIONALS

Non-EU nationals must have a visa and permit to work. You must first secure work before arriving, get written proof from your employer, and approval from the aliens authority nearest to your intended place of work, and then you can apply to your embassy for your work/residence permit. The application process can take six weeks. Swiss and US citizens can apply after they arrive in Germany if they have not already started work.

Council on International Educational Exchange run a Work in Germany exchange programme for American students. Check out **www.ciee.org** for more information.

Bundestag Internship Program (**www.bipaa.org/**) is a fully funded fellowship for an academic year during which participants spend one semester studying at the Humboldt University in Berlin and one semester as an intern in the office of a member of the German Parliament. Internships are available to the French, East Europeans and Americans.

HEALTH

If you are an EU national, you can enjoy all the benefits of living in an EU member state which entitle you to the same basic rights as German nationals. One of these benefits includes an EC agreement that entitles you to get urgent medical treatment free in Germany. In order to do this, you should get hold of the form E111 before you leave the UK from any post office or benefits office. Once in Germany you must then register at the *Allgemeine Ortskrankenkasse* (AOK or local health insurance fund) for a *Krankenversicherungskarte* (health insurance card) and a *Sozialversicherungsausweis* (social insurance card). Your health insurance card also covers basic dental treatment.

WORK OPPORTUNITIES

TOURISM

Germany's tourism industry is heavily reliant on foreign workers and as such there should be plenty of work available at campsites, holiday camps, hotels, fast food joints and theme parks. Typical jobs around include waiter and waitressing, washing up dishes and scrubbing floors. Germany has strict health regulations so it needs plenty of cleaners. You can find names and addresses of hotels from holiday brochures.

Head for Munich, Berlin, the Alps, the Black Forest, seaside resorts and ski resorts on the Austrian border. It's also a good bet to try the trade fairs such as the Frankfurt Book Fair and the Munich Beer Festival, both in October. The German work ethic and discipline is legendary and not just a national stereotype, so expect to work long shifts and cope with demanding employers.

Europa Park (**www.europa-park.de/deut/f_index.htm**) is a theme park employing 1,860 seasonal employees.

OTHER OPPORTUNITIES

There are plenty of other opportunities such as in nursing and the skilled building trade. The industrial centres of Stuttgart, Dusseldorf, Munich and Hanover should offer plenty of manufacturing work in hard labour, warehouses and factories. Be aware that jobs can be advertised anywhere, and may not be as glamorous as they sound. Jason Cobbing found work in the *Artists' Newsletter*, advertising for 'scenic artists' to work at a Warner Brothers' movie theme park near Dusseldorf. When he got there he found they were nothing but 'glorified labourers' doing painting and construction work.

TEACHING ENGLISH

Germany doesn't have many opportunities for teaching work, particularly for fledgling Tefl teachers. Experiences and good references are paramount in securing posts, and speaking German is also a distinct advantage. There is however a strong market for Business English, particularly in the big cities of Berlin, Munich and Frankfurt, where American English is favoured for international negotiating. There is also a strong presence of all the big chains here, such as Berlitz and Linguarama, so contact the main players for school addresses before you leave. Private work should be easy to find, as long as you have experience and good references. (See Tefl section in Chapter 6, Teaching English).

You can find vacancies by checking the job section of the English language magazine *Munich Found* (**www.munichfound.com**) for Tefl vacancies.

AU PAIR

Like France and the UK, Germany has many opportunities for fixing up au pair work. Under the law, au pairs in Germany should be between seventeen and twenty-four years old, have a basic knowledge of German and childcare experience.

Some Au Pair agencies online are:
Au-pair Agentur am Bodensee
(**www.home.t-online.de/home/aupair-Bodensee**)
Au-Pair Agency Anette B. Wandres (**www.aupair-vermittlung.de**)
Au-Pair-Vermittlung Reinhard Krohn
(**www.home.tonline.de/home/Reinhard.Krohn/english.htm**)

AGRICULTURE

Fruit picking work is available in the Altes Land between Stade and Hamburg in north Germany. During the summer you may find work picking cherries in July and August, while September is the time for apple picking. The German vineyards also require workers to help with the grape harvest in October and November. Head for south-west Germany, particularly along the Rhine valley.

The German Wine Page (**www.winepage.de**) includes a guide and map to the German wine regions.

Working Holidays (**www.workingholidays.de**) arrange jobs all the year round on German farms or in country hotels, living with the family, looking after children and/or horses and farm animals. The project Happy Hands is suitable for gap-year students from Britain, and all students from EU countries wishing to perfect their knowledge of the German language and help the families. Work typically lasts for three to six months and includes accommodation, meals and some pocket money.

VOLUNTARY WORK

Many of the voluntary organisations such as Concordia, International Voluntary Service and UNA Exchange run placements and camps in Germany. (See Voluntary Work chapter for addresses.) To arrange voluntary work on an organic farm contact WWOOF who have a branch in Germany (WWOOF-Deutschland, Postfach 210259, 01263 Dresden, Germany).

THE JOB SEARCH

As a member of the EU and EEA, the Employment Service in the UK has details of vacancies throughout the EU, supplied to it through the EURES network. You can speak to one of their Euroadvisers via local Employment Jobcentres. For job vacancies on the EURES website, go to **www.europa.eu.int/jobs/eures**.

You can also visit the German jobcentre *Arbeitsamt*. There are more than 800 jobcentres throughout the country – you can find the address of your nearest one in the German Yellow Pages *Gelbe Seiten*.

Private agencies are listed in the Yellow Pages under *Arbeitsvermittlung*.

German national newspapers such as the *Frankfurter Allgemeine Zeitung*, *Die Welt*, *Handelsblatt* and *Frankfurter Rundschau* carry job advertisements, particularly on Sundays. Local newspapers such as *Westdeutsche Zeitung* and *Stuttgarter Zeitung* carry job ads on Wednesdays and Saturdays. A list of German newspapers is available from the German embassy.

For opportunities for seasonal work on farms, in hotels and in vineyards, write in German to: Zentralstelle fur Arbeitsvermittlung (ZAV), Villemombler Strasse 76, D-53123 Bonn, Germany, Tel: 0049 228 7130.

Keep an eye on the job section, *der Stellenmarkt*, in German newspapers such as *Berliner Morgenpost*, *Die Welt*, or *Frankfurter Allgemeine Zeitung*.

Try the international employment agencies such as Manpower, Robert Walters and International Secretaries, which can be contacted in the UK before leaving.

If you are a professional, the CEPEC Recruitment Guide may be of some use. It lists recruitment agencies and search consultants in the UK, many of which deal in overseas placements, for professional, manager and executives. You should be able to find this in your local reference library or alternatively contact: CEPEC Ltd, 13 Hanover Square, London W1R 9HD, Tel: 020 7629 2266.

Applying on spec is also common in Germany and worth trying. Try German firms with an office or presence in the UK, or UK firms with an office or presence in Germany. Applications should be typed in German and come with a photo and covering letter. The Chambers of Commerce (www.bccg.de/about/bccgInfo.htm) publish lists of British companies with associates in Germany.

EU national students can try looking at the *studentische arbeitsvermittlung* in German universities, where they can find advertised casual work.

USEFUL ADDRESSES

German Embassy, 23 Belgrave Square, London SW1X 8PZ, Tel: 020 7824 1300 or Bundesverwaltungsamt, Marzellenstrasse 50 56, 50668 Koln, Tel. 00 49 221 7582748), Bundesverwaltungsamt, 50728 Koln (for postal enquiries); 4645 Reservoir Road, NW, Washington DC, 20007, USA, Tel: 202 298 4000, **www.germany-info.org**

Auf Weidersehn Net (**www.pagemagic.net/expat**) has information for the British expat living in Germany

Germany Online (**www.germany-info.org/f index.html**) also has lots of useful information for travellers and students provided by the German embassy and the German Information Centre

The UK Overseas Placement Service produce a *Living in Germany* leaflet. Write to Employment Service, Overseas Placing Unit, Rockingham House, 123 West Street, Sheffield S1 4ER

TRAVELLERS' STORIES

Darren Cooper worked in an electronics company in Germany for a year, as part of his Electronic Engineering degree. The placement was optional and came on the condition that he attended a year's duration of German lessons, every morning at 6.30 in the morning. He says that speaking German was crucial in adapting to life there. 'The company was based about twenty miles outside Berlin and in what was the old Eastern bloc region so everyone spoke Polish, Russian and German. There were no other foreigners, and no one spoke English, so I was very much on my own, but the people were really friendly. Everyone went out of their way to make me feel at home, and every weekend, my colleagues would organise an outing for me. My boss would even arrange afternoons off and take me out to visit local places. I did a lot of travelling while I was there because it was an excellent base to explore other regions. I went to the Czech Republic, Poland, France and Holland as well as seeing most of Germany.'

The one thing Darren did find hard to adapt to was the working culture. 'We were expected to work long hours and it took some getting used to. I started work at 6 a.m., so had to leave my room at 5 a.m., and would work on until about 6.30 in the evening. It was a very strict regime. We would have breakfast and lunch at exactly the same time each day. But we were paid extremely well and the standard of living was good.'

17 GREECE AND TURKEY

GREECE

Greece is teeming with opportunities for working travellers, and with a lower cost of living than the UK combined with the notoriously stunning landscape, you can see why there is such a high percentage of Britons living here. However, there are also downsides. While many people have a fantastic time in Greece, tales abound of unscrupulous employers, so it is imperative that you know your rights.

VISA AND REGULATIONS

Greece is part of the EU so if you're an EU national you won't need a working visa to work there. The official line is that you should register with the local police within eight days of arriving, but that said, many people work all summer without any kind of permit or registration. Once your first three months is up, you should do as you do in all EU member states, and apply for a residence permit from your local police station or Aliens Department (*Grafeio Tmimatos Allodapon*). Take with you your passport and a letter from your employer.

- **Aliens Bureau, 173, Alexandras Avenue, 11522, Tel: 01 770 5711 17**

- **Aliens Centre, 37 Iroon Politechniou Str., Piraeus 185 10, Tel: 01 412 2501, 424 1333, 412 8607**

- **Aliens Centre, 25 Tsimiski Str., Thessaloniki (Salonika), Tel: 521 067**

- **Aliens Centre, Athens Suburbs, 73 D. Gounari, Maroussi, Tel: 01 802 4808**

Non-EU nationals can obtain a work permit in Greece if a vacancy matching their qualifications exists. The work permit is valid for a specific period of time and only for a specific position. Contact your nearest Greek consulate office or embassy for details.

Greece has been known to adopt a fairly relaxed attitude to 'unofficial' work without the necessary documentation, but it's best to err on the side of caution. Immigration officers do make checks – particularly in harvesting areas – and fines can be heavy if you do not have the right permit.

KNOW YOUR RIGHTS

One of the most common problems foreign workers encounter in Greece is not getting paid. Greek employers have a reputation of being a little, hmm, unscrupulous, and while there are many who are fair minded and decent, it's best to make sure you are protected. The best thing to do is ask your employer to pay you at the end of every day. That way you can avoid being one of the countless number who have worked for weeks in advance only to receive no payment.

Another thing to do is make sure your employers register you with the Greek social security system (IKA), which they are legally obliged to do. This isn't popular with many employers as they have to fork out around sixteen per cent of your earnings, but without it you will be classified as an illegal worker and could risk being taken to court. Your employer will face a pretty hefty fine too.

Registering with the IKA is also a measure of insurance. Not only does it entitle you to free medical care, but if your employer refuses to pay you and you threaten to go to the IKA, he should soon change his mind – even if you're not registered.

WORK OPPORTUNITIES

Greece is one of the best countries to just turn up and find work. This is for two reasons. The first is that casual work is easy to find in Greece, whether it's picking oranges or teaching English or looking after children. The second is that with the dubious reputation of its employers, it's a good idea to meet them in person and check them out first.

TOURISM

Your best bet for finding work is to head for the package holiday resorts at the beginning of the season (the holiday season lasts from May to September). Women in particular should be able to pick up work easily in the numerous bars and tavernas, although not necessarily for the best reasons. Men can often find work building, or helping to paint, fix roofs and such like.

You can fix up seasonal work before you leave through the usual British tour operators who have holidays in Greece. Mark Warner recruit over 1,500 staff for the Alps and the Med each year. Applicants must be over nineteen and hold an EU passport. (See Chapter 7, Tourism).

Working on boats and yachts is also popular although most of the work tends to be offered by hanging around the harbours or contacting yacht agencies and brokers. Blue Sails Yachting (**www.bluesails.com**) and Polco Yachts (**www.polco.net**) both offer crewed charter yachts.

Alternatively, you can fix up work before you arrive by contacting the big sailing holiday operators. Sunsail (**www.sunsail.com**) employ 'team players' in the Med, while Sunworld Sailing, a large water-based leisure firm, part of Thomas Cook, offers summer jobs on land and sea during April to end October. Contact (**www.sunworld-sailing.co.uk**).

CASUAL WORK

In Athens you may be able to find work in hostels – either helping out cleaning and such like or acting as a 'runner', which involves waiting at the stations and drumming up customers. Outside the main tourist areas, you can sometimes pick up casual work fruit picking, working on farms and building, by turning up at the main village square where locals congregate. Other ways of finding work are to talk to fellow travellers. Some Greek employers put ads in newspapers but make sure you meet them and get a good idea of the kind of work and conditions offered before agreeing to anything. The other option is to just walk the streets and knock on doors. Kevin Pritchard went on holiday to the Greek island of Ios and ran out of money after two and a half weeks. 'I'd seen some English-looking people around pushing wheelbarrows so knew there was work for English people. I went round every restaurant and bar in the area, and after ten places met an Australian woman and her Greek husband who were opening a watersports shop the next week and needed someone to help them get the space ready. I worked for them for three days, clearing rubble, moving furniture and painting, and then found another four days' work with her friend, doing more painting and labouring. The pay was terrible – about £10 a day – but it was just enough money for me to live off.'

AGRICULTURE

Greece is famed for its succulent olives and luscious fruit so it's not surprising that many people head off in search of casual fruit-picking work. However, competition for seasonal jobs is high and according to the website **www.anyworkanywhere.com**, applicants will improve their chances of employment if they apply for work after arriving in the country.

Head for the local square, or you could try visiting local bars frequented by farmers and asking around for work. Learn a few key Greek phrases.

The following guide is provided by **www.anyworkanywhere.com** who also run ads for job vacancies. They stress that this is only a rough guide, as harvest times vary according to weather conditions, and it is advisable to check at the employment agency first.

Harvest Guide For Greece

Oranges	Western Crete	Jan–Apr
Olives	Central Peloponnese	Jan–Apr
Tomatoes	Southern Crete	April–June
Apricots	Navplion, in the eastern Peloponnese	April–June
Cherries	Between Argos and Tripolis in the central Peloponnese also to the west of Thessaloniki, Macedonia	April–June

Pears	Between Argos and Tripolis in the central Peloponnese	April–June
Melon	Around Patras	June–Oct
Tobacco	To the west of Thessaloniki, Macedonia	June–Oct
Grapes	Central Peloponnese, on Crete and Rhodes	June–Oct
Apples	To the west of Thessaloniki, Macedonia, Pilion peninsula	June–Oct
Pears	Pilion peninsula, west of Volos	June–Oct
Nuts	Pilion peninsula, west of Volos	June–Oct
Peaches	Pilion peninsula, west of Volos	June–Oct
Oranges	Eastern Peloponnese	Nov–Feb
Olives	Rhodes	Nov–Feb

TEACHING ENGLISH

There are also countless private English language schools called *frontisteria*, which can be a stable source of work for native English speakers. Not all will demand to see Tefl certification, but most will expect you to be an EU graduate and to see proof. Write to the British Council for lists of schools and agencies. Most agencies require a Tefl certificate and interview in Greece and the UK.

Anglo-Hellenic Teacher Recruitment (**www.anglo-hellenic.com/**) is the foremost agency for English teachers in Greece, providing employment, training and support. Their address is PO Box 263, 201 00 Corinth (Tel/fax: 0741 53511, jobs@anglo-hellenic.com).

Cambridge Teachers Recruitment (33A Makryanni Street, New Halkidona, 143 43 Athens Tel/fax: 01 218 5155) is a huge agency placing eighty to one hundred teachers per year.

TURKEY

Turkey marks the crossover between the East and West and as such, offers a fascinating glimpse into two colliding cultures. Working here is illegal without a work permit, but there is plenty of unofficial work around, particularly in the tourist areas such as Istanbul and the south-west coast. Pay tends to be low by western standards, but on the upside, it is also very cheap to live. Travellers are reminded that Turkey is a Muslim country, so expect – and respect – religious and cultural differences.

VISAS AND REGULATIONS

As Turkey is outside the EU, the ease with which UK travellers can move around Europe stops here. Like all foreign nationals, if you want to work in Turkey you must get hold of a work visa from a Turkish consulate in your country of residency before you leave.

Getting a work permit is not easy – you will need a contract of employment and in some cases a letter of approval from the relevant authorities. English teachers must have a degree and Tefl certification. Work permits are required for all work including au pair and voluntary work. The processing time can take about two to three months so bear this in mind before booking your flight.

Once you arrive in Turkey, you must also obtain a residence permit from the local police within a month of your arrival. Any UK national is also advised to have a minimum of six months validity on their passports from the date of entry into Turkey. For more information contact your nearest Turkish consulate or embassy.

You will also need to check with your local travel clinic, or doctor, which injections are advised for travelling to Turkey.

TEACHING ENGLISH

Turkey is a Mecca for English teaching work and can be the ideal starting place for Tefl teachers eager to get on the first rung of their teaching career. The jobs also come with some good packages including free accommodation and flights. Pay varies from around $700 to $1,300 a month for roughly 26 contact hours a week, although some schools may expect you to work more. Most schools pay in Turkish lira – check that your pay is linked to the dollar rate every few months as the Turkish lira is very unstable and devalues suddenly.

Most language schools are based in the big cities like Istanbul, Ankara and Izmir, although such is the demand there will be plenty of work in other areas. Finding work is more difficult in universities and private high schools as they don't advertise so much and usually ask for more than just a Tefl certificate, such as three or four years' experience.

Many teachers turn up and find work, relying on the usual method of cold-calling schools and looking for vacancies in the *Turkish Daily News*. The best time to come is August and September, when schools may be looking for last-minute staff to make up for teachers not turning up.

To find work look in the usual sources, such as the *Guardian*, and write to the British Council for a list of language schools. Also try the school agencies in Turkey.

Turkeng Recruitment (Ayanoglu Mah, 1284 Sok No 8, Varsak, Antalya Tel: 242 325 2662, Fax: 242 326 6778, Website: **www.angelfire.com/biz/turkeng** and

UK branch: 3 Peck Close, Norwich NR5 9NF) recruits native English speaking teachers for schools and private language schools for adults, private universities and private high schools in Istanbul, Bursa, Izmir and Antalya.

Typically their contracts last from nine to twelve months. Teaching duties usually include between 24 and 30 guaranteed teaching hours per week with the opportunity to do overtime if wished. Teachers are usually required to work evenings and/or weekends. The school provides rent-free accommodation in addition to a salary of around US$600–US$1000 per month depending on qualifications, experience and the cost of living in the particular city.

TRAVELLERS' STORIES

Kate Barlow has worked at International House in Suadiye, Turkey, for one and a half years. Before training to be a Tefl teacher, she was a journalist working on regional newspapers but 'got sick of the low pay and had a bad case of itchy feet'. She says that living in Turkey is not as hard as people think: 'Some of my friends still think I live somewhere like Afghanistan but if they could see my school next to Marks and Spencer's, Motherworld and Burger King. In fact I feel it is too westernised at times, although I do appreciate being able to drink alcohol so don't complain too much.

There is a good expat community here, with plenty of places to go in the evening and things are relatively cheap – teachers are relatively rich by Turkish standards.'

There, are, however, cultural differences of which she has to be aware, and which some people might find difficult.

Generally, my students are great – they're talkative, keen to learn, funny and warm. However, they are quite set in their ways in some respects. Generally, you can't mention Kurds or Cyprus, because they are all very sensitive to the European attitudes to this. They can be racist about Kurds and Arabs, and it's important to remember they are not horrid people but their history and education and upbringing has left them with no alternative ways of thinking.

Basically, it's a love–hate relationship with this place. Usually, just before I go on a trip home to the UK, I'm desperate to escape the crazy traffic, the noise, the people and men who just see dollars and sex when they look at me. Then after about three days back in England I start to miss the vibrance, the smells, and the warm smiles from some old random shopkeeper who is pleased I spoke Turkish to him. My advice for people coming here is, be relaxed, flexible and don't expect everything to be the same here. It sounds stupid but the number of people who complain about trivial things like having to change a gas bottle for their shower or not having a plug. It's not like home here – and I'm thankful for that!

AU PAIR

With learning English at such a boom, there are plenty of wealthy families in Turkey looking for English-speaking au pairs and nannies. However, Turkey is a Muslim country and prospective au pairs and nannies are urged to think carefully about living with cultural differences so close to home. Look in *The Lady* for advertisements (see Au Pairing and Childcare chapter) or contact the following agencies.

ICEP (2 Innes Lodge, Iglemere Road, London SE23 2BD, Tel: 0800 074 6502, Email: london@icep.org.tr) offers an au pair programme in Turkey for three to twelve months.

Anglo Nannies London (20 Beverley Avenue, London SW20 0RL, Tel: 020 8944 6677, Website: **www.anglonannies.com**) specialises in placing professional English-speaking nannies and teachers in Turkey.

TOURISM

Apart from the bustling city of Istanbul, job seekers should head for the Aegean coastal resorts such as Marmaris and Bodrum where they may find work in bars, restaurants and hotels. The yachting resorts can also be a good source of work, particularly Marmaris: find work in the hotels, restaurants and bars, or hang around the boats and cold-call for work.

There is also work for qualified diving instructors along the south-west coast, although it is better to fix up work with a diving centre or activity holiday company before you go out. Check out the websites **www.twarp.com/diving.htm** and **www.turizm.net/bluecruise/diving.html** for details of diving centres in Turkey.

Some active holiday companies such as Neilson require staff in Turkey, including hotel and kitchen staff, nannies, skippers, P.A.D.I. qualified diving instructors and R.Y.A. qualified sailing and windsurfing instructors. Interviews are held in July and August. Go to **www.neilson.com** for more information, or write to: Neilson Overseas Personnel, Locksview, Brighton Marina, Brighton BN2 5HA, UK.

THE JOB SEARCH

Look on **www.jobsites.co.uk** and **www.overseasjobs.com** which may have job vacancies.

In Turkey, check the job adverts in the English language newspaper the *Daily News*.

Some British holiday companies run holidays in Turkey. Try Sunsail (Port House, Port Solent, Portsmouth PO6 4TH) and Mark Warner (see Tourism chapter for address).

USEFUL ADDRESSES

Embassy of Greece, 1a Holland Park, London W11 3TP, UK, Tel: 020 7229 3850; 2221 Massachusetts Avenue, NW, Washington DC 20008, USA Tel: 202 939 5800, Website: **www.greekembassy.org**

Turkish Embassy, 43 Belgrave Square, London SW1X 8PA, UK, Tel: 020 7393 0202; 1714 Massachusettes Avenue, NW, Washington DC 20036, USA, Tel: 202 659 8200, Website: **www.turkey.org/turkey**

18 HOLLAND AND BELGIUM

HOLLAND

Holland has much to attract the working traveller. English is spoken widely and fluently, so there are few language barriers and work for non-Dutch speakers, in the tourist sector at least, is easy to obtain. It also has one of the lowest unemployment rates in the EU and the tourist industry and bulb fields can provide a rich source of work. The standard of living is also high and wages can be good – according to the website **www.visitholland.com**, a recent comparative study of major European cities showed that after Lisbon and Athens, Amsterdam is the least expensive city for a short stay. Luxembourg, Dublin, Copenhagen, Brussels, Helsinki, Oslo, Vienna, Paris, Frankfurt, Zurich, Stockholm, Milan, Madrid and London all proved to be more expensive.

VISAS AND REGULATIONS

The same rule as with all EU member states applies: EU nationals are free to enter Holland to look for work for up to three months. However, you may be asked to prove that you have adequate means for the duration of your stay and that the cost of your return journey is secured. Once you are there, EU/EEA citizens must register with their local foreign police registration office (*Vreemdelingenpolitie*) within eight days of arrival. If you are intending to look for work (and are without a work contract) you will be asked to show your passport at the Foreign Police registration office to get a police permit.

If you are a first-time jobseeker in the Netherlands you will also need to obtain a SOFI number (Social Welfare/Taxation) from the local tax office (*Belastingdienst*) – you will need to show your passport and the police permit.

If you wish to work for more than three months, you must apply for a residence permit (*Verblijfsvergunning*) from the town hall or community office – *Stadhuis* or *Gemeente*. You will need to present your passport, police permit, SOFI number, two photographs, a full version of your birth certificate, and in some cities (for example, Amsterdam) proof from your landlord that you have a permanent address.

Contact the Netherlands embassy in your own country before you leave for more details.

NON-EU NATIONALS

Visitors from Australia, Canada, Japan, New Zealand and the USA don't need a visa to enter the Netherlands for stays of up to ninety days. They are also allowed to work for less than three months but must report to the foreign police within three days of arrival. Their employer must also obtain an employment permit for them (*tewerkstellingsvergunning*), although this is rarely issued for casual work.

If you wish to stay for more than three months you must first obtain a work permit before entering the country. Work permits can be difficult to get hold of for non-EU nationals and you may have to show proof of return fare and sufficient funds to support yourself.

ACCOMMODATION

You can find accommodation advertised in local newspapers, in the Wednesday edition of daily newspaper *De Telegraaf* or on shop/supermarket notice boards. Otherwise contact the Netherlands Estate Agents Federation (NVM).

AGRICULTURE

Many people manage to find work in flower bulb factories in the summer, and from mid April to October there may be work available picking asparagus, strawberries, gherkins, apples and pears. Visit the nearest jobcentre for details.

Harvest Guide For The Netherlands

Flowers	Coastal Noord-Holland and Zuid-Holland, towns and villages between Leiden and Haarlem, also the Noordostpolder, Friesland and Groningen	May–July
Bulbs	Coastal Noord-Holland and Zuid-Holland, towns and villages between Leiden and Haarlem, also the Noordostpolder, Friesland and Groningen	June–Oct
Cucumbers	Western province of Zuid-Holland, the area between Den Haag, Rotterdam and Hoek van Holland	April–Nov
Peppers	Western province of Zuid-Holland, the area between Den Haag, Rotterdam and Hoek van Holland	April–Nov
Lettuce	Western province of Zuid-Holland, the area between Den Haag, Rotterdam and Hoek van Holland	April–Nov

Tomatoes	Western province of Zuid-Holland, the area between Den Haag, Rotterdam and Hoek van Holland	April–Nov
Strawberries	Western province of Zuid-Holland, the area between Den Haag, Rotterdam and Hoek van Holland	June–Aug
Cherries	De Betuwe, the area between the Rhine and Waal rivers, including the towns of Buren and Culemborg, also the southern province of Limburg	June–Aug
Apples	De Betuwe, the area between the Rhine and Waal rivers, including the towns of Buren and Culemborg, also the southern province of Limburg	Aug–Nov
Pears	De Betuwe, the area between the Rhine and Waal rivers, including the towns of Buren and Culemborg, also the southern province of Limburg	Aug–Nov

This is a rough guide and harvest times vary according to weather and conditions. For more details look at the jobs on their website or contact the Eures Office in your chosen region. Details can be found at **www.europa.eu.int**. This information is taken from the website **anyworkanywhere.com**.

VOLUNTARY WORK

Holland has many opportunities for voluntary work. Contact the big voluntary organisations or try Service Civil International (**www.planet.be/asbl/sci**) for volunteer workcamps.

AU PAIR

While au pairing in Holland is not so popular as in other countries, there are some agencies who can help you find work.

Au Pair Discover Holland (C. Barendregtlaan 9-F 3161 HA Rhoon) runs au pair programmes and can help you fix up and secure work.

House of Orange Au Pairs (**www.house-o-orange.nl/**) is a Dutch au pair/nanny agency looking for native English speakers (UK, Aussie, Kiwi, South African, US, Canadian). Applicants must be aged between eighteen and thirty, single and non-smokers or social smokers only. Positions start all the time and commitment can vary from one to twelve months.

TOURIST WORK

Amsterdam's numerous hotels, restaurants and bars have much to attract the working traveller. You can find a list of hotels by contacting the Amsterdam Hotel Guide (**www.medialink.nl/amsterdam/hotelguide.html**) and ask around the hotels for work. Casual work is easy to find.

TRAVELLERS' STORIES

Iain Rudgyard worked in Holland for four months, arriving in February. 'A friend of mine was having a baby in Holland so we thought we'd go over and help. My original plan was to find work in IT, but when I arrived there, there weren't any IT jobs available, not for non-Dutch speakers anyway. In the end, I targeted the agencies and found work through them – I even sat a typing test in Dutch and came out with 36 words a minute, although I can't speak a word of the language!'

Finding work was tricky, and apart from handing out flyers for clubs, there weren't many opportunities open to him. Two weeks later, one agency eventually found Iain work in a DHL factory in Schipol, near Amsterdam. 'I was working for the logistics company DHL and most of the work was picking up pallets and moving boxes around. I was the only English person there, and apart from two Spanish girls, everyone else was Dutch. Initially, I felt a bit out of place, but I soon settled in and found it easy to integrate into the Dutch community.'

Iain says that, despite the fact that the Dutch speak excellent English, out of season it can be difficult to find work if you don't speak the language. 'There was some bar work around but it was mostly for women. My wife worked as a barmaid in Amsterdam and didn't speak any Dutch, but it was called The London Bridge and full of English people! I don't think it was a particularly good time to find work in February and it would probably be much easier to find work in the summer.'

THE JOB SEARCH

Check out the EURES Network (European Employment Services) (see Chapter Three).

The Dutch jobcentres, *Arbeidsbureau* (AB), are available to EU nationals after completing the entry formalities listed above. For addresses look in the Yellow Pages (*Gouden Gids*) or contact Central Bureau voor de Arbeidsvoorziening, Boerhaavelaan 7, Postbus 883, Nl-2700 Aw Zoetermeer, Tel: 31 79 371 2000, Fax: 31 79 371 2099, Koninklijke Algemene Vereniging voor Bloembollencultuur.

There are also many private employment agencies such as Manpower, Randstad and ASB, which can help you find unskilled work in supermarkets or factories, for example. Look for *uitzendbureaus* in the Yellow Pages.

The press and word of mouth are very important media for job-hunting in Holland. Most Dutch national and regional newspapers such as *De Telegraaf*, *Het Algemeen Dagblad* and *De Volkskrant* carry job advertisements, especially on Saturdays. There is also *Intermediair*, a weekly paper for graduates. Check the classified advertisements under 'Personeel Gevraagd' ('Personnel Wanted').

Some useful job search websites are:

JobbingMall (**www.jobbingmall.nl**)
JobNews (**www.jobnews.nl**)
Vacaturebank (**www.vacaturebank.nl**)
Jobcenter (**www.jobcenter.nl**)

BELGIUM

Belgium is often neglected by the working traveller as a viable place to find work. However, like Holland, it has a good minimum wage and prides itself on its egalitarian attitude to looking after its workers. There is also a good expat scene – not surprising in a country where almost a third of the population is made up of foreigners. As the centre for the European Union, Brussels has plenty to offer for English speakers, although outside here, you will need to speak some of its three official languages: Dutch in Flanders, French in Wallonia and German in the Eastern cantons.

VISAS AND REGULATIONS

Belgium is notorious for its red tape, but if you're an EU national, the same EU rules apply. EU nationals are free to work and live in the country, but if you intend to stay for over three months you should register within eight days at the local town hall. Here you will be issued with a temporary *certificate d'immatriculation*, valid for three months, or a *certificate d'insciption au registre des etrangers*, lasting for one year. You should also be able to get hold of a copy of its magazine *Newcomer*. Although this is mainly aimed at the professional or managerial people relocating to Belgium, it has some useful information for anyone wishing to live there.

NON-EU NATIONALS

Non-EU nationals must first find work and get hold of a work permit and residence entry visa before arriving in Belgium. But because of high unemployment, this isn't as easy as it sounds. According to Belgian law, your prospective employer must first prove that there is no local source of labour or skills in the Belgium labour force to fill the job. If you are in any doubt, contact your Belgian embassy or the nearest Belgian consulate for details.

AU PAIR

Belgium has stricter rules for au pairs than many other countries, so check the situation thoroughly before arriving. Details about the regulations can be found on the government website www.meta.fgov.be/pc/pce/pcea/encea01.htm.

Under Belgian law, au pairs must be aged between 18–23, and be enrolled on a government-authorised language course of one of Belgium's regional languages, with certificates to prove this.

The host family must also meet strict rules; as well as covering the costs of medical insurance and any repatriation, they must also give the au pair at least one day off a week, pay a minimum allowance per month and employ the au pair for more than four hours a day and twenty hours a week. They must also apply for an employment authorisation from the consulate.

For placements in Belgium try Almondbury Au Pair & Nanny Agency (**www.aupair-agency.com**) and Au Pair Europa (**www.au-pair-europa.be**).

THE JOB SEARCH

Belgium's coastal resorts boast many hotels and eateries which can provide plenty of work opportunities. The Belgian theme park Bobbejaanland (**www.bobbejaanland.be/en/index.html**) employs around four hundred people. Eurocamp (**www.eurocamp.co.uk**) also requires campsite couriers in both Holland and Belgium. If you have languages and secretarial skills you might well be able to find work temping in the many multinational companies Brussels affords, particularly if you are a bilingual secretary.

Contact the main employment agencies such as Manpower and International Secretaries. Robert Walters (**www.robertwalters.com**) has offices in both Holland and Belgium and is good for temp and permanent vacancies in banking and finance, accountancy, secretarial and call centres. You can also try the employment agency ORBEM (**www.orbem.be**).

Read *The Bulletin* and local papers, particularly the weekend editions for work. *The Bulletin* has a 'Situations Vacant' column or go to **www.xpats.com** for job vacancies.

Belgium also hosts a Welcome Fair in late September which offers job services as well as information on all aspects of life in Belgium – for more information visit **www.welcomefair.be**.

USEFUL WEBSITES

www.expatica.com.belgium.asp
www.citizens.eu.int

USEFUL ADDRESSES

The Belgian Embassy, 103 Eaton Square, London SW1W 9AB, Tel: 020 7470 3700; 3330 Garfield Street, NW, Washington DC 20008, USA, Tel: 202 333 6900, Website: **www.belgium-emb.org**

The Ministère de l'Emploi et du Travail can supply you with information and application forms for work permits. Contact Ministère de l'Emploi et du Travail, 51, rue Belliard, 1040 Brussels, Tel: (02) 233 41 11, Fax: 02 233 44 8851

Royal Netherlands Embassy, 38 Hyde Park Gate, London SW7 5DP, UK, Tel: 020 7584 5040; 4200 Linnean Avenue, NW, Washington DC 20008, USA, Tel: 202 244 5300, **www.netherlands-embassy.org**

You can get the free booklets *Working in the Netherlands* and *Working in Belgium* from Employment Service, Overseas Placing Unit, Rockingham House, 123 West Street, Sheffield, S1 4ER.

19 ITALY

Italy's complicated red tape can make working in Italy difficult. There is also high unemployment particularly in the south, which means you could be in competition with natives for jobs. Ideally, you should speak Italian and have marketable skills. Although there is plenty of cash-in-hand work to be had, beware of working without the necessary permission. The government has recently cracked down on illegal immigrants, issuing the real threat of arrest and deportation.

VISAS AND REGULATIONS

If you hold an EU passport you are legally entitled to work in Italy. However, the complicated Italian bureaucracy might make things more time consuming than you expect. You will also need to apply for a temporary resident's permit (*una Ricevuta di Segnalazione di Soggiorn*) at the main police station (*Questura Centrale*), which entitles you to stay for up to three months. For this, you will need to take a valid passport and some proof of employment or financial resources (for example, bank statements, tax returns or a contract). If you wish to stay any longer you need to apply for a resident's permit, *un Permesso di Soggiorno*. Once you have your work and resident's permits, you will also need to get an employment number from the tax office. You may also have to get a *Libretto di Lavoro* (work registration card), although in the case of EU nationals, this doesn't happen much.

NON-EU NATIONALS

Non-EU nationals will find the whole process much more difficult. The official line is that non-EU nationals can only get hold of work visas in their own country of residence and typically need an authorisation to work from the Ministry of Labour and from the local police. The red tape is complicated and procedure can vary, so travellers are advised to look into it in some detail first. Furthermore, despite the fact that unofficial work has been reported to be relatively easy in the past, a strict clampdown on illegal workers has made the situation much more risky now.

TIPS

- **Learn the lingo**
- **Try to fix up work before you go**
- **Make contacts in Italy before you arrive**

• **Make sure you have all the necessary documentation as the red tape can be time consuming and complicated, even for EU nationals**

WORK OPPORTUNITIES

TOURISM

Despite high unemployment, the growing markets of tourism, catering and commerce can offer good opportunities for work. Seasonal work in the tourist industry is probably your best bet, although if you don't speak good Italian it might not be easy to find jobs. Restaurants, hotels and tourist resorts recruit plenty of seasonal staff to help during the major tourist periods (summer for seaside and lake resorts; summer and winter for mountain resorts) so if you persevere you may be lucky.

As usual, this can be found either on the spot or by writing first from your own country to the hotels, campsites, restaurants and tourist villages. You can get a list of hotels from tourist offices, and at the *Informagiovani* (see below in the job search section).

Eurocamp (**www.eurocamp.co.uk**) employs people as campsite couriers in Italy and other European countries, and according to Eddy Martin, is a good starting place from which you can hunt for other work. After two months putting up tents, he found work in a campsite restaurant despite not speaking much Italian. 'The work didn't pay much but the owner gave me a caravan to stay in. I started off doing anything, like making sandwiches, working behind the bar and selling ice creams, until eventually I was promoted to pizza chef.'

Tourist villages are a particularly Italian phenomenon and recruit seasonal staff to entertain the masses. Skills such as acting, swimming, dancing, tennis, windsurfing, and horse riding can all help you find a post. The main organisations that manage tourist villages are:

Club Med, Via Pascoli 60, 20123 Milano, Italy
Alpitour Italia, Viale Maino, 42 20129 Milano, Italy
Valtur, Viale Milano 42, 00184 Roma, Italy
Francorosso International, Via C. Colombo 440, 00145 Roma, Italy

Alex Rayner worked as a windsurfing instructor for a Mark Warner hotel in Sardinia for six weeks. He had previously trained as a windsurfing instructor with the Royal Yachting Association and after an interview in Kensington, London, in July, was flown off last minute to the Capo Testa resort in Sardinia. Alex says it was generally really a good experience, but there were drawbacks, such as being roped into dodgy Red Coats-style cabarets.

There were no major incidents but the employers didn't treat the staff that well. They were very clear about the behaviour that was expected of us. For example, we were expected to eat dinner with the guests and often had to entertain them in the evenings like Red Coats. This wasn't obligatory but we were heavily cajoled into joining in – one night we did a production of Grease and a version of the TV programme Blind Date. We had to wear a beach uniform while we were working and dress in a different manner when we picked up the guests from the airport. There was a lot of emphasis on customer service skills which I wasn't so comfortable with. It was a sackable offence to sleep with any of the guests, although many people did and the employers didn't seem to find out.

TOUR OPERATORS

Another option is to try and fix up work with one of the many tour companies that operate in Italy. The website Tour-Web (**www.tour-web.com**) lists Italian travel agencies and tour operators, or you can contact the following companies which specialise in tours to Italy:

Club Toscana (**www.clubtoscana.com**) is a tour operator that specialises in leading small groups on hiking, walking and cycling trips through the regions of Italy.

Experience Italy (**www.experiencetravel.com**) runs specialised group tours through Italy.

Italy Travel Tours (**www.onestepcloser.net**) has information on tour packages to major destinations in Italy.

Italy Vacation Packages – Orbitz (**www.orbitz.com**) provide a number of guided tours as well as vacation packages for trips to Venice, Florence, Milan, Rome, and other major Italian cities.

Magic Trips (**www.magictrips.it**) specialise in tours of Italy's Tyrrhenian and Ionian coasts, as well as culinary tours of rural Italy.

SKI RESORTS

The big ski resorts of Cervinia, Cortina d'Ampezzo, Courmayeur and Selva can also throw up plenty of work opportunities for ski instructors, technicians, kitchen and hotel staff. Contact the big ski companies well in advance, sending your CV and a photo. Crystal Holidays Ltd offers some work in the Italian Alps, as do many other holiday companies (see Ski resorts section in Chapter 7). You can find a list of ski tour companies by contacting the Italy Ski Vacation Package Destinations at **www.snowpak.com** or the tour operator Ski Italy (**www.skiitaly.com**), which provides details on hotels and restaurants in the various ski areas. Alternatively, turn up on spec at the beginning of the season and ask around the many hotels and eateries.

AGRICULTURE

There are also opportunities to be found working on farms during Italy's harvest seasons, although this isn't as easy to find as in other countries. Contact the farms directly or do some research at the jobcentre (*ufficio di collocamento*). Remember that most work can be found on the grapevine.

A Harvest Guide For Italy

Strawberries	Emilia Romagna	May–Aug
Cherries	Emilia Romagna	May–Aug
Peaches	Emilia Romagna	May–Aug
Plums	Emilia Romagna	May–Aug
Apples	Emilia Romagna, Piemonte and Trentino	Sept–Oct
Pears	Emilia Romagna, Piemonte and Trentino	Sept–Oct
Grapes	Emilia Romagna, Lazio, Piemonte, Puglia, Trentino, Veneto and Toscana	Sept–Oct
Olives	Puglia, Toscana, Liguria, Calabria and Sicilia	Nov–Dec
Tobacco	Umbria, Puglia and Campania	Nov–Dec
Flowers	Liguria, Toscana, Lazio, Puglia	Nov–Dec

This is a rough guide and harvest times vary according to weather and conditions. For more details look at the jobs on their website or contact the Eures Office in your chosen region. Details can be found at **www.europa.eu.int/comm/employment_social/elm/eures/en/about/network.htm**. This information is taken from **anyworkanywhere.com**.

AU PAIRING

Au pairing in Italy is a popular way of working and seeing the sights, and there are various agencies and associations that can help you find work with families. However, there are certain conditions put in place by A.R.C.E. (*Attività Relazione Culturali con l'Estero*) which families and au pairs should adhere to. These are designed to protect au pairs from exploitation so try to ensure that your host family is at least aware of them. According to the rules, au pairs should be aged between eighteen and thirty and stay for a maximum of twelve months. There must also be a written agreement specifying the duties of the guest. In any case, there should not be more than five or six hours per day of light housework which should generally end by early afternoon, so that the guest can pursue their own interest in their free time. An au pair should have one day off, with two to three evenings free each week and should be treated as a member of the family as much as possible. The host family must provide private insurance against accidents or illness, as well as room and board and a predetermined sum, which would be agreed upon prior to the work stage.

If you are interested in au pair work in Italy you can write to the following agencies:

Au Pair International, Via S. Stephano 32, 40125 Bologna, Tel: 051 267575/ 38320.

Euro Au Pair, Borgo S. Croce 4, 50122 Firenze, Italy, Tel: 00 39 55 241 181, Fax: 00 39 55 241 722.

Elizabeth Lenihan, Piazza De Amicis, 10126 Torino, Italy, Tel:00 39 11 678 906, Fax: 00 39 11 545 000.

TEACHING ENGLISH

There is a huge demand for English teachers in Italy, as it is widely thought that Italy is behind other European countries in English proficiency. Most cities and towns have many private language schools where you should be able to find work easily. Usually a Tefl certificate is required, although you may be able to find work without one. In any case, knowledge of Italian will considerably improve your chances.

Long-term contracts are hard to find, and most teachers work part-time and face constant job insecurity. This is largely because, under Italian law, employers are required to pay social security contributions for their workers, so many schools avoid the extra cost by hiring teachers on a freelance basis.

Pay tends to vary between the north and the south – expect more in the north where you will have to meet higher living costs. According to a message posted on esl-lounge.com by EFL teacher Martine Aulton, 'Pay varies enormously in the northern cities from hourly rates of between 15–35 euros. You need to be looking at a take-home pay of about 1000 euros a month to be comfortable, bearing in mind that a shared rent is around 350–400 euros monthly, much less if you get accommodation out of Rome. For private, cash-in-hand work you can get between 20–35 euros an hour.'

Italy has a wide range of schools and institutions including international school chains such as Linguarama, Berlitz and Inlingua, which also provide in-house training. The more respectable schools in Italy tend to belong to

AISLI (*Associazione Italiana Scuole di Lingua Inglese*), and/or to EAQUALS (a pan-European association of language training providers), which are both tightly regulated and have good conditions for their teachers (pay, contracts, teaching hours). However, there are also some private institutions which have a rather dubious reputation, so be extra vigilant about payment.

There are also opportunities in Italy's universities, where foreigners may find work as *lettori*. These lecturers teach English to students, in addition to other subjects. Work may be found by applying directly to the universities. It is also worth nothing that, in the past, there have been problems with non-Italian *lettori* being denied the same rights as native Italian teachers. The situation is reported to be better now, but it's worth being aware of the history.

FINDING EFL WORK

For pre-arranged work, look through the usual sources such as the *Guardian* (Tuesday) and the Tefl websites (see Tefl section of Chapter 6).

Saxoncourt Recruitment and English Worldwide sends EFL teachers out to institutions such as the British Schools, which have over seventy branches across the country. See Tefl section of Chapter 6 for contact details.

It is also possible to turn up on the spot and find work once you're there. Bear in mind that competition will lessen if you are out of the big tourist centres such as Rome, Florence, Pisa and so on. You can find the addresses of English schools by looking in the Yellow Pages (*Pagine Gialle*) listed under '*Scuole di Lingue*'.

There are also vacancies listed in regional papers – the fortnightly English-language magazine *Wanted in Rome* often advertises Tefl jobs, which you can also see online at **www.wantedinrome.com**.

The website Teaching English in Italy (**www.teachingenglish.net**) contains some information on working as an English teacher.

TEFL Net Nation (**www.teflnetnation.com/index.html**) includes an I-Zine, for teachers and students of English in Italy.

VOLUNTARY WORK

Many voluntary organisations operate in Italy. Here are some:

Servizio Civile Internazionale, Via Laterani 28, 00185 Roma, Italy, Tel: 00 39 6 7005367

Mani Tese, Via Cavenaghi 4, 10149 Milano, Italy, Tel: 00 39 2 46971888

Europe Conservation Italia (**www.agora.stm.it/eco.htm**) runs spring and summer conservation projects in Italy.

Summer Camps (**www.rosenet.it/summercamps**) runs a programme where people can provide an English language immersion experience to Italian children who cannot afford to spend the summer in a foreign English-speaking country

THE JOB SEARCH

The best way to find work in Italy is to make good contacts and keep your ear to the ground. In this country, the normal routes of employment agencies (both private and state) and reading the local and national press do not tend to be as fruitful as in other European countries. Speaking good Italian certainly helps and you'd be well advised to learn a bit of the lingo before arriving. That said, there is plenty of seasonal and cash-in-hand work around – it's just a case of being in the right place at the right time.

Wanted in Rome is a fortnightly publication that appears in newsagents in Rome and contains jobs for English speakers and other expatriates. There are a wide variety of jobs listed including teaching English, nannying and cafe/bar work. See **www.wantedinrome.com**.

Informagiovani is a Youth Information Scheme that provides information on jobs, scholarships, enrolment to universities, as well as a database on the availability of work. It is accessible nationwide and on the internet. A complete list of *Informagiovani* is available at the Italian Cultural Institute for consultation. Here is a list of the *Informagiovani* addresses in the main Italian cities:

Agenzia Informagiovani, Via Captain Bavastro 94, 00154 Roma, Italy, Tel: 00 39 6 575 6759, Fax: 00 39 6 574 7623.

Informagiovani, Via Marconi 1, 20123 Milano, Italy, Tel: 00 39 2 62085215, Fax: 00 39 2 865067.

Centro Informagiovani, c/o Centro Civico Lame Via Marco Polo 53, Quartiere Navile, 40131 Bologna, Italy, Tel: 00 39 51 6345550.

Servizio Informagiovani, Vicolo S. Maria Maggiore 1, 50123 Firenze, Italy, Tel: 00 39 55 218310, Fax: 00 39 55 292056.

USEFUL ADDRESSES

Italian Embassy, 14 Three Kings Yard, London W1Y 2EH, UK, Tel: 020 7312 2200, Website: **www.embitaly.org.uk**; 1601 Fuller Street, Washington DC 20009, USA, Tel: 202 328 5500.

20 SCANDINAVIA

Despite its high standard of living, Scandinavia isn't exactly brimming with opportunities for the foreign worker. Denmark, Norway and Sweden have the most potential for finding work but most of the vacancies that exist are for skilled professional people and casual work can be hard to find. Your best bet is to try and fix up work before you arrive. English is spoken widely, but it's still advisable to learn a little of the language of the country you intend to visit. Despite these setbacks, working in Scandinavia can be a good option, if only because it will help you finance your travels in a region that is notoriously too expensive to travel around.

VISAS AND REGULATIONS

Denmark, Finland and Sweden are all members of the EU so in theory EU nationals can enjoy all the benefits their membership affords. Norway and Iceland are outside the EU but as members of the EEA, EU nationals are still free to enter to look for work for three months.

All countries require you to apply for a residence permit from the local police once you have found work and got hold of a confirmation of employment from your employer.

Unfortunately, foreigners outside the EU and EEA have hardly any prospects to find work. Not only will they have to obtain a work permit before leaving home, but this meets with some strict regulations. For more information contact the department of immigration or the consulate of the country you would like to visit.

Despite these difficulties there are, however, some schemes open to non-EU/EEA nationals. The American–Scandinavian Foundation (Exchange Division, 58 Park Avenue, New York, NY 10016, Tel: 212 879 9779, Fax: 212 249 3444, Website: **www.amscan.org**) has a year-long Tesol programme in Finland. It also fixes up placements for 21–30-year-old American trainees in engineering, chemistry, computer science and business posts in Scandinavian companies for the summer.

Australians can apply for the Working Holiday Maker programme (WHM) which allows Australians to work legally for up to twelve months in eleven participating countries, including Denmark and Norway. Contact the Australian embassy for details.

DENMARK

Denmark may be small but it certainly knows how to do some moving and shaking. It is a wonderfully forward-thinking country and the driving force behind much of the legislation in the European Union. It also holds the European record for most women on the labour market and looks after its workers well with good social security. However, the Danes have to pay a price for this as they also pay the heaviest taxes and take home less of their pay than almost any other European.

TOURISM

The best chances of finding work are to target the small tourist industry in Copenhagen where you may be able to find work in the hotels, bars, restaurants and fast-food joints cleaning, washing dishes, working behind the bar and such like. You can find work before you leave or when you arrive, although your main chances will be in Copenhagen. There are also two theme parks you may be able to find work, although you might have to speak Danish: Legoland (**www.lego.com/legoland/billund/default.asp**) and the Danish theme park Tivoliland (**www.tivoliland.dk/gb/html/hoved.html**).

AU PAIR

Au pair work is also a growth area, and many of the worldwide au pair agencies fix up placements to Denmark.

Try Anderson Au Pairs & Nannies (**www.childcare-europe.com**) or visit the website for 100s Au Pairs (**www.100s-aupairs.co.uk**) for agencies that place au pairs in Scandinavia.

You won't need a work permit for au pair work, but you will need a residence permit, and to get one as an au pair there are a number of conditions. The applicant must be 17–29 years of age and have the linguistic and cultural background necessary to benefit from the stay. There must be one or more underage children in the host family. The host family must be able to communicate Danish culture to the au pair, which generally means that at least one of the host parents must be a Danish national. Duties must be part of the daily housekeeping, and apart from free board and lodging in the home of the host family, the au pair must receive a minimum of DKK 2,500 per month (gross) in pocket money. Daily working hours must not exceed five hours, and the au pair is entitled to at least one weekly day off plus the freedom to attend religious ceremonies. Moreover, the au pair must be given the opportunity to cultivate her interests during the entire stay. It is up to the host family to make sure that the au pair is registered with the public Health Insurance Scheme. For more information contact the Danish Immigration Service, Ryesgade 53,2100 Copenhagen Ø or visit their website **www.udlst.dk**.

AGRICULTURE

Another popular alternative is farming and fruit picking: picking tomatoes, strawberries, cherries in the summer and apples during early autumn.

Exis (Postbox 291, 6400 Sonderbørg, Tel: 74 42 97, Fax: 74 42 97 47, info@exis.dk) is an au pair agency that also recruits EU nationals for the strawberry-picking season. The Danish WWOOF (VHH) can also find you placements on their organic farms. Contact WWOOF for more details (see Agriculture chapter).

THE JOB SEARCH

The best methods of finding work are to go through the normal channels of information. There are some private employment agencies (look in the Yellow Pages under *vikarbureauer*) although you will probably have to speak Danish for them to be of use to you. Private employment agencies may be able to find you casual, admin or secretarial work. Or, if you speak a little Danish, try the state employment agency *Arbejdsformidlingen*. Students can try the *Studenternes Arbejdsformidlingenn* (Student Employment Agency) for casual work. The free Copenhagen paper *Sondagsvisen* (out on Sundays) carries ads for casual work. Other more skilled vacancies are advertised in *Berlingske Tidende* although you will have to speak Danish.

You can also try the youth information centre Uselt, Rädhusstraede 13, 1466 Copenhagen K (Tel: 33 73 06 20, Fax: 33 73 06 49, Website: **www.useit.dk**) which can provide some useful tips on finding work and is a good first port of call. You should also be able to get hold of a copy of a free booklet *Working in Denmark*.

FINLAND

As a small country, Finland has a shortage of experienced and qualified professional people so if you have special skills to offer in a professional capacity you may be able to find openings before you leave. Generally, however, Finland is off the map for working travellers. Casual work opportunities are few, although there are openings for au pairing and childcare, and teaching English. You can find out more by reading the EFL web article on 'Teaching English as a Foreign Language in Finland' on **www.eflweb.com/experience/finland.htm**. For au pair vacancies contact the agencies listed in the Au Pair and Childcare chapter, including Nannies Now, which sometimes places au pairs in Finland. Visit **www.nanniesnow.uk.com** for details.

The Finnish Family programme is a scheme where native English-speaking families can live with a Finnish family for up to a year and teach English on a regular basis. For more information contact: The Ministry of Labour, PO

Box 30, 00100 Helsinki 10 or in the UK, the Education and Training Group, 10 Spring Gardens, London SW14 2BN.

The Centre for International Mobility specialises in study and training placements to Finland and runs a number of official EU programmes. Go to **www.cimo.fi** for more information.

Agricultural openings aren't as easy to find as in Denmark; however the International Student Exchange Centre (Isec) runs an agriculture exchange programme in Finland – see Norway section for more details.

For voluntary work contact WWOOF Finland at Partlala Information Services for Organic Agriculture, Huttulantie 1, 51900 Juva (Tel: 15 321 2380).

NORWAY

As Norway is not a member of the EU and most foreign workers (except EU nationals) are banned, it doesn't exactly welcome you with open arms. However, EU citizens do not need to get work permits and, actually, there is plenty of casual work around, particularly in farms, tourism and factories. However, immigration rules are strict and the Norwegians do have a reputation for not exactly falling over themselves to employ non-natives, so it's best to set up work before you arrive. There are some skills shortages in Norway's manufacturing industries as well as nursing and teaching so if you are skilled and qualified and go through the right channels, you may find an opening.

For more information on working in Norway visit the Norwegian Directorate of Labour's website **www.aetat.no:80/english/index.html** which offers information on using their, and other, services to find a job or study in Norway.

WORK OPPORTUNITIES

Norway has a thriving winter tourism scene where you may be able to target some of the hotels and restaurants. Many of the towns have their own website containing skiing information and lists of hotels. Try Beitostolen on **www2.skiinfo.no/beitostolen/sommer/uk/index.html**, Gaustablikk on **www2.skiinfo.no/gaustablikk/english/main.html** or head for the Tourist Information. Remember you are more likely to hit gold if you speak a little Finnish.

You could also try your hand at strawberry picking during the summer. Working travellers can apply for casual work through the Work Guest Programme which offers farm work to people aged between eighteen and thirty. Contact Atlantis-Norwegian Foundation for Youth Exchange, Director International Programs, Rolf Hofmosgate 18, 0655 Oslo 6.

The International Student Exchange Centre run agriculture programmes in both Finland and Norway. Visit their website **www.isecworld.co.uk** for more information or write to them at 35 Ivor Place, London, NW1 6EA, Tel: 020 7724 4493, Fax: 020 7724 0849.

Atlantis runs an au pair programme for eighteen- to thirty-year-olds in Norway for contracts of at least six months. Their website **www.atlantis-u.no** carries full details or else contact them at Atlantis Ungdomsutveksling, Kirkegata 32, 0153 Oslo, Tel: 22 47 71 70, Fax: 22 47 71 79, Email: post@atlantis-u.no.

THE JOB SEARCH

In order to find work, you can try the state employment service: *Arbeidsdirektoratet*, Holbergs Plass 7, Postboks 8127 Dep, Oslo 1, Tel: 02 11 10 70 or the daily newspaper *Aften Posten* carries job adverts. Addresses of private temp agencies can be found by looking up *Vikarutleie* in the Yellow Pages. Try the usual international agencies like Manpower. It's also worth mentioning that despite not being an EU member, Norway participates in the EURES (European Employment Services) network.

Norway has its own Uselt centre on Møllergata 3, 0179 Oslo, Tel: 22 41 51 32, Fax: 22 42 63 71, Email: post@unginfo.oslo.no, Website: **www.unginfo.oslo.no/streetwise**.

SWEDEN

In Sweden the same rule applies as to the rest of Scandinavia: the best tactic is to fix up work before you arrive. That said, some of the hotels rarely hand out work in advance and you may be better off turning up on spec as you would do in other European countries. Tourism work offers plenty of chances for seasonal work – particularly in Stockholm, Göteburg and some of the coastal resorts. You may also be able to find 'informal' jobs like fruit picking, especially in Skane.

WORK OPPORTUNITIES

Tefl posts in Sweden are not so easy to get hold of, particularly on the spot, but if you are a qualified teacher, it's well worth looking into. As always, get hold of a list of Swedish schools from the British Council (see Tefl section of Chapter 6) or you could try sending a CV and letter to Folkuniversitetet which has various teaching posts ranging from public courses to adults, courses commissioned by companies, or government-backed training programmes. Applicants should have a first degree or recognised teaching qualification or initial TEFL certificate with classroom experience.

Contact Folkuniversitetetatt, at: Peter Baston, Box 2116, S-220 02 Lund, Sweden, Tel: 46 46 19 77 00, Fax: 46 46 19 77 80,

Email: peter.baston@folkuniversitetet.se,
Website: **www.peter.baston@folkuniversitetet.se**.

There are also some opportunities for au pair work, although you will have
to check the regulations first (you can download PDF files on working
regulations for au pair work in Sweden from
www.migrationsverket.se/pdiffiler/aupair).

Two Swedish au pair agencies are AuPair and Language Center, Sweden
KB, Nedre Långvinkelsgatan 36, 25234 Helsingborg, Sweden, Tel: 46 42
126045, Fax: 46 42 126025, Email: sweden@aupaircenter.com, Website:
www.aupaircenter.com and Scandinavian Au-Pair Center Saturnusgatan
240, 260 35 Ödåkra, Sweden, Tel: 46 42 20 44 02, Fax: 46 42 32 82 39, Email:
scandinavian@aupair.se, Website: **www.aupair.se**.

For voluntary work, contact the Swedish branch of WWOOF: Andeas
Hedren, Hunna, Palstorp, 340-30 Vislandia (Tel: 0470 75 43 75).

THE JOB SEARCH

The best places to find work once you are there is through the Swedish
state employment service *Arbetsmarknadsstyrelsen*, at Kungstensgatan
45, 113 99 Stockholm, Tel: 08 5860 6000, Fax: 08 5860 6499. Alternatively,
the Swedish Labour Market Administration (*Arbetsmarknadsverket*) has
about 380 employment offices or *Arbetsformedlingen*, offering placement
and job counselling services. One of their main offices is in Stockholm at
Arbetsförmedlingen City, Box 534, Vasagatan 28–34, S-5101 30 Stockholm,
Tel: 46 8 21 43 00. Opening hours: Monday to Friday 09.00–15.00.

You can also pick up employment magazines here, like *Platsjournalen* and
Nyttjobb, which contain vacancies and useful information about the labour
market in Sweden, or check out the jobs available on the website
www.amv.se.

To find addresses of private agencies, which may be able to find you office
work, look up the entry *Arbetsformedlingar* in the Yellow Pages or the
phone directory.

Newspapers in Sweden are also a very important resource for job seekers.
Check the national newspapers like *Dagens Nyheter*, *Svenska Dagbladet*
and *Dagens Industri*, as well as local and regional newspapers, for the
latest vacancies, particularly on a Sunday.

EMBASSIES

Finnish Embassy, 38 Chesham Place, London SW1X 8HW, UK, Tel: 020 7838
6200; 3301 Massachusetts Avenue, NW, Washington DC 20008, USA, Tel:
202 298 5800, Website: **www.finland.org**.

Swedish Embassy, 11 Montagu Place, London W1H 2AL, UK, Tel: 020 7917 6400, Email: embassy@swednet.org.uk, Website: **www.swedish-embassy.org.uk/embassy/index.html**; 1501 M Street, NW, Washington DC 20005, USA, Tel: 202 467 2600, Website: **www.swedenemb.org**.

Royal Danish Embassy, 55 Sloane Street, London SW1X 9SR, UK, Tel: 020 7333 0200; 3200 Whitehaven Street, NW, Washington DC 20008, USA, Tel: 202 234 4300, Website: **www.denmarkemb.org**.

Royal Norwegian Embassy, 25 Belgrave Square, London SW1X 8QD, UK, Tel: 020 7591 5500, Email: morten@embassy.norway.org.uk, Website: **www.norway.org.uk**; 2720 34th Street, NW, Washington DC 20008, USA, Tel: 202 333 6000, Website: **www.Norway.org**.

TRAVELLERS' STORIES

Olesja Okatjeva from Latvia worked as an au pair in Denmark for two families, the first in a town called Vedbaek for six months, and the second in Hellerup, 10 km from Copenhagen.

My sister was working in the International Student Exchange Centre and asked me if I would like to go somewhere. I was finishing school that year and didn't really know what I wanted to do after graduating, so decided to work abroad as an au pair. I didn't want to go to the USA because it's too far, so, in the end, decided on Denmark. I'm not sure why I chose it, but after arriving here, I remembered that it was my childhood dream!

When I arrived I was very surprised that the families are usually huge and they all stay together. I was taken to the host father's family party and there were about sixty people there.

In the first family I had a very good relationship with the host father and the child, so the host mother became very jealous. She was working all the time and saw her own one-year-old daughter for about two hours a day. My duties were to look after the children and to clean the house for around five hours a day. But the first family cheated me and I started to work for eleven hours a day, and they wanted me to do everything.

In the end, after six months, I decided to leave and find work with another family. I moved to Hellerup, not far from Copehhagen, where I have been for seven months. This town is also on the shore but there are more shops and I can see my friends more often.

Generally, it's not difficult to find a job here looking after children, but other positions are very hard to find. It's a mistake to come to Denmark without a job and think that you can find a job easily. That is not true – it is very hard, even for those who have been living here for some time. It is better to apply for a programme in the home country and only leave when you have arranged a position.

21 SPAIN AND PORTUGAL

SPAIN

Despite high unemployment, Spain has a high percentage of foreign workers in its labour force. That said, don't let this lull you into a false sense of security as finding work can be harder than you think. Madrid, in particular, is expensive, so make sure you have good contacts and plenty of money before you set off. There is also plenty of illegal work, mostly doled out by employers who want to avoid high social security contributions and consequently offer poor pay and working conditions. Bear in mind that if you are caught working illegally, you and your employer could face heavy fines.

VISAS AND REGULATIONS

Living and working in Spain is relatively easy. As part of the EU, all EU citizens are free to live and travel there, although if you intend to stay there for longer than three months you will have to get a residence card (*a tarjeta de residencia*) and tax/fiscal number (*el NIF or Número de Identificación Fiscal*). You can apply for these from the Foreigners' Department *el Departamento de Extranjeros*, which should be done within thirty days of arriving. Forms are available from the Ministry of the Interior (**www.mir.es/extranje/guiap.htm**) – you will need a valid UK passport, four passport photos, medical certificate from your home doctor, proof of financial resources (such as, bank certificates from your home bank) and proof of health insurance.

If you're an EU national, your residence permit should entitle you to find employment so you won't need a separate work permit. For non-EU nationals it's a complicated and tricky procedure – first you must get hold of a *visado especial* from the Spanish embassy in your country. This requires setting up work before you leave. In order to apply for the visa, you will need to provide a copy of your contract and documentation such as medical records and qualification certificates. To find out more, contact your Spanish embassy.

TOURISM

Most of the opportunities for short-term casual work come in Spain's incredibly popular tourism industry. English speakers are an important part of the mix as Spain is chock-a-block with British holidaymakers not exactly in search of the authentic Catalan experience. Whether it's DJ-ing in superclubs in Ibiza, promoting clubs on the street by distributing flyers, working in bars on the Costa del Sol or selling ice cream on the beach in Benidorm, thousands of Brits flock to Spain every year to work during the day, party at night and top up their tans on their hours off. There is also a burgeoning expat scene with retired couples by the score, and Spain is becoming particularly popular for buying property.

The winter ski resorts in the Pyrennees can provide all the employment opportunities of ski resorts, both in casual and pre-arranged jobs through the ski tour companies (see Tourism chapter). If you're fixing up work when you arrive, make sure you get there before the season starts or just at the beginning of the season in mid-November. Summer work in the Costa del Sol, however, is probably the easiest place to find work, for all kinds of catering jobs from hotel managers to cleaners. Accommodation can be pricey as you'll be competing with seasonal tourists, so if you can find work with board thrown in, so much the better. There are also some opportunities to be had selling Time Share in Andalucia (Costa del Sol) or on some of the resort islands such as Gran Canaria. You may be able to find work on the spot or keep an eye open in *Overseas Jobs Express*, where vacancies are occasionally advertised.

Many British tour companies operate in Spain and Portugal, where you may be able to find work as a courier or tour representative. However, these jobs usually require Spanish or Portuguese fluency and tend to favour older employees. You can find out which companies operate in Spain by checking the brochures in the travel agents. Competition can be intense, so apply well before the summer season starts.

Eurocamp (**www.eurocamp.co.uk**) has summer vacancies in Spain, as does The Magic Travel Group (**www.magictravelgroup.co.uk**) tour operators in Spain and Portugal.

Panorama and Manos Holidays (Vale House, Vale Road, Portslade, East Sussex BN41 1HG, Tel: 01273 427000, Fax: 01273 427149) organises holidays in the Algarve, Cyprus, Ibiza, Gran Canaria, Majorca and Tenerife, and requires overseas representatives.

SAILING

If sailing is your thing, you may be able to pick up work crewing or manning yachts, on one of the many boats that are moored in the Costa del Sol. Even those with no sailing or crewing experience may be able to find cash-in-hand work cleaning the decks – cold-call the boats and ask them for work.

Alternatively, if you want to fix up work before you arrive, Sunworld Sailing (**www.sunworld-sailing.co.uk**), a large water-based leisure firm, part of Thomas Cook, offers summer jobs in Spain.

CLUBS AND BARS

Bar work is a universal job and requires little more than a friendly manner, a steady hand, and a working knowledge of the native language. Madrid's and Barcelona's numerous Irish bars can be a good source of work for British, Americans and Australians, while Spain's tourist resorts have a huge number of clubs and bars. Ibiza is a particular hotspot for drawing working travellers so bear in mind that competition can be tough. Hours are supposed to be long for little pay, but clubbers insist it's all part of the Ibizan experience.

Like many people, Karl Evans arrived in Ibiza on his holidays and liked it so much he decided to stay, finding work behind a local bar. He says, 'Timing is crucial. You've got to get there just before the season starts in early March, when people are hiring. Otherwise, you'll end up with promo work selling flyers on the beach, which is really badly paid.'

For information about working in Ibiza, check out **www.gapwork.com** which has listings of clubs you can contact. Other useful sites are **www.balearic-jobs.com** and **www.resortjobs.com**.

TRAVELLERS' STORIES

Anita Westmorland has been working in Barcelona for four months. She originally arrived in January and found there was no work around.

Finding work depends on the time of the year – in the summer there are plenty of jobs around in bars although you will have to speak some Spanish. For any kind of work in Barcelona you will need a CV with a photograph, even to work in an Irish or English bar. There are lots of foreigners here so finding work can be quite competitive but if you're friendly and determined enough, you'll find something quite soon. I'm now teaching English and working for a marketing company on a freelance basis where I entertain business people who come over to Barcelona for conferences. The work is bizarre and can be a ridiculous at times – last week I supervised a raft-building competition and have also led a midnight ghost walk and judged sandcastle competitions.

THE JOB SEARCH

One of the best places to look for a job in the Costa del Sol area is *SUR* in English, which has an extensive classifieds section and is published every Friday. To subscribe to *SUR* in English, write to Circulation Department, *SUR* in English, Avda Dr Marañon 48, 29009, Malaga.

The Entertainer, a free newspaper published each Thursday, has a similar classified section covering Costa Almeria as well.

You can also try *Island Connections* (**www.ic-web.com**), an online version of the Canary Island's fortnightly English language newspaper or *Island Sun* (**www.island-sun-newspaper.com**), a newspaper for the Canary Islands.

The Paper (**www.thepaper.net**) and *Tenerife News* (**www.tennews.com**) are fortnightly Tenerife newspapers.

The website Spainalive (**www.spainalive.com**) also includes a 'Jobs in Spain' section.

VOLUNTARY WORK

In addition to the main voluntary organisations such as Concordia and UNA Exchange, the following organisations run volunteer placements in Spain:

Sunseed Desert Technology (**www.sunseed.org.uk**) organises volunteer placements to help with the charity's work on semi-arid land. Work includes research into appropriate technology, semi-arid land management and organic gardening as well as helping communities to live in such environments. You can either pay to take part in a working holiday in an idyllic Spanish village or become part of the staff for a small weekly allowance.

British Trust for Conservation Volunteers (**www.btcv.org.uk**) organises international conservation working holidays in both Spain and Portugal. Call 01491 821600.

Atlantic Whale Foundation, (St Martin's House, 59 St Martins Lane, Covent Garden, London WC2N 4JS; **www.whalefoundation.f2s.com**) allows volunteers to help on whale and dolphin conservation and research projects in the Canaries. Participation costs £95 a week including half-board accommodation and training.

AU PAIRING

There is a big demand for au pairs in Spain, fuelled in part by the burgeoning need to speak good English. English-speaking au pairs are placed in high esteem, but may also be seen as a cheap way to hire a live-in English teacher, as some au pairs have found out to their peril. The best time to look for an au pair position is before the beginning of the school year in September, as most families require an au pair for at least the whole school year from September to June.

The following agencies recruit au pairs for Spain:

Jolaine Agency (**www.jolaine.com**)

Nannies Now (**www.nanniesnow.uk.com**)

International Educational Services (**www.ies.ciberia.com**) runs au pair and study programmes in Valencia, and places au pairs throughout Spain and western Europe

Centros Europeos Principe. S.L. (C/Principe, we, 6A – 28012 Madrid, Spain, Tel: 34 91 532 72 30, Fax: 34 91 521 60 76) places au pairs in Spain and runs exchanges between Spanish and British students aged 12–25 for two to four weeks

Many of the big holiday companies and tour operators also recruit nannies and childcare couriers/assistants for those with childcare qualifications.

Try the big names such as Club Med and Mark Warner, and Panorama and Manos Holidays (Vale House, Vale Road, Portslade, East Sussex BN41 1HG, Tel: 01273 427000, Fax: 01273 427149).

TEACHING ENGLISH

There is a huge demand for English teachers in Spain, although most private schools insist on a Tefl qualification. Those without, however, may be able to find work in one of the international chains such as Linguarama and Berlitz, who run in-house teacher training courses. However, prospective teachers are warned that these courses are unpaid, and can last up to a week, so bring extra money to tide you over. August is a particularly dead time to come out, particularly in the international business centres of Madrid and Barcelona. The new school season starts afresh in October, so arrive in September if you want to fix up work on the spot.

Most people fix up work before arriving, and there is plenty of scope to do this. However, many of the smaller schools only advertise locally so most of the work you can find in your home country will be with the larger schools and institutes. Check the usual sources of work (see Tefl section of Chapter 6) and contact the British Council for a list of schools in Spain. You can also get a list of schools from the Spanish embassy as well as a leaflet *Teaching English as a Foreign Language* (The Spanish Embassy Education Department, 20 Peel Street, London W8 7PD, Tel: 020 7243 8535).

Americans can organise language assistant programmes in Spain through InterExchange (161 Sixth Avenue, New York, NY 10013, **www.interexchange.org**).

You can also get information about language schools in Spain by writing to Centros de Enseñanzza de Idiomas, Calle Sagasta, 27, 28004 Madrid.

Language schools are also listed in the local Yellow Pages (*Las Paginas Amarillos*) under 'Escuelas Idiomas'.

Business English is particularly popular in Madrid and Barcelona, and teachers can often find work teaching English to the business community, often for schools on a freelance basis. Again, it is very common to find part-time work in a private school and supplement your income with private tuition. You can advertise for services on notice boards in universities, schools and so on. Private tuition can be hard to build up so it's better to have already secured work in a language school first. Pay can be high for private tuition, particularly for Business English. You can also exchange

English lessons for Spanish lessons with a native, whereby you meet up for a coffee and spend half the time talking English and half the time Spanish. Look out for adverts for Intercambio (Exchange) on university notice boards.

Teaching children is also particularly popular. Jo Rea came over to Madrid originally intending to work as a bilingual secretary but found work easily as a nursery teacher in a bilingual school instead.

PORTUGAL

In contrast to Spain, Portugal has one of the lowest rates of unemployment in Europe. Most of the jobs are in the tourist season (May to September) although there is also voluntary and au pair work, and plenty of opportunities for English teachers.

VISAS AND REGULATIONS

EU nationals are free to live and work here, although, as is usual, you will need a residence permit if staying longer than three months. For details and application form, contact your local immigration office (*Servico de Estrangeiros e Fronteiras*), the British Embassy in Portugal, Rua de S.Bernardo 33, 1249-082 Lisbon, Tel: 21 392 40 00, Fax: 21 392 41 88) or your Portugese embassy or consulate.

Non-EU nationals have to fix up work before being granted a residence visa – contact your nearest Portuguese consulate for more information.

TOURISM

If you fancy working in Portugal, your best bet is to head for the Algarve which, like Spain, has thousands of hotels, bars and restaurants to cater for the millions of Britons and Europeans who arrive every summer.

Many tour companies operate here, so if you want to secure work before you arrive, these are a good place to start. See the Tourism chapter for companies to contact and read the Spanish section, as many of the companies that operate there also operate in Portugal.

Powder Byrne International (**www.powderbyrne.com**) need many summer staff for the Algarve and now have an online job application and job description section.

TEACHING ENGLISH

There are also plenty of opportunities for English teachers, particularly in Lisbon and Oporto, and the historic towns. Wages tend to be low, but if you don't have a Tefl (but do have a degree), you might find it easier to find work than in Spain. There is a particularly burgeoning market for teaching of young learners, with children learning English from a very early age. Here, the same rules apply: look in the Yellow Pages for lists of language schools and look in the English-language newspaper *Anglo-Portuguese News*.

International House has nine schools in Portugal but is usually only interested in recruiting experienced and IH-trained and qualified teachers.

Cambridge School recruits abroad for qualified Tefl teachers. Contact Cambridge School, AV. Da Liberdade, 173 – 1250-141, Lisboa, Portugal, **www.Cambridge.pt**.

THE JOB SEARCH

EU nationals can use the national employment service *Centro de Emprego*. Look in the Yellow Pages (*Las Páginas Amarelas*) for addresses.

Portugal also has many private employment agencies including international agencies such as ManPower and Adecco.

You can also try Select, Avenida João Crisóstomo, 54 – B, 1069-079 Lisbon. Tel: 21 317 3200, Fax: 21 315 2968, Website: **www.select.pt**.

Portuguese speakers can check out the online job site StepStone Portugal **www.stepstone.pt**.

Check out the English-language papers such as *Anglo-Portuguese News* and *The Algarve* that both carry job adverts.

USEFUL ADDRESSES

Spanish Embassy, 39 Chesham Place, London SW1X 8SB, UK, Tel: 020 7235 5555; 2375 Pennsylvania Avenue, NW, Washington DC 20037, USA, Tel: 202 452 0100, Website: **www.spainemb.org**.

Portuguese Embassy, 11 Belgrave Square, London SW1X 8PP, UK, Tel: 020 7235 5331, Website: **www.portembassy.gla.ac.uk**; 2125 Kalorama Road, NW, Washington DC 20008, USA, Tel: 202 462 3726, Website: **www.portugal.org**.

Expatriate Cafe **www.expatriatecafe.com** has articles and information for teachers of English in Spain.

You can get a free booklet *Working in Portugal* from Employment Service, Overseas Placing Unit, Rockingham House, 123 West Street, Sheffield, S1 4ER.

22 SWITZERLAND AND AUSTRIA

SWITZERLAND

The first thing to say about working in Switzerland is that it doesn't exactly welcome foreigners to work with open arms. One of the most frequently quoted reasons for this is that in order to preserve its spectacularly low unemployment rate, it needs to impose strict work regulations. It's not that there isn't much work around – there is, particularly in the tourist industry – it's just that you need a work permit to do any kind of work (including au pair and voluntary work) and getting one isn't easy. Switzerland is a tightly regulated country and there are some petty laws you might find difficult to adjust to, such as you cannot wash the car on a Sunday. If you live in a flat there are set times when you can use the washing machine. You can't flush the loo after 10 p.m. You can't put batteries in the rubbish.

VISAS AND REGULATIONS

The Swiss residence permit covers both the right of abode and employment so you need to get one in order to do any kind of work. You must have secured a job before entering the country and the permit can only be applied for from outside Switzerland (allow six to eight weeks processing time).

FREEDOM OF MOVEMENT

The good news is that it is all set to change. Despite not being a member of the EU, Switzerland has recently signed a bilateral treaty on free movements with the European Union, granting EU nationals the right to live and work in Switzerland. The legislation is due to come into effect in 2003: for more info go to **www.europa.admin.ch**.

In the meantime, if you want to work in Switzerland you will have to

- **Secure work before you get there.**

- **Make sure you have the relevant residence and work permit. This must be applied for by your employer on your behalf. EU passport holders can get an A permit for seasonal work up to nine months in the tourist and building industry. For a specific job lasting up to one year, you will need a B permit, although this is much more difficult to obtain.**

- **Apply for a visa from the Swiss embassy once you have been granted your permit.**

- **On arriving in Switzerland, you should register with the Aliens Police before starting work and within eight days.**

- **The country is notorious for its complicated bureaucracy so once you've secured work and your work permit, make sure you have all the correct documentation that you require *before* arriving in Switzerland.**

The Canada–Switzerland Young Workers' Exchange Program gives Canadians the opportunity to work in Switzerland for a period of four to eighteen months. Contact International Youth Experience, The Canada–Switzerland Young Workers' Exchange Program, 12, rue Laval, Aylmer, Qc., Canada, Tel: 819 684 9212, Fax: 819 684,5630 for more details.

WORK OPPORTUNITIES

TOURISM

Despite the difficulties in obtaining work permits, there are some opportunities around for the working traveller. These mainly exist in Switzerland's healthy tourist industry, particularly in the summer (July to September) and winter (December to April) seasons, where you should be able to find work as bar staff, chambermaids, porters and waiters/waitresses in the resorts of Arosa, Champery, Crans Montana, Davos and St Moritz. The work can be hard – the Swiss have a reputation for being one of the most industrious of European nations – but the wages are supposed to compare favourably with the UK, although Americans may feel more short-changed.

Write to the big hotels and tour operators, which you can find in any holiday brochure. You can find details on thousands of Swiss hotels in the Swiss Hotel Guide (**www.swisshotels.ch**), which you can then write to requesting work. Speaking Swiss German is usually required, and sometimes French or Italian – remember Switzerland is divided into three language zones (German (Swiss German), French and Italian) so bear in mind that the dominant spoken language will depend on whichever region you find work.

The Swiss Hotel Association (Mobijoustrasse 130, 3001 Bern. Tel: +41 31 370 43 33, Fax: + 41 31 370 43 34, Website: **www.hotel.job**) has a section called HotelJob which places EU students, aged 18+, in Swiss hotels and restaurants in German-speaking parts of Switzerland. Placements last for around three months and run from June to September. Candidates must have excellent spoken German.

Jobs in the Alps Agency (17 High Street, Gretton, Northants NN17 3DE, Email: alan@jobs-in-the-alps.com) places hotel staff such as porters, waiters/waitresses, chamber staff, kitchen staff etc. in Swiss hotels, restaurants and cafes.

AGRICULTURE AND VOLUNTARY WORK

There are also some opportunities working on farms and during the grape harvest in early to mid October, but again only if you have a work permit. The main grape harvesting areas are in the Vaud north of Lake Geneva, Valais and the Lausanne area and the harvest is quite short, lasting one week to ten days.

You can secure farm work before you arrive by arranging a working stay on a Swiss farm. UK voluntary organisation Concordia fix up work as farmer assistants through the non-profit-making organisation Landdienst-Zentralstelle (Postfach 728, CH-8025 Zurich, Switzerland, Tel: 1 261 44 88, Fax: 1 261 44 32, Email: admin@landdienst.ch, Website: **www.landdienst.ch**). Wages are around £190 per month plus free board and lodging. Send a sae to Concordia, Heversham House, 20/22 Boundary Road, Hove, East Sussex BN3 4ET.

Like France, there are also opportunities for voluntary work. Concordia and International Voluntary Service run international work camps where you can find yourself doing anything from renovating an old church to planting trees. Contact Swiss WWOOF for more details. See the chapter on Voluntary Work and Gap Year.

AU PAIRING

To be an au pair in Switzerland, you need a work permit, and should normally speak German and undertake a minimum of language lessons. Many agencies place au pairs in Switzerland – for more information see the Au Pair and Childcare chapter.

Perfect Way is a Swiss agency that places British girls in au pair work and pledges to provide ongoing support. Contact Perfect Way, Integration Services Karen Schatzmann, President, Steinweg 12b, 5303 Würenlingen, Switzerland, Tel: +41 56 281 39 12, Tel from Switzerland: 056 281 39 13, Fax: 056 281 39 14, Email: info@perfectway.ch, Website: **www.perfectway.ch**.

THE JOB SEARCH

In order to work in Switzerland, you should have fixed up work before you leave your country. However, that said, people may be able to pick up casual work in the ski resorts, washing up in restaurants, cleaning or working behind the bar. You can also register with the tourist offices, which may be able to find you work.

AUSTRIA

With its low unemployment rate and thriving tourist scene, Austria has much to offer the working traveller. A good level of German is generally required, although with the increasing importance of English, there may still be opportunities for non-German speakers. The cost of living is comparable to the UK.

VISAS AND REGULATIONS

As Austria is a member of the EU, all EU nationals have the right to live and work in Austria without a visa for no longer than three months. EU citizens who intend to stay longer than three months should register with the Aliens Adminstration Office within three days of arrival. They do not, however, require a work permit.

Non-EU/EEA nationals who want to live and work in Austria, should apply for a work and residence permit, normally outside Austria. Work permits can be hard to obtain unless you work for an international organisation or have essential skills that Austrians and EU citizens can't provide. Contact your Austrian embassy for details.

TOURISM

Austria's ski scene provides countless opportunities for casual work. Head for the big resorts such as St Anton, Kitzbhuel and Mayrhofen, where you should be able to find work in the many hotels, bars and restaurants. German is normally required although if you head for a predominantly English resort such as Kitzbhuel, you may be able to find work without the language. You can try to fix up work through the big hotels or large skiing companies, or else get there at the beginning of the season in November and go round asking for work. Casual workers should be able to find work as dishwashers, kitchen porters or behind the bar.

Eddy Martin found work as a pizza chef in the resort of Solden, Austria, after unsuccessfully looking for work in Switzerland. He says,

It was much easier to find work in Austria. I was staying in a hostel in the Tyrol region, and the people there told me to go to the local Arbeitsmarkt (jobcentre). It was dead easy – I just went to the desk for guest visitors and they printed out a list of jobs. The worse thing was phoning round all the hotels and having to speak German, but eventually I struck lucky and found work in a bar as a pizza chef. I had picked up some experience making pizzas in a campsite in Italy so could make a mean pizza! The work was well paid and at the end of the month I came away with around £1,000, which was after eating out and drinking every night. It was a great life, I could afford to party all the time and I wasn't even earning that much money compared to most other people.

AGRICULTURE

Austria's grape picking season can provide casual short-term work. The grape harvest starts early autumn in Austria, to the west of Vienna and around the Hungarian border. For voluntary work contact WWOOF Austria (**www.wwoof.welcome.at**) which can arrange working holidays on organic farms in Austria.

TEACHING ENGLISH

Native speakers without formal teaching qualifications can often find work giving private English lessons and at adult education institutes (*Volkhochschulen*). You will find these listed in your local telephone book or by visiting the website of the association of Austrian adult education institutes (**www.vhs.at**) (*Verband Österreichischer Volkshochschulen*). A list of private language schools is available on the British Council website (**www.britishcouncil.at**).

THE JOB SEARCH

The Austrian public employment service, the *Arbeitsmarktservice*, provides information in English and has an online job search on its website (**www.ams.or.at**).

Local and national newspapers, such as *Die Presse* (**www.DiePresse.at**), *Kurier* (**www.kurier.at**) and *Der Standard* (**www.derStandard.at**), contain supplements on job vacancies in their weekend editions.

Check out main agencies for work – you can find the private employment agencies in the local Yellow Pages under *Personalberatung* (personnel advice) or on *Gelbe Seiten* on-line (**www.gelbeseiten.at**).

ACCOMMODATION

You can find accommodation in estate agents (although you may have to pay a small fee) and most weekend editions of local and national newspapers, such as *Die Presse* and *Der Standard*.

USEFUL ADDRESSES

The Overseas Placement Unit (which is part of the UK Employment Service) produces a leaflet *Working in Austria*. It is available from Jobcentres and Euroadvisers in the UK or by writing to: Overseas Placing Unit, Rockingham House, 123 West Street, Sheffield S1 4ER.

Euro Practice (**www.euro-practice.com**) organises placements for European students in Austria and has offices in France, England, Germany and Spain.

Simply Ski (**www.simply-travel.com**) is a small specialist ski company which offers high quality chalet and hotel holidays to Verbier in Switzerland and St Anton in Austria.

Swiss Travel Service (**www.swisstravel.co.uk**) is a ski tour operator with online application form for overseas work.

Village Camps (**www.villagecamps.com**) arranges work for the summer in multiactivity language children's camps in Austria and Switzerland – contact Village Camps, rue de la Morache, 1260 Nyon (Tel: 022 990 9405, Fax: 022 990 9494).

EMBASSIES

Austrian Embassy, 18 Belgrave Mews West, London SW1X 8HU, Tel: 020 7235 373, Website: **www.austria.org.uk**; 3524 International Court, NW, Washington DC 20008, USA 9, Tel: 202 895 6700, Website: **www.austria-emb.org**.

Swiss Embassy, 16–18 Montagu Place, London W1H 2BQ, Tel: 020 7616 6000, Fax: 020 7724 7001, Email: swissembassy@Lon.rep.admin.ch, Website: **www.swissembassy.org.uk**; 2900 Cathedral Avenue, NW, Washington DC 20008, USA, Tel: 202 745 7900, Website: **www.swissemb.org**.

23 THE UNITED KINGDOM AND REPUBLIC OF IRELAND

UNITED KINGDOM

The United Kingdom is booming in work opportunities for travellers, particularly in seasonal work. It's a good job – with the increasing popularity of English as the international language of commerce, the country is filled to groaning point with an influx of language learners every year. Many of these head for the retail and tourism sector – London's workforce in particular has a huge proportion of foreign workers especially in shops and catering outlets. That said, the type of work you end up with may vary enormously, and many backpackers in London find work in higher paying jobs such as banking, computing or accountancy.

VISAS AND REGULATIONS

Despite not so far having signed up for the euro, the United Kingdom is part of the EU so EU and EEA nationals can enjoy all the advantages being in the European Union brings and do not need a work permit.

Most non-EU nationals, except those who fulfil certain criteria, need a work permit to work in the UK. Work permits can only be obtained by a UK employer and will not cover 'low level or unskilled jobs' (for example, manual craft, clerical, secretarial or domestic work such as nannies or housekeepers). However, they are easily obtained if you fulfil criteria to work in one of the skills shortages industries, such as engineering, healthcare (doctors and nurses), vets, IT specialists and teachers.

Commonwealth nationals aged between 17 and 27 with no dependants over the age of five can obtain working holiday visas. These permit holders to work in Britain for up to two years. As the working holiday visa is primarily geared towards holiday and travel within the UK, work is only permitted for half of your stay and should be no more than 25 hours a week. Apply for the visa in your home country before travelling and be prepared to show proof of a return airfare and sufficient funds for your stay.

The government website **www.workpermits.gov.uk** is an excellent source of information and includes leaflets on a wide range of relevant topics which you can download. Another good website is the British Council's on **www.britishcouncil.org/eis/workuk** which answers frequently asked questions about working in Britain.

SPECIAL SCHEMES AND VISAS

A new initiative was also launched this year called the Highly Skilled Migrant Programme (HSMP) which allows individuals with 'exceptional personal skills and experience' to come to the UK to look for work. The system operates on a point system, with varying points awarded for fulfilling certain criteria. For more details write to: Highly Skilled Migrant Programme (HSMP), Work Permits (UK), Integrated Casework Directorate, North Home Office, Level 5, Moorfoot, Sheffield S1 4PQ, Tel: 0114 259 1113, Fax: 0114 259 1392, Email: hsmp.workpermits@wpuk.gov.uk.

Another type of work permit, the Training and Work Experience Scheme (TWES) enables foreign students to do work-based training for a professional or specialist qualification, or work experience. The training or work experience offered should be for a minimum of thirty hours per week (excluding study) and the TWES is granted on the understanding that the person intends to leave the UK at the end of the agreed period to use their new skills and experience. For more details, contact the British embassy or look on the website www.workpermits.gov.uk which has comprehensive information.

Non-European Economic Area students can now work in the UK without a permit. Since 21 June 1999, international students over the age of sixteen who are not nationals of an EEA country, and who have in their passports a stamp prohibiting them from working 'without the consent of the Secretary of State, are no longer required while studying in the UK to obtain the Secretary of State for Education and Employment's permission on an individual basis. However, there are certain restrictions on the type of work they may do. Work should be of no more than twenty hours per week during term time, except where the placement is a necessary part of their studies and agreed to by the education institute. They must not engage in self-employment, business or working as a sportsperson or entertainer, or fill a full-time permanent vacancy.

US students can take part in the Work in Britain programme which allows full-time college students and recent graduates over the age of eighteen to look for work in Britain. Participants can work for a maximum of six months – jobs may be pre-arranged or found on arrival. Before leaving the US they must obtain a Bunac card which acts as a work permit and allows entry into the UK. Contact Bunac for more details (see gap year organisations listed in Chapter 12).

Canadian students, graduates and young people can take advantage of the Student Work Abroad Programme (SWAP), which is organised by the Canadian Universities Travel Service. For more information visit their website www.swap.ca.

Alliances Abroad provide many and varied opportunities for arranging shorter term jobs, internships, and teaching positions for all nationalities in several countries. Visit the website **www.alliancesabroad.com** for more details.

NATIONAL INSURANCE

Under UK law, everyone legally working in the UK must pay National Insurance contributions. You do not need one while you are looking for work, but once you have started work, you must apply for an NI number at the local Benefits Agency office. This requires proof of identity (such as a passport) and a letter from your employer confirming your job. You can apply on the spot, but the process can take some time to come through, sometimes around sixteen weeks. However, while you wait, you can carry on working as normal.

WORK OPPORTUNITIES

Prospects for work in the United Kingdom (encompassing England, Scotland, Wales and Northern Ireland) are generally good, particularly in London, Edinburgh, the South Coast and tourist areas such as the Lake District. Bear in mind that in some sectors, such as catering, pay can be low, although you shouldn't be paid less than the minimum wage (which is £3.60 for 18–21 year olds and £4.20 for those over 21). Visit the government website **www.adviceguide** for information regarding employment rights and regulations.

Be aware too that the high cost of living in London detracts slightly from the ready availability of work. Rent is particularly high (expect to pay at least £80 a week), although you may find something cheaper if you head for the less salubrious quarters of south-east London. London landlords have a dubious reputation with some travellers – South African Tracey Hesom was shocked to find her landlord backdated a standing order and took three months worth of rent from her bank account without even telling her. Fortunately, such cases are rare but the cost of rent can be shocking to some visitors.

TOURISM AND RETAIL

Restaurants, cafes, bars, pubs, hotels and fast food joints can all be good places to find work. Most employers will require you to speak good English, but if you've got the basics, working in these establishments and dealing with the public can be a great way to hone your language skills. Many shops will also advertise their vacancies in shop windows, and you may be able to find work in the department stores. The London department store Harrods regularly recruits, particularly for the big January and summer sales. Contact the Harrods Recruitment Department on 020 7893 8793; you will need to wear 'smart black and whites' and be able to speak good English.

If you've plenty of muscle power, another option is security work, as many clubs and pubs require men with a bit of clout to stand on guard outside their doors. Most of this work comes through word of mouth and by asking around clubs, although you may be able to find adverts in Jobcentres and local papers.

The other main tourist areas to head for are the Lake District, and the coastal resorts such as Brighton and Bournemouth. The big cities should usually be safe bets, particularly Edinburgh, and Scotland's ski resorts Aviemore (Cairngorm) and Aonach Mor (the Nevis Range), where ski bums should be able to pick up work easily. Look out for work in the job centres and local papers.

You may also be able to find work as an assistant in a youth hostel – contact the Youth Hostels Association (England and Wales), National Recruitment Department (Hostel Staff), PO Box 11, Matlock, Derbyshire DE4 2XA, Website: **www.yhao.org.uk**.

Try the big holiday camps and theme parks such as Butlin's Holiday World which has five centres in England, Scotland and Wales (Minehead, Bognor Regis, Pwllheli, Skegness and Ayr). Call the jobs hotline 01243 224 206 for more information.

The theme park Alton Towers offers over 1,000 seasonal jobs between the end of March and the end of October. Check out **www.alton-towers.co.uk**.

Activity holidays provide seasonal work opportunities for qualified sports and outdoor instructors. PGL Travel is one of the largest employers. Write to them at Alton Court, Penyard Lane (847), Ross-on-Wye, Herefordshire HR9 5NR.

TRAVELLERS' STORIES

Tracey Hesom moved from South Africa to London in 1998 and has so far worked as a sales assistant, window dresser in fashion retail outlets and is now assistant buyer for Burberry and Windsmoor. She says that London has many opportunities for working travellers and can be a good place to launch a career.

I came to the UK to find work in the fashion industry after doing a fashion course in South Africa. It was quite tough to get started, but it was so interesting living in a foreign country. The first thing I noticed was the size of the pigeons – I remember thinking what do they feed them with here? I was also quite fascinated with the tube and all the different accents I'd hear in the streets. I was constantly listening to them and trying to place them.

Initially, I could only find work in retail or as a waitress and even then it took me two weeks before I found work. I saw an advertisement in the window of Oxford Street Gap for a sales assistant so went in to offer my services. At first I didn't have much luck but I kept going back until I met one manager who was from South Africa. He hired me on the spot!

The work was mostly boring and involved serving customers, unpacking stock and folding T-shirts and so on. It was also quite tiring and I worked for long hours starting at 7 a.m. and working until 6 p.m. But I like the large international staff – there were people from US, Canada, Bulgaria and Spain, Germany and Australia.

It took me a while to break into the fashion industry. Employers assumed I'd be returning to South Africa, but after I'd been here for eighteen months they agreed to interview me. I targeted everyone in the fashion industry, sending spec letters out to head offices of the major fashion retailers, designer houses and style magazines until I eventually landed a job with Burberry and Windsmoor.

Finding work is easy here if you're prepared to do anything in the beginning. Generally, there are lots of opportunities particularly if you're skilled in IT or banking. Many of my friends have landed good jobs in IT, sciences and teaching and are earning good salaries. As long as you persevere, you'll find something.

BUSINESS AND CLERICAL

There is also plenty of casual temp work around, although secretarial agencies may want to see evidence that you intend to stay for some time. Every city boasts a good selection of employment agencies such as Manpower, Alfred Marks, Adecco and Office Angels.

There are also plenty of telesales jobs around – beware those that pay on a commission-only basis as it could be days, even weeks, before you see any money. Regional newspapers and magazines, such as London's *Evening Standard*, *TNT* magazine and the *Manchester Evening News*, carry advertisements for a huge variety of work including telesales jobs, shop jobs and other casual opportunities.

AU PAIRING

With more and more women choosing to return to work after starting a family, the UK has plenty of au pair work around. The quality of these positions will vary as much as they do anywhere, but do beware of working overlong hours. The British guidelines are that au pairs should be aged 17 to 27 (although this is not set in stone) and live for up to two years as a member of an English-speaking family. In return for working a maximum of five hours per day with at least two full days off per week, they should receive a reasonable allowance of a weekly £45 and the use of a room of his or her own. These are only guidelines, however, and with British people spending longer at work (a recent news story in *Overseas Job Express* said that around four million people in Britain work for more than 48 hours a week) many au pairs may find themselves expected to work far longer hours. Try to guard against this by negotiating an agreement with your employers and agency before your arrive. You can download a leaflet on working as an au pair in Britain from the government website **www.workpermits.gov.uk**.

There are many au pair and nanny agencies in the UK.

Domestic Angels recruit nannies, mothers' help and carer positions in London.

The UK & Overseas Nanny Bureau finds work in London and throughout Europe for nannies or au pairs. Contact them at 1st Floor, 89 Regent Street, London W1R 7HF (Tube: Oxford Circus), Tel: 020 7494 2929, Fax: 020 7494 2922.

HARVEST AND AGRICULTURE WORK

Like many countries, the UK's agricultural industry thrives on help from foreign workers, particularly when it comes to fruit picking. Remember that there are many other jobs available in the production of 'soft fruits', from packing to technical positions. The website **www.fruitfuljobs.com** has plenty of information on fruit picking in the UK and should be your first point of call. According to the website, backpackers can earn more money outside London, bearing in mind the extra cost of accommodation. Work is available from April to November. To find work, the website **anyworkanywhere.com** lists some UK farms who are looking for workers, or try the Jobcentres. Alternatively, target the harvests at the appropriate time, and ask around at the farms.

Harvest Guide For The UK

Flowers	Cornwall, East Sussex, Shropshire	March–July
Vegetables	East Sussex, Kent, Shropshire, Cambridgeshire	May–Oct
Asparagus	Kent, Essex	May–July
Plums	Somerset, Kent, Gloucestershire	May–Aug
Peas	Kent, Somerset, East Sussex	May–Aug
Strawberries	Kent, Somerset, Suffolk, Aberdeen, Perthshire, Essex, Herefordshire, Suffolk	June–Oct
Cherries	Suffolk, Kent	June–Oct
Berries	Norfolk, Somerset, Dorset, Herefordshire, Aberdeenshire, Perthshire	June–Oct
Hay	Lincolnshire	Aug–Oct
Pears	Kent, Somerset, Gloucestershire, Suffolk	Aug–Oct
Hops	Kent, Worcestershire, East Sussex	Aug–Oct
Apples	Kent, Essex, Suffolk, East Sussex, Gloucestershire	Aug–Oct
Mushrooms	All over the UK	All Year

This is a rough guide and harvest times vary according to weather and conditions. For more details look at the jobs on their website or contact the Eures office in your chosen region. Details can be found at **www.europa.eu.int**. This information is taken from the website **www.anyworkanywhere.com**.

The Seasonal Agricultural Workers Scheme (SAWS) is a British government-sponsored scheme which enables full-time students of Eastern and Central European countries to carry out harvest work including fruit picking jobs on farms throughout Great Britain. The scheme is operated on behalf of the government by organisations such as Concordia and HOPS. If your university does not have an arrangement with one of these organisations, the British embassy may be able to put you in touch with local agents. There is a limited number of places available and they are filled very quickly. You usually need to apply in October or November to have any chance of obtaining a place for the following year.

TEACHING ENGLISH

As you might expect, finding work teaching English in the UK is no mean feat. Natives tend to dominate the Tefl scene, and despite the huge amount of language schools, overseas Tefl teachers will be hard pushed to find work. It's not impossible – I taught with a German teacher at a language school on Tottenham Court Road in London who was so paranoid about not being a native English speaker that she told all her students she was English. (This was particularly galling for me when some students praised her 'Queen's English' in comparison to my slight Manchester accent.) However, you will have to have strong selling points – such as good teaching experience, a Tefl certificate and English fluency, of course. That said, some London language schools can be overstretched at the height of the summer season in July and August, and you may strike lucky if you turn up with a CV and introduce yourself in person. You could also target the summer schools and find out if there is work in the social activities programme. For a list of British Council accredited UK language schools, contact Arels at 56 Buckingham Gate, London SW1E 6AG (Tel: 020 7802 9200). Outside London, there are many schools in Edinburgh, Oxford, Cambridge and along the south coast such as in Brighton and Bournemouth.

THE JOB SEARCH

There are many resources in the United Kingdom which can help with your job search. Remember if you are a non-EU national and don't have a work permit, your chances of turning up and securing work are slim. Companies employing foreign nationals now face steep fines if they are not legally allowed into the UK so will be unlikely to take risks.

There are plenty of employment agencies in the UK which serve a wide range of professions including security work, cleaners, au pairs and nannies, caterers and professions such as teachers and nurses. The British Nursing Association is a nursing agency which supplies nurses and healthcare workers to hospitals: 115 Kingston Road, Wimbledon, London SW19 1LT, Tel: 020 8542 9949.

Many other general employment agencies are more geared to the needs of working travellers. Acer Recruitment has been known to have vacancies for vegetable harvesters and packers, telesales staff and cleaners. Acer Recruitment, 2nd Floor, Victoria House, 20 Hougton Street, Southport, Merseyside PR9 0NX, Tel: 01704 549771, Fax: 01704 539895, Website: **www.acer-recruitment.co.uk**.

Hotrecruit.co.uk is an online recruitment agency aimed particularly at students aged between 16 and 28, including working travellers. It doesn't list many jobs but is worth checking out to see the 'wacky' jobs on offer, from stilt-walking at a club night to playing Santa Claus in shops for children.

Check out the British newspapers for vacancies. The magazine *TNT* carries many vacancies, as do the regional newspapers such as London's *Evening Standard*. For more professional posts, try the *Guardian*, *The Times* and the

Financial Times (for accountancy and banking) although these are obviously much more competitive.

VOLUNTARY WORK

British Trust for Conservation Volunteers runs week- or weekend-long conservation projects in Britain. Write to British Trust for Conservation Volunteers, 36 St Mary's Street, Wallingford, Oxfordshire OX10 0EU, Tel: 01491 821600, Fax: 01491 839646, Website: **www.btcv.org**.

Conservation Volunteers Northern Ireland is a registered charity involved in practical conservation work throughout Northern Ireland. Task projects include a diverse variety of activities such as tree-planting, dry-stone walling, path creation, river clearance and pond construction as well as office work. For a list of addresses of their offices in Northern Ireland go to their website **www.cvni.org**.

Community Service Volunteers, 237 Pentonville Road, London N1 9NJ, Tel: 020 7278 6601, Website: **www.csv.org.uk** runs projects in the UK for Brits and foreigners.

British Waterways, Willow Grange, Church Road, Watford WD17 4QA, Tel: 01923 201 120, Website: **www.britishwaterways.com/site** maintains Britain's old industrial canals and has voluntary work opportunities.

OTHER OPPORTUNITIES

This guide is just scratching the surface – many other opportunities exist such as a courier work, from driving vans and minicabs to couriering parcels or delivering pizza. Look under 'Courier Services' in the Yellow Pages for companies, or contact pizza delivery chains such as Pizza Hut. You could also act as a 'human guinea pig' and offer yourself for medical tests/experiments, although a recent article in London's *Time Out* revealed that some people had died taking part in these experiments. Glaxco Wellcome at Northwick Park Hospital is one clinical research unit who use volunteers. Phone 020 8864 3322, or look for details on hospital notice boards.

There is also a huge demand for cleaners – check out 'Cleaning and Maintenance Services' in the Yellow Pages and phone round companies asking for work.

REPUBLIC OF IRELAND

The Irish economy has been booming of late and has a reputation for being one of the best places in Europe to find work. However, according to the *Irish Times*, the last year has seen something of a slow down. Although unemployment is still good at 4.2 per cent, compared to the EU average of 7.6 per cent, it is at its highest since 2000 with the IT sector and executive positions being particularly affected. However, work opportunities still abound. Dublin in particular is good for working travellers and with a huge proportion of its workforce under 26 years old, the city is famous for its young, relaxed and European atmosphere. The minimum wage at the time of writing is just over €6.35.

VISAS AND REGULATIONS

EU and EEA nationals are allowed to work in Ireland without a work permit but will need to apply for an RSI number to register with the Revenue Commission before they can work legally. Once you have an RSI number, you can earn around €110 per week (depending on your situation) before paying tax. For a full description of the Irish taxation system, visit **www.revenue.ie**.

NON-EEA STUDENTS

Non-EEA students in Ireland are allowed to take up casual employment of up to twenty hours part-time work per week (or full-time work during vacation periods) without a work permit. However, it is a primary condition of entry into Ireland that they are in a position to support themselves while they are studying there, and this shouldn't include earnings from casual work.

There are also reciprocal agreements with the USA, Canada, Australia and New Zealand.

Postgraduate students do not need a work permit where the work is an integral part of the course of study being undertaken, such as doctors and dentists. To find out more contact the Irish embassy or consulate in your country. The website **www.gov.ie/iveagh** has plenty of information.

Non-EU nationals can only obtain a work permit by finding employment first. Then the potential employer must apply for the work permit for you, and prove that the vacancy cannot be filled by an Irish citizen or EU national. The process takes around six weeks, during which time you cannot work, so the employer must be willing to hold the position open. A work permit will normally allow you to stay in Ireland for a maximum of one year, although some visas only last for a month depending on your circumstances. Once you have received a work permit, you must then take it to the local immigration office and apply to get a green book. This registers you as a legal alien.

WORK OPPORTUNITIES

TOURISM

Ireland's beautiful, lush countryside and famously relaxed atmosphere draws tourists like a magnet, so there is plenty of tourist work around. The tourist industry in Dublin and on the coast have the best offers of seasonal work. Check out the hotels in a good hotel guide and if you're eligible for work, write or phone enquiring about opportunities. Dublin has a staggering array of bars, pubs and restaurants to cater for its young and lively population – look out for vacancies advertised in shop windows. You can also head for the tourist areas in Galway, Kerry and East and West Cork. Killarney in Kerry is one of the biggest tourist centres in Ireland, while East Cork is famed for its gourmet excellence. The small upmarket yachting resort of Kinsale in East Cork has many top quality restaurants and hotels where you may be able to find work.

AGRICULTURE

Despite the fact that there are many farms in Ireland, paid farm work is not easy to find. Your best bet is to call round the farms and ask if they are looking for helpers – some may exchange free board or camping in exchange for work. WWOOF (Willing Workers on Organic Farms) runs a scheme in Ireland. Contact the Irish Organic Farmers and Growers Association – Organic Farm Centre, Harbour Road, Kilbeggan, Co. Westmeath, Ireland, Tel: 353 506 32563, Fax: 353 506 32063, Website: **www.irishorganic.ie.**

VOLUNTARY WORK

Conservation Volunteers Ireland organises environmental working holidays. Contact Conservation Volunteers Ireland, The Green, Griffith College, South Circular Road, Dublin 8, Ireland (Tel/fax: +353 0 1 454 7185.)

Simon Community of Ireland requires volunteers to work alongside homeless men and women in Ireland in Cork, Dundalk, Dublin and Galway. Contact Simon Community of Ireland, St Andrew's House, 28–30 Exchequer Street, Dublin 2, Ireland (Tel: 353 0 1 671 1606, Website: **www.simoncommunity.com**).

AU PAIRING

Irish immigration law states that only nationals of EEA countries, Iceland and Switzerland can be accepted as au pairs in Ireland. However, American, Canadian, Australian and New Zealand students can get round this usually by applying for the Exchange Visitor Programme Work Permit.

There are several language schools in Dublin that run offshoot au pair placement services, but if you are studying English, you may be expected to study there. Try the Dublin School of English and the Swan Training Institute. For a list of agencies throughout the world that send au pairs to Ireland, consult the *Au Pair and Nanny's Guide* (Vacation Work Publications).

BUSINESS AND CLERICAL

Dublin is booming with office and temp work, where many travellers report receiving good salaries. However, the IT sector is one area which has experienced job losses, so if you are looking for a secure IT job you will need a strong CV and good experience. Dublin has many employment agencies so look in the Golden Pages (Yellow Pages) for addresses. Top Secretaries recruits 'office specialists' and will expect you to provide references and sit a skills test before they take you on. Richmond Recruitment has branches in Dublin, Limerick, Cork, Galway and Naas, while The Recruitment Business recruits for financial, IT, accountancy and the legal professions.

THE JOB SEARCH

EU nationals can use Ireland's state employment service, FAS (Foras Aiscanna Saothair), or can register at the European Employment Services Eures for advice on job opportunities. The Irish Eures branch is at 27–33 Upper Baggot Street, Dublin 4 (Tel: +353 1 6070500, Website: **www.fasjobs-ireland.com**).

Uslt Now (19–21 Aston Quay, O'Connell Bridge, Dublin 2) has a notice board advertising jobs.

All the major papers carry classified job ads such as the *Irish Times*. The *Evening Herald* newspaper has a job section each day, while other papers feature jobs on certain days.

Check out the *Irish Jobs Page* (**www.exp.ie**) and *Top Jobs* (**www.topjobs.ie**) for work. The website Nixers.com (**www.nixers.com**) specialises in short-term and part-time jobs

There are a number of recruitment websites and agencies in Ireland. The website Go Ireland (**www.goireland.com**) has a comprehensive list – go to **www.goireland.com/low/visitorsguide/work**.

You can also contact the Department of Trade and Enterprise for a list of agencies – Davit House, Adelaide Road, Dublin 2.

If you want to find temporary work for over two months, you can register for free with **www.irishjobsearch.com** for work in the hospitality and leisure industry. Key in your details on the website's database so employers can contact you if any suitable positions arise.

The website **www.ireland.com** has a good jobs section and links to the *Irish Times*.

EMBASSIES

British Embassy, 3100 Massachusetts Avenue, NW, Washington DC 20008, USA, Tel: 202 588 6500.

Employment Service, Glen House, 22 Glenthorne Road, London W1 0PP, UK, Tel: 020 8210 8184.

Irish Embassy, 17 Grosvenor Place, London SW1X 7HR, UK, Tel: 020 7235 2171; 2234 Massachusetts Avenue, NW, Washington, DC 20008, USA, Tel: 202 462 3939.

The booklet *Working in Ireland* is available from the Overseas Placement Service from Employment Service, Overseas Placing Unit, Rockingham House, 123 West Street, Sheffield, S1 4ER.

Get hold of the booklet *London, Edinburgh and Dublin Guide* published by the London-based travel magazine *TNT* (TNT Guides, 14–15 Child's Place, London SW5 9RX, Tel: 020 7373 3377); send a sae with 70p. Look out for their free pocket-sized regional guides at airports, stations and backpackers' hostels. If you're outside the UK, contact your post office for details about sending international postage vouchers.

REST OF THE WORLD

24 AFRICA AND THE MIDDLE EAST

AFRICA

Despite its atmospheric and majestic beauty, Africa has few opportunities for the working traveller. Work visas are generally hard to come by and, unless otherwise listed, finding paid work in Africa is rare. That said, many travellers fall in love with this vast continent and come back home eager to return. If you are planning to travel to some of the developing countries, be prepared to endure conditions which may be shocking and disturbing. Be aware that there are some countries in Africa, such as Nigeria, that are not safe for independent travellers. It is also essential to take out the right health care and carry all the necessary precautions such as your own sterilised needle kit and medication. Statistics on the website for Students Partnership Worldwide, an international development charity, put it into perspective. Over two million children die each year from diarrhoeal diseases in developing countries. In Nepal, the cutting down of trees to expand agricultural land without replanting has resulted in widespread deforestation. Over ten million children in Africa have already lost their parents to AIDS and HIV infection rates are rising steeply among fifteen- to nineteen-year-olds.

Unsurprisingly, then, the easiest way to work in developing Africa is to sign up for voluntary work. Much of the continent is still heavily reliant on aid work, and there are numerous opportunities with charities and religious organisations from helping farmers to teaching English.

VOLUNTARY WORK

Many of the big voluntary and gap-year organisations run placements in Africa such as UNA Exchange, VSO, Cross-Cultural Solutions, Student Partnership Worldwide, Gap Activity, Gap Challenge, Project Trust, Teaching and Projects Abroad, and Travellers Worldwide. WWOOF requires volunteers for work in Ghana and Togo while Christians Abroad organises missionary work.

Work can include anything from teaching (English or other subjects) to working on game reserves to conservation work studying biodiversity. There are also plenty of voluntary and conservation organisations that specialise in sustained development in Africa. The following are only a brief guide – for more information read *World Volunteers* edited by Fabio Ausenda and Erin McCloskey (published by Green Volunteers Publications), which is a highly comprehensive directory of volunteering organisations in developing countries.

Africa and Asia Venture send hard-working students to Africa and Asia to spend four to five months teaching or working on conservation projects, followed by an exciting safari. Go to **www.aventure.co.uk** for more information.

Greenforce requires volunteers to work on wildlife research projects in Fiji, the Bahamas, Borneo, Peru and Zambia, such as helping to conserve endangered habitats. Go to **www.greenforce.org** for more information.

Project Trust sends volunteers to 24 developing countries for 12 months as volunteers on teaching, caring, conservation, medical and outdoor education projects. Go to **www.projecttrust.org.uk** for more information.

Quest Overseas specialises in combining exciting, worthwhile projects and expeditions in Africa and South America. Go to **www.questoverseas.com** for more information.

African Conservation Experience (**www.afconservex.com**) runs varied voluntary work on game reserves in southern Africa. Tasks may include game capture, wildlife veterinary work and alien plant control.

Save the Earth Network (PO Box CT 3635, Cantonments-Accra, Ghana, West Africa, Tel: 233 21 236362, Fax: 233 21 231485) organises voluntary work in Ghana for maths and English teachers, tree nursing and planting in the tropical rainforest, and conservation work on agro-forestry farms or harvesting fruit.

Volunteer Africa (PO Box 24, Bakewell, Derbyshire DE45 1TA, Website: **www.volunteerafrica.org**, Email: admin@volunteerafrica.org) places volunteers in community-based initiated projects in Tanzania.

Skillshare Africa (126 New Walk, Leicester LE1 7JA, UK, Tel: 0116 254 1862, Fax: 0116 254 2614, Email: info@skillshare.org, Website: **www.skillshare.org**) organises voluntary placements in Botswana, Lesotho, Mozambique, Namibia, Swaziland, South Africa, Tanzania and Uganda.

Africa Inland Mission (2 Vorley Road, Archway, London N19 5HE) provides English teachers.

The website **www.idealist.org** has a huge database of volunteer organisations and also runs a subscription-only newsletter with details of up and coming volunteer work.

PAID WORK

Apart from voluntary work, chances of finding paid work are slim in most parts of Africa. Teaching English represents the biggest opportunity but with English as the medium of instruction in many state schools, many of the posts are taken up by natives or filled by gap-year organisations and charities.

If you are a qualified expedition leader or have extensive experience of travelling in developing countries, you may be able to find work in one of the numerous overland tour companies. However, most overland operators demand a commitment of at least eighteen months and extensive experience travelling around Third World countries. For more information go to **www.go-overland.com** (see Working a Passage chapter).

EGYPT

Egypt is one of the easiest places to find work in Africa, although the search can still be hard. Cairo and Alexandria have plenty of language schools where you should be able to find work teaching English if you have a Tefl certificate, but it could be difficult otherwise. There also may be some seasonal work available in Hurghada and the Red Sea area in private schools supporting the tourist industry.

TEACHING ENGLISH

Many teachers do turn up and find work when they arrive, but this will be pretty difficult if you are not Tefl qualified. Also, legally, you need to be sponsored by your employer in order to work, and can only get a tourist visa to enter the country without work. All the main organisations require at least Tefl certification. The British Council require a Cambridge CELTA or recognised equivalent, *plus* a minimum of one year full-time post qualification experience for freelance work. You should also be a native speaker (or IELTS Band 9) and hold a UK or Egyptian passport.

Most teachers use the Internet to find work, or look for job adverts in the BCA magazine (British Community Association) and sometimes the weekly *Cairo Times*. The British Council has a notice board for staff to advertise private tuition but it doesn't carry information about other organisations, although students may put up requests for qualified teachers. You can look up addresses of language schools listed under 'Schools Language' in the Yellow Pages or **www.egyptyellowpages.com.eg**.

The best place to start your search is to head for the British Council. They have three centres in Egypt. The addresses are:

9 El Batalsa Street, Bab Sharki, Alexandria, Egypt, Tel: 20 3 486 0199, Fax: 20 3 484 6630.

4 El Minya Street, off Nazih Khalifa Street, Heliopolis, Cairo, Egypt, Tel: 20 2 452 3395/6/7, Fax: 20 2 258 3660.

192 El Nil Street, Agouza, Cairo, Egypt, Tel: 20 2303 1514 (8 lines), Fax: 20 2 344 3076, Email: **british.council@britishcouncil.org.eg**.

CASE STUDY

ELT teacher Andrew Dobbie has been working for International Language Institute (ILI) in Cairo, part of the International House chain of language schools, for one year. He says that although many teachers do turn up and find work, the more teaching qualifications and experience you have the easier the job search.

It's a lot easier if you already know someone here, or start mixing with teachers who can give you advice on where to try. Generally, the quality of work you find will depend on your experience and qualifications. If you work for one of the less reputable language schools, you may not get paid on time. There may also be opportunities at the international schools (primary), but without a PGCE you'll be working for schools at the lower end of the bracket, with fewer resources and less support for staff and you may also be asked to teach subjects other than English. Once you're established, however, it is fairly easy to set up private tuition, if you're attached to a school and you let your colleagues know you're looking for private students. Otherwise, you're going to have to go out and get it. Many teachers charge between 50 and 100LE an hour for private lessons, so it can make a significant difference to your lifestyle.

Andrew enjoys his work but says working in Egypt can take some adjustments.

Don't sign up for a two-year contract without knowing what it's like to live here. You can get a great deal out of being here, but for some people it's not what they want. You do have to be culturally sensitive with the students as you'll come across opinions voiced in the classroom which are diametrically opposed to what you believe. There is also a general lack of international awareness, of what's going on and has gone on outside Egypt and the Middle East. Compared to Istanbul, Cairo is a much more Islamic city. Religion is taken very seriously here and Ramadan is strictly observed. It's a very safe country but foreign women do get a lot of unwelcome attention in the form of stares, hisses and comments, even if dressed modestly.

OTHER OPPORTUNITIES

Apart from teaching, there are some opportunities in journalism and working in the tourist resorts. Many foreigners find work in journalism – be it writing articles, copy-editing or working full-time for one of the English language magazines or newspapers. Pay may not be good but it can be a great experience for fledgling journalists.

Outside Cairo, the tourist resorts of Luxor, Aswan, El Gouna and Hurghada can be a good source of work, although Egypt's currently high unemployment rate means there are plenty of Egyptians, especially graduates, looking for work in tourism who are prepared to work for very little. In addition to this, the more expensive hotels are restricted in the number of non-Egyptians they can hire.

Qualified diving instructors should head for the Red Sea, particularly Sharm El Aheikh and Hurghada which are known for their diving sites and watersports. You can find a list of dive centres from Travel Egypt's Red Sea Virtual Diving Centre. Go to **www.redseavdc.com/redsealinks.htm**. Some online diving magazines are **www.aquanaut.com** and **www.exploreuw.com** and for scuba diving, try **www.scuba.about.com**.

MOROCCO

For a totally unique taste of working in Africa, you could try Morocco. This beautiful, vibrant country marks the crossroads between the East and the West and offers a fascinating collision of African and European life. You will have to obtain a work permit before finding work, which your prospective employer will have to obtain from the Ministry of Labour, but you can apply for one in Morocco providing you have found work. Also bear in mind that you will probably need to speak French to do well in your job search.

TOURISM

Morocco's expanding tourism industry, which is known for its magnificent beaches, may throw up a few opportunities, especially if you target the most popular resorts of Agadir, Marrakech and Tangier. There are many holiday companies and tour operators who run holiday programmes here – contact the Moroccan Tourist Board for more information.

Qualified ski instructors could also try their luck in the skiing resorts close to Marrakech, especially Oukaineden, which boasts the highest ski lift in North Africa. The season typically lasts from February to early April.

Morocco's mountainous terrain is also ideal for trekking and there are some outdoor adventure holiday companies which operate here. If you are a qualified mountain or expedition leader, you may be able to find work. Keep an eye out in the mountaineering magazines *On the Edge*, *High Magazine*, *Climber* and *Trail Magazine* for any suitable vacancies.

SOUTH AFRICA

South Africa is currently enjoying a surge of interest from travellers. From January to May 2002, it was the best performing tourist destination in the world with UK visitors comprising much of that market. In the same period, the number of British visitors rose by 20.6 per cent. So how does South Africa fare for work? For the right skilled people, work can be found easily – an exodus of doctors, teachers, nurses and IT people, lured to the UK by the strong pound (known as the 'brain drain') means that the country has a great need to import skilled staff such as nurses and IT workers.

However, on the downside, work permits for non-nationals are hard to come by with so many natives unemployed. Applicants must have fixed up work first, and the prospective employer must prove that no South African can undertake the work.

In addition to this, most of the population in South Africa live in abject poverty and experience working conditions we privileged westerners can barely imagine.

Bunac run a work and travel programme in South Africa for full-time students and recent graduates under the age of 27. Call 020 7251 3472 or go to **www.bunac.org** for more details.

The agency Foreign Placements can arrange short-term casual work in South Africa as well as contracts for medical staff and skilled workers. Contact Foreign Placements CC, PO Box 912, Somerset West 7129, South Africa.

JCR SA Intercultural Exchange Programs (Pty) Ltd is a cultural exchange organisation in South Africa and offers legal au pair and student exchange programmes for most nationalities wishing to visit South Africa. For more details, check out their website **www.jcr.co.za** where you can also apply online.

Many travellers work on the three-month tourist visa, finding casual work, usually in Cape Town. Backpacker hostels are reputed to be good places to find unofficial work, both for working in the hostel and finding out about local employers. However, the reprisals for illegal work can be intense with some casual workers facing prosecution or deportation. Some au pair agencies send nannies to South Africa, although they may take a while to find.

TRAVELLERS' STORIES

Suze Ingle stayed for one year in Happy Acres, an outdoor field centre for children about one hour's drive west of Johannesburg, as part of her degree course. The centre had a small zoo and glasshouse, housing a number of species used in the school curriculum in Magaliesburg.

We were based in a beautiful mountain area used as a retreat by those working in the city, hence the number of well-equipped local hotels on our doorstep. The kitchen and maintenance staff were all black Africans, mostly local, although a few had come from other countries. One man called Jo came down from Mozambique. He went home one day to visit family and never came back, so I don't think he had a passport. After I left I heard that a member of the kitchen staff I knew had died from AIDS. This was a great shock to me.

Happy Acres was owned and run by a British family and some of the teaching staff had visited the centre when they were younger. The rest of us were British, five of us in all. We all lived on site, in various houses. The kitchen and maintenance staff lived in small communities on the edge of the property. This seemed unfair to me, however everyone seemed to work together very well.

Happy Acres was quite an isolated environment. We were based in a very rural area well away from Johannesburg and were advised where to go and not to go when we went out. Even visiting friends, sport facilities and shopping malls were tightly controlled so it took some getting used to.

I managed the zoo, which I really enjoyed, met lots of lovely people and generally had a great time. Being more interested in animals I was enthusiastic about being part of the zoo, but also learnt to love plants and still have a real interest in them. I soon got used to handling snakes daily, as well as rats, locusts, African snails and chameleons. Teaching was fun most of the time and exhilarating when the students really understood. To have a group of one hundred or more children sing for you was moving. Unfortunately, sometimes with the very bad schools it was depressing – children weren't interested and nor were the teachers.

Road accidents were something that I will always remember, witnessing many with varying degrees of severity and hearing of others in the local area. Often 'black cabs' were involved, which were small minibuses. They were always overcrowded and when involved in an accident, the crashes were horrible. I received the odd speeding/parking ticket myself and was given the option to bribe the policemen.

THE MIDDLE EAST

In the past, the Middle East has been a magnet for professionals such as oil engineers and doctors, lured by the tax-free high salaries, lucrative packages, in some cases including villas, and the dream of lounging by your private pool all day. Much of that boom is now over, of course, although there is still well paid work in Saudi Arabia for nurses, nannies, oil and construction workers. Some agencies place au pairs in the Middle East – consult the *Au Pair and Nanny's Guide* (Vacation Work Publications) for more details. *The Lady* also has the occasional advert. No tax is deducted in Saudi Arabia but you should check for any possible tax liability in your home country.

However, despite the high pay – and even this is becoming less of a certainty – living in a strict Islamic society can come at a cost and women are urged to be particularly careful. According to the Amnesty International website there are countless stories of western women being arrested, and even beaten, on suspicion of prostitution or for not adhering to the strict dress code. If you do brave the strict segregation of sexes, follow the guidance given by the Saudi Embassy in Washington, D.C: 'dress in a conservative fashion, wearing ankle-length dresses with long sleeves, and . . . [don't] wear trousers in public. In many areas of Saudi Arabia, particularly Riyadh and the central part of the Kingdom, Mutawwa pressure women to wear a full-length black covering known as an Abaya and to cover their heads.'

ISRAEL

At the time of writing, the violence in both Israel and Palestine is reaching crisis point so travel to either territory would be inadvisable. In fact, the British Foreign Office's website lists Israel and the Occupied Territories as 'countries not to travel to'. In more peaceful circumstances, however, Israel does have some work opportunities for foreign travellers – particularly in Tel Aviv, Jerusalem and the Red Sea tourist resorts. Diving instructors can target the popular diving resort of Eliat, which is known as the Riviera of Israel and said to be the one town in Israel that hasn't heard a shot fired in anger in 55 years.

That said, working in Israel isn't easy. Work permits are required for all paid work and are generally hard to come by. You must have a job first and your prospective employer must prove that the job cannot be filled by an Israeli national. Immigration is open to all Jews (by the 'Law of Return') and normally also to their spouses whom they have married outside Israel, even if their spouses are not 'Halachically' Jewish.

THE KIBBUTZ

Most people who want to work in Israel choose to work on kibbutzim or moshavim. Kibbutzim are generally well understood: volunteers work in a self-sufficient communal society for usually around eight weeks. Most volunteers receive free room and board and a small amount of pocket money in return for the labour.

Moshavim operate on a similar principle, but are less communally minded: property is privately owned, unlike kibbutzim where the property is owned collectively, and volunteers on moshavim are in fact paid.

For both types of work you need a B4 Volunteer Visa, which you can apply for in Israel once you have found work. The visa expires after three months and can be renewed only once (under current regulations) allowing you to stay for a maximum of six months.

Lara Silverston spent two months in a kibbutz near Tel Aviv, working in the kitchen and fruit picking. 'I had a great time although the work could be hard. We got up at four or five every morning and by six we would have started work, until 2 p.m. when we'd finish and have the rest of the day free. I shared a room with two other girls who I really got on with and it was a great way to meet people. The kibbutz was made up of mixed nationalities, including Canadians, South Africans, Brazilians, and of course Israelis, but not so many Europeans. I wanted a cheap holiday where I could experience a difference culture in a safe environment, and this turned out perfectly for me.'

Her only regret was that she didn't use it as an opportunity to go travelling. 'Lots of other people went travelling together after the kibbutz, but I came home instead. If I could do it again, I'd make the most of that opportunity.'

The website **www.kibutz.org.il** has details of agencies all over the world which can fix up kibbutz placements, as well as extensive information on life as a kibbutz volunteer. In the UK, contact Kibbutz Representatives: 1A Accommodation Road, London NW11 8ED (Tel: 020 8458 9235) to organise a placement. Costs £60 for administration fee and pay for your own flights.

American applicants can contact the Kibbtuz Aliya Desk (633 3rd Avenue, 21st Floor, New York, NY 10017, Tel: 212 318 6130). Some agencies offer a package including flights, placement, insurance, transport to the kibbutz and the B4 visa for around £400.

Alternatively, you can turn up and find work. Tel Aviv has some agencies that will place you in kibbutzim and moshavim. There is also the official Kibbutz Program Centre where you can visit its Volunteer Department (18 Frishman Street, Cnr. 90 Ben Yehuda Street, Tel Aviv 61030). You will have to pay for registration (around $60) and supply various documentation such as passport, proof of insurance, return airflight tickets and a medical certificate.

EMBASSIES

Kenyan High Commission, 45 Portland Place, London W1B 1AS, UK, Tel: 020 7636 2371; Kenyan Embassy, 2249 R. Street, NW, Washington, DC 20008, USA, Tel: 202 387 6101, Website: **www.kenyaembassy.com**.

Nigerian High Commission, Nigeria House, 9 Northumberland Avenue, London WC2N 5BX, UK, Tel: 020 7839 1244.; Nigerian Embassy, 1333 16th Street, NW, Washington DC 20036, USA, Tel: 202 986 8400.

South African High Commission, South Africa House, Trafalgar Square, London WC2N 5DP, UK, Tel: 020 7312 5000; 3051 Massachusetts Avenue, NW, Washington, DC, 20008, USA, Tel: 202 232 440, Website: **www.southafrica.net**.

Zimbabwe High Commission, 429 Strand, London WC2R 0JR, Tel: 020 7836 7755; 1608 New Hampshire Avenue, NW, Washington DC 20009, USA, Tel: 202 332 7100, Website: **www.zimweb.com/Embassy/Zimbabwe**.

Zambian High Commission, 2 Palace Gate, Kensington, London W8 5NG, Tel: 020 7589 6655; Zambian Embassy, 2419 Massachusetts Avenue, NW, Washington DC 2008, USA, Tel: 202 265 9717, Website: **www.statehouse.gov.zm**.

Egyptian Embassy, 2 Lowndes Street, London SW1X 9ET, UK, Tel: 020 7235 9777, Website: **www.egypt-embassy.org**; 3521 International Court NW, Washington DC 20008, USA, Tel: 202 966 6342.

Moroccan Embassy, 49 Queen's Gate Gardens, London SW7 5NE, UK, Tel: 020 7581 5001; 1601 21st NW Washington DC 20009, USA, Tel: 202 462 7979.

Israel Embassy, 2 Palace Gate, London, W8 4QB, UK, Tel: 020 7957 9500, Website: **www. Israel-embassy.org.uk/London**; 3514 International Drive, NW Washington DC 20008, USA, Tel: 202 364 5500, Website: **www.israelemb.org**.

USEFUL WEBSITES

www.africaonline.com has job listings and links to other African job listings sites. It also has the latest visa requirements for each African country.

www.africaguide.com/work has job vacancies and links to websites on working in Africa.

25 ASIA

Working in Asia might bring to mind the idea of sunning yourself on exotic beaches and loitering with the locals over Pad Thai and corn cakes, but the reality is that there are few opportunities for paid employment. Voluntary work is the main way to experience life in Asia and western travellers are urged to consider fully the implications of taking much-needed paid employment from locals.

TEACHING ENGLISH

There are, however, notable exceptions. Teaching English is the obvious one. Despite many of Asia's struggling economies, English teachers are in huge demand and native speakers can often turn up in places like Taiwan, Korea, Thailand and Nepal without even a Tefl qualification and find work. Check out the local press – most countries have at least one English language paper – or leaf through the Yellow Pages and contact the British Council. With the explosion in demand for spoken English, there is also a big market for private tuition. Pay varies but don't expect to be left prospering on what often amount to developing world salaries. In rural locations conditions can also be basic and teaching materials hard to come by, so be prepared to be resourceful. Also bear in mind that even in Asia, big cities can be expensive places to live.

JAPAN

TEACHING ENGLISH

Head for Japan for the big bucks. Despite their economic problems, teachers can still land lucrative posts, sometimes with added bonuses like apartments thrown in, although, at the very least, you'll be expected to be university educated. For the best deals, fix up work before you leave. If you've got a Tefl qualification, so much the better – check out *EL Gazette*, the newspaper for Tefl teachers, the *ELT Guide* and the Education pages of the *Guardian* (Tuesday) to find posts. Other schools can set you up in positions before you leave, although they're only likely to give work to qualified teachers.

GEOS Language Limited (St Martin's House, 16 St Martin's Le Grand, London EC1A 4EN) recruits fluent English-speaking teachers for its five hundred schools in Japan. Posts come with visa, furnished apartment, health insurance and ongoing training.

Saxoncourt Recruitment and English Worldwide (124 New Bond Street, London W1S 1DX, Tel: 020 7491 1911, Fax: 020 7493 3657) places teachers in schools in many countries including Japan.

AEON recruits individuals to teach English in one of its 280 schools throughout Japan. Contact AEON, 230 Park Avenue, 1000, New York, NY 10169 or go to **www.aeonet.com**.

The Japan Exchange and Teaching (JET) Programme, run by the Japanese government, places graduates from over 39 countries in teaching and administrative positions throughout Japan. UK graduates should contact CIEE, Council on International Educational Exchange, 52 Poland Street, London W1F 7AB, Tel: 020 7478 2010, Fax: 020 7434 7322, Email: JETinfo@councilexchanges.org.uk. Website: **www.councilexchanges.org.uk**. Placements last one year, and participants receive remuneration of 3,600,000 yen (£23,000) per year, a return ticket to Japan, training and help in finding accommodation. Programmes start in mid to late August – application forms are available from October each year and must be returned by 7 Dec.

US applicants should contact the Embassy of Japan at 2520 Massachusetts Avenue NW, Washington DC 20008 (Tel: 202 939 6772). Other nationalities should contact the Japanese embassy in their country.

VISAS AND REGULATIONS

In order to obtain a work permit, you must have a position secured before entering the country. However, there are Working Holiday Visas available for British, Australian, Canadian and New Zealand passport holders. These must be applied for at the Japanese embassy of your home country. The rules are generally the same as Australian Working Holiday Visas and are intended primarily for holiday purposes for twelve months from date of entering the country. However they are single-entry so if you leave Japan, you must obtain a re-entry permit before leaving to re-enter the country.

CHINA

TEACHING ENGLISH

Teachers in China are in huge demand and there are many vacancies in provincial schools and universities that are left unfilled. You can fix up work before you go by applying through the relevant channels, or find work once you're there in the numerous private language schools in Shanghai and Beijing. Prospective teachers will not necessarily need a Tefl certificate, although it will certainly help. Teachers should have a degree and the Chinese authorities will usually expect to see evidence of this before entering the country.

Advertisements for native speaker teachers can be found at the Chinese Education Association for International Exchange (CEAIE), 37 Damucang Hutong, Beijing,100816, Tel: 10 664 16582/16583/14933/18220, Fax: 10 66416156, Email: ceaieipd@public3.bta.net.cn, Website: **www.ceaie.org**.

Alternatively, contact the Education and Training Group, 10 Spring Gardens, London SW1A 2BN (Tel: 020 7389 4431, Fax: 020 7389 4426).

Again, the CIEE run a Teach in China scheme for graduates. Placements last between five to ten months and for a cost of £625 plus flights, include one-week training on arrival in Beijing. In the UK email TiC@councilexchanges.org or ring 020 7478 2018 for further details.

There are also opportunities for teaching other subjects. Frank Baker is teaching Economics in Beijing as part of a foundation level course to 45 Chinese students who will be studying at Manchester University next year. He says, 'The teaching experience here is far more rewarding than in England. The students here are all products of the single child family policy, whose parents have plenty of money; Communist China has embraced capitalism with a gusto that is impossible to describe. The students are desperate for an English education and are very keen to learn and get to the UK. An English University education is very highly valued here, and with one the sky is the limit so motivation is no problem.'

Despite the fact that finding work without a work permit is illegal in China, once you have arrived there is plenty of unofficial work teaching English privately and in institutions, or even in TV work. Says Frank, 'Once you are in the country, the Chinese may not be quite as fussy regarding references. It is all a question of who you know, and being in the right place at the right time. Everyone wants to learn English – I have even been approached by people wanting lessons in parks and Tianamen Square.'

VOLUNTARY WORK

Many of the voluntary organisations listed in the Voluntary Work chapter run programmes to Asia. Also look at the Latin American section, or read World Volunteers (published by Green Volunteers and distributed in the UK by Vacation Work Publications).

INDIA

Despite being such a Mecca for backpackers, like the rest of Asia, India has few opportunities for paid employment. With a population of one billion, most Indians are more than happy to work in jobs that, to the westerners' eyes, are very low paid. On the upside, the country is also incredibly cheap – a meal in a local eatery costs around 60p. There are also countless tales about the natives' famous generosity. Says one traveller, 'Wherever you go, people want to give you food, no matter how poor they may be,' and maybe it is this altruism, combined with the beautiful lush scenery and exotic tastes and smells, that continues to lure the hundreds of travellers here year after year.

VOLUNTARY WORK

If you really want to experience working in India, the best thing is to opt for voluntary work, and there are many organisations such as UNA, Africa and Asia Ventures, Teaching and Projects Abroad and Travellers Worldwide that can arrange placements in conditions which are certainly guaranteed to open most westerners' eyes. See Voluntary Work chapter for more details.

Indian Volunteers For Community Service (IVCS) (12 Eastleigh Avenue, South Harrow, Middlesex HA2 0UF, Tel: 020 8864 4740, Website: **www.ivcs.org**) runs three-week visitor's programmes at a rural development project in India.

You can also try to fix up your own voluntary work. Many people help out at Mother Teresa's Missionaries of Charity in Calcutta. You can either turn up and speak to one of the Sisters at Shishu Bhavan, 78 AJC Bose Road, Calcutta, or contact the London office at 177 Bravington Road, London W9 3AR (Tel: 020 8960 2644) for more information.

Jilly Coombes worked as a volunteer for six months in an orphanage in Delhi. She decided to volunteer after visiting the orphanage with some rich donators when she was on holiday in India.

I loved the work but it could be quite upsetting at times to see some of the conditions they lived in. The children were up to five years old and were mostly babies whose parents were either unmarried or had died from AIDS. The babies were colour-coded so we could see which ones' parents had died from AIDS, and there were children up to four who were still stuck in cots. Many children were orphaned out but it was always the pretty docile ones who managed to find foster parents. Our work involved playing with the children and feeding and changing them, working from nine in the morning until lunchtime. We grew very close to the children over time and it was hard to leave them at the end, but it was still a wonderful experience.

VISAS AND REGULATIONS

Under Indian visa regulations, all non-Indian nationals should have a tourist visa before entering the country. If you are planning to stay over three months, you should register with the Foreigners' Regional Registration Office within fourteen days of arrival and provide evidence of how you intend to support yourself. If you intend to take up paid employment, you should have a valid work permit before you enter the country. Apply to the nearest Indian consulate, enclosing a copy of your contract.

That said, the reality on the ground can be a million miles from the regulations. As one expat said who, despite living there for a year and having a work permit, still hasn't registered at the Foreign Regional Registration Office, 'India is very bureaucratic but nobody bothers to follow the rules.'

For voluntary work lasting over three months, send details of the scheme to the Indian consulate when applying for a visa at least two months in advance. If you do not intend to work for the voluntary scheme for that long, enter India on a student or employment visa.

BOLLYWOOD

Aspiring actors and film workers can head for Bollywood in Mumbai (Bombay). According to Lindsey Hulme who has been living in Mumbai for the last eighteen months, film-extra work is a popular and lucrative way for foreigners to make money. She says the work can be boring, particularly working on a film where you could be hanging around a set all day, but can be very well remunerated. Extras can earn an average of 1,000 rupees a day, which in India goes a long way (approximately £12 a day).

Modelling is another popular alternative, and occasionally model coordinators will scour the tourist resorts looking for the right kind of western face. 'You don't have to be beautiful,' says Lindsey, 'but clear, white skin and dark hair usually helps as it fits the classic Indian definition of beauty. Freckles are considered weird but are still tolerated. Czech girls with beautiful porcelain complexions are hugely popular at the moment.'

If you fancy yourself as a future Kate Moss, the best thing is to contact the model coordinators: you can get a list of these, as well as TV stations and production houses, from Mumbai's photography shops. Pay varies and you have to be careful. The model coordinators should officially only take around twenty per cent but tend to take much more. Lingerie shots and condom adverts are particularly lucrative. Pay can be as high as 100,000 rupees (over £1,200) and the model coordinators will actually go looking for westerners as no Indians would be willing to be in bikini or lingerie shots.

Lindsey says the best thing is to state your price and make sure you get your money in cash on the day, preferably before you do the work. You can also negotatiate as you go along, depending on what you do or don't want to do.

Lindsey Hulme has been working in Bollywood as a make-up artist for eighteen months. After doing a BBC make-up course, she landed in Mumbai on a tourist visa and went round all the production houses with her portfolio, introducing herself. She says,

Formal qualifications don't count for much in Bollywood. Film producers want to see evidence of the work you've done so I showed them my portfolio. It took a few weeks before they offered me work and then over the last year I have gradually built up work on films, TV and magazines. It's easy to get through the door but generally people in Bollywood don't like to take risks so you have to persevere. Employers also like to pigeonhole you. I'm typically called out to work on modern western-style films and TV, and that's really my niche.

You also have to be strong to survive in the big cities like Mumbai and Delhi. There are many frustrations working in Bollywood, and the cities can be incredibly grim places to be. The conditions are terrible, the dirt and the heat is appalling, and as soon as you walk out of the door, you are surrounded by people, poverty and disease. But it's also amazing and there are many opportunities. Things are booming at the moment. Radio stations are starting up and it would be easy to find work as a DJ or disc jockey as it's still in its infancy.

MODELLING AND HOSTESS WORK

Never underestimate the lure of a Caucasian face and a native English accent. Registering with the advertising agencies in Thailand and Japan can lead to being paid a daily rate of around £80. You don't have to be beautiful, although blonde hair can certainly help.

Hostessing is a common way of earning your keep in Tokyo, although the tragic murder of 21-year-old British woman Lucie Blackman has recently highlighted the dangers. However, across the big Asian cities Western women have been offering flirtatious conversation (and not sex) with businessmen, or Salaries, as they are known in Japan. Pay can be good – expect around 5,000 yen (£30 an hour) in Tokyo – but be warned: the case of Lucie Blackman has uncovered many other disappearances from these establishments. In Tokyo, head to Ginza for a classier clientel, while the area Roppongi is more seedy and some of its clubs are rumoured to have gangster connections.

JOURNALISM
Native English speakers can also lend their voices to English radio programmes. Visit the local radio stations and TV stations, and ask around

the expat bars and cafes. Wannabe hacks can make a beeline for the English language newspapers and magazines where you may be able to find freelance work, writing reviews or articles.

HONG KONG

Hong Kong has probably the best reputation for finding work. Before the birth of the Hong Kong Special Administrative region (HKSAR) of the People's Republic of China in 1997, British people could find work easily and thrived in the former colony's economy. Although opportunities have slimmed considerably since, and the regulations say you can only have a work visa with pre-arranged work, there are still stories of working travellers finding work without visas in expats bars and restaurants.

VISAS AND REGULATIONS

Most visitors to Hong Kong still don't need a visa. British citizens who hold UK passports can stay for up to six months without a visa, while citizens of Commonwealth countries and most western European countries are also permitted to stay for three months without a visa. Americans, Japanese, South Africans and Germans (and the majority of Latin American countries) do not require visas for a visit of one month or less.

Obtaining a work visa however is a different story – work permits are hard to come by. The Hong Kong Immigration Department requires proof that you have been offered employment, usually in the form of a contract. The prospective employer is also obliged to show that the work you plan to do cannot be performed by a local. Apply to a Chinese consulate for details. For more information in Hong Kong, contact the Hong Kong Immigration Department, 2nd floor, Immigration Tower, 7 Gloucester Road, Wan Chai (Tel: 2824 611 1, Fax: 2877 771 1, Email: enquiry@immd.gcn.gov.hk, Website: **www.info.gov.hk/immd**).

EMBASSIES

Bangladesh Embassy, 28 Queen's Gate, London SW7 5JA, UK, Tel: 020 7584 0081.

Chinese Embassy, 31 Portland Place, London W1B 2QD, UK, Tel: 020 7631 1430; 2300 Connecticut Avenue, NW, Washington DC 20008, US Tel: 202 328 2500, Website: **www.china-embassy.org**.

Indian High Commission, India House, Aldwych, London WC2B 4NA, UK, Tel: 0906 8444 544; 2107 Massachusetts Avenue NW, Washington, DC 20008, Tel: 202 939 7000, Website: **www.indianembassy.org**.

Indonesian Embassy, 38 Grosvenor Square, London W1X 9AD, UK, Tel: 020 7499 7661; 2020 Massachusetts Ave NW, Washington DC 20036, US, Tel: 202 939 7000, Website: **www.indianembassy.org**.

Japanese Embassy, 101–104 Piccadilly, London W1V 9FN, UK, Tel: 020 7465 6500; 2520 Massachusetts Avenue, NW, Washington DC 20008, US, Tel: 202 238 6700, Website. **www.cmbajapan.org**.

Korean Embassy, 60 Buckingham Gate, London SW1E 6AJ, UK, Tel: 020 7227 5500; 2450 Massachusetts Avenue, NW, Washington DC 20008, US, Tel: 202 939 5600, Website: **www.mofat.go.kr/en-usa-htl**.

Malaysian Embassy, 45 Belgrave Square, London WC2N 5DU, UK, Tel: 020 7235 8033; 2401 Massachusetts Avenue, NW, Washington DC, USA, Tel: 202 328 2700.

Nepal Embassy, 12a Kensington Palace Gardens, London W8 4QU, UK, Tel: 020 7229 6231.

Philippine Embassy, 9A Palace Green, London W8 4QE, UK, Tel: 020 7937 1600; 1600 Massachusetts Avenue, NW, Washington DC 20036, USA, Tel: 202 467 9300.

Sri Lankan Embassy, 13a Hyde Park Gardens, London W2 2LU, UK, Tel: 020 7262 1841.

The Royal Thai Embassy, 29–30 Queens Gate, London SW7 5JB, UK, Tel: 020 7589 2944, ext.117; 1024 Wisconsin Avenue, NW, Washington DC 20007, USA.

Vietnamese Embassy, 12–14 Victoria Road, London W8 5RD, UK, Tel: 020 7937 3222.

26 AUSTRALIA AND NEW ZEALAND

AUSTRALIA

Australia is a hugely popular destination for working travellers, which is hardly surprising when you consider how many opportunities there are. Whatever you want to do, you should be able to find it here, providing you use a little motivation and ingenuity. The cost of getting here makes it an unsuitable destination for short-term work lasting only a few weeks, so to make the most of your ticket (and the fact you are eligible for only one working holiday visa) it's best to aim for a long stay of at least a few months.

WHEN TO GO?

The fact is any time is good for travelling round Australia although spring and autumn are the best times. Summer (December to February) can be very hot and is also the wet season in the north.

VISAS AND REGULATIONS

THE WORKING HOLIDAY VISA

Every nationality except New Zealanders need a visa to enter Australia, but the working holiday visa is one of the main reasons it is such a popular choice for travellers. The visa can only be issued once and entitles you to stay for a maximum of twelve months (starting from the day you enter Australia), but as the main purpose of the visit is to travel, you cannot work for more than three months for any one employer, or undergo studying or training for more than three months. If you break the conditions of your visa, you may be asked to leave. It is also worth noting that if you leave Australia within the twelve months of the visa's permit, your visa still expires on the original date, so don't expect to recover any months you were absent from the country.

In order to be eligible for the Working Holiday Visa you must be aged between eighteen and thirty (inclusive) at the time of the application, have no dependent children with you, and hold a valid passport from one of the following countries: the UK, Canada, the Netherlands, Ireland, Japan, Korea, Malta, Germany, Sweden, Denmark, Norway and Hong Kong. However Australia is currently negotiating the same working holiday arrangement with other countries – to check which ones, look on the DIMA website **www.immi.gov.au** or check with your nearest Australian government office.

OVER 30S

Once you have turned 31, you are no longer eligible for a working holiday visa, and can only work there if you meet the requirements for another type of temporary residence visa. Generally, you need special skills (such as nursing) which are in demand in Australia and to be sponsored by an employer in Australia. Successful applicants should score over 115 points – the points awarded are based on criteria such as job (for example, lawyers score 60 points and journalists score 50), age, professional qualifications and so on. People wishing to emigrate to Australia, however, should be warned that demand for employment visas is strong, and according to the Australian High Commission, applications will take eighteen months to process. Contact the Australian embassy for more details.

HOW TO APPLY FOR THE WORKING HOLIDAY VISA

Application for the visa must be lodged outside Australia, where you should also be granted it. Fill in Form 1150 available from the Australian consulate, embassy or high commission. Since November 2001, applications for working holidaymaker visas cannot be lodged in person at the Australian High Commission London, but can only be lodged by post. It can also be downloaded from the Australian Department of Immigration and Multicultural Affairs' website **www.immi.gov.au** or call the Australian and Citizenship Information Line on 09065 508900 (calls charged at £1 per minute).

For more information contact the Australian government offices.

HOW LONG WILL IT TAKE AND WHAT EVIDENCE WILL I NEED?

Begin the application process well in advance of your travels as Australia is such a popular destination, there can be a limit on the number of working holiday visas issued. Generally the process takes four to five weeks and it's recommended that you don't book your flight until your visa has been granted. You don't need to show a return ticket but proof will be asked that you have sufficient money for a return or onward journey (around £2,000 for UK citizens). There are also strict health standards and in exceptional circumstances, you may be asked to have a medical examination or X-ray as part of your application.

Once you have been granted the visa, you have twelve months to travel to Australia. You can apply for another visa while you are in Australia should you meet the requirements. Working holiday visa holders may be able to apply for a visitor visa to enable a longer stay in Australia but only in exceptional circumstances.

TAX

In order to work in Australia you have to obtain a tax file number which you quote when applying for work. You can apply for this online at the Australian

Taxation Office website. Despite paying tax, you are not entitled to most government services such as healthcare so it's a good idea to fix yourself up with good insurance before you leave.

Working holidaymakers are taxed at the non-resident rate of 29 per cent – for more information check out the Australian Taxation Office website **www.ato.gov.au**.

WORK OPPORTUNITIES

The fierce competition in Australia detracts slightly from the huge range of jobs on offer, so it's a good idea to look away from the big cities, and check out the smaller, rural destinations. That said, the big cities such as Melbourne and Sydney throw up numerous opportunities in retail and business work. Temping work can be easy to come by – register with one of the secretarial agencies if you have secretarial skills.

Australia has a famously high standard of living, and many UK travellers in particular are amazed to find just how far their pay actually goes. However, while there is much work there, there are also a lot of jobseekers, so it's important to get out there and do it, instead of just waiting around. The first thing to do is to get on the Internet as this can be a rich source of work vacancies. Before leaving, register free with **www.gapwork.com** which has regularly updated lists of vacancies for working holidaymakers.

Other general purpose employment websites are:

Employment.com.au
MyCareer.com.au

BUSINESS

For urban work in bars, restaurants, offices and factories check out the private employment agencies such as Bligh, Adecco and Drake Personnel. Others are: Hamilton James & Bruce, Hays Personnel Services, IPA Personel, Manpower, Medistaff, Michael Page, Morgan Consulting Group, Recruitment Solutions and Kelly Services.

Temp work is generally easy to find and, if you are lucky, can place you in interesting environments. Cath Mortimer took a year out and travelled through south-east Asia, before living in Sydney for nine months. As soon as she arrived she registered with Sydney's numerous temping agencies.

My favourite was TMP Worldwide who got me some brilliant placements. I worked in an ad agency for some time, and the Sydney radio station Nova. The work was just basic admin stuff but it was a brilliant environment to work in. I got to meet loads of DJs and came up with ideas for radio shows and promotions. After this, the agency found me work for the record company Festival Mushroom records whose artists include Kylie Minogue, Ash and Garbage. I worked on the reception and helped other departments, organising parties, packaging up CDs and sorting out press cuts. Again, I loved it – I met lots of artists and had a great social life. There were free gigs and album launches all the time. I knew loads of backpackers, of course, so the free bar really came in handy!

AGRICULTURE

One of the easiest ways to pick up work is to head for the harvest fields. Australia has an extensive range of crops and harvest work is available in the fruit, vegetable, cotton, seed, grain and wine producing areas. Generally work is easy to find – there are countless websites listing harvest dates and areas – although it's wise to remember that Australia's summer is our winter, so July and September aren't the best months to look for work. Many backpackers, of course, find work fruit picking, but there is also work available for pruners and trimmers, chippers, farmhands and labourers, farm machinery operators, packers and truck drivers.

Bring a tent if you intend to fruit pick, as many farmers allow you to camp on their ground. You can typically earn around A$9 an hour doing harvest work although this can vary and some lucky pickers manage to up this considerably. Generally, many farmers tend to pay full-time work with free board (food and lodgings) plus a small daily rate, and part-time work with free board.

Ian Maidens picked fruit throughout his travels in Australia, including raspberries, grapes, bananas, eggplant and pumpkins. He says, 'It's easy to make some money in fruit picking but you have to be in the right place at the right time. Pay can be OK – we made A$300 a week picking bananas although you have to be careful of the spiders and snakes falling on you as you do your work! You can also be in competition with the locals, who work very quickly, so you have to work hard to keep up. Hours can be long in some places – I know one farm where the pickers worked twelve hours a day.'

You can get hold of a booklet from many campsites in suitable harvesting areas in Australia – *Fruit Picking Around Australia* (114 Hazelton Way, Waterlooville, Hants PO8 9DW) or in Australia for A$10 from Pickpack 11 Coral Street, Saudners Beach, Queensland 4818. Or check out **www.cix.co.uk/~yama.fruit**.

TNT magazine also carries details of the harvest calender and fruit-picking work.

For details about Australia's harvest calender, go to **www.nomadsworld.com/oz/work/about/harvest_c.html**.

For harvest work in Tasmania, check out the Tasmanian government's website **www.dsd.tas.gov.au/publications/harvest.html** which has many useful links including the National Harvest Trail where you can find details of where work is available **www.jobsearch.gov.au/harvesttrail.asp**.

The Employment National website has a regularly updated page on harvest work or call 01300 720 126. Visiting one office will link you to harvest opportunities in more than 200 offices in other regions of the country.

For details of the National Harvest Trail, check out **www.jobsearch.gov.au.**

OTHER USEFUL WEBSITES
www.backpackingaround.com
www.greyhound.com.au
www.waywardbus.com.au/seaswork
www.countrylink.nsw.gov.au
www.yha.com.au
www.backpackers.com.au
www.immi.gov.au/allforms/temo.whm.htm
www.riverinatourism.com.au

FINDING WORK
Work can also come easily through word of mouth, especially if you are staying in a hostel. There is a huge network of backpackers' hostels in Australia, many of which employ travellers themselves. Payment is typically low but free board and lodging will be provided and many hostels provide plenty of information of local opportunities.

Most people who travel around Australia pick up a wide range of work, although you may have to scour the jobcentres and newspapers to find it. Most travellers say that meeting and speaking to people is crucial, as most jobs come through word of mouth. Angela Haddow, who worked in a banana plantation, an ice cream store and as a chambermaid, says, 'The best thing about travelling with no money is that you'll do absolutely anything. You're not worrying about your career and no one judges you on that basis.'

The other thing to do is read the classifieds in the main Australian newspapers and magazines – *The Advertiser* (Adelaide), *The Age* (Melbourne), *The Australian, Australian Financial Review, Canberra Times* (Canberra), *Courier Mail* (Brisbane), *The Mercury* (Tasmania), *Sydney Morning Herald* (Sydney) and *Queensland Country Life* magazine (Queensland).

TRAVELLERS' STORIES

Mark and Lynda Whittaker travelled around Australia after saving up by working in Pizza Hut for eighteen months. Says Lynda,

'The first thing we did when we arrived was head for Brisbane. Mark had an uncle there who was away for a month, so we looked after the house for him. We then bought a car, and then after three weeks found work delivering pizzas – I drove and Mark had to find the roads for me. We had no idea where we were and it felt a bit surreal delivering pizzas to all these houses in a strange new country. We did that for three weeks, and then drove up the coast stopping off at places for about one or two weeks, until we ended up in Magnetic Island, off the coast of Townsville. There we found work in a backpackers' hostel called Geoff's Place, where we worked for two months. I worked as a receptionist and Mark was a barman. It was hard work, but a fantastic experience – we met some brilliant people. The money wasn't great – we just worked for bed and food and around A$10, but we still managed to save up enough money to do a week-long dive course to become qualified open water divers.

After that, it was on to Cairns. 'We sold the car there and spent two weeks in the rainforest white-water rafting. Then we flew to Darwin and didn't work for a while. After a few months, we ran out of money and we had to choose to either go back home or continue absolutely skint. So we decided to stay put – we were having such a great time having no money seemed bearable, and for about two months we were living off jam sandwiches.'

By the time Mark and Lynda arrived at Sydney they had only A$10 and their ticket home. Lynda says, 'I remember going to the jobcentre only to be told there was nothing available. We were just about ready to give up and book our passage home, when a man came in and said, "Are you looking for work?" He took us to his muffin shop and we ended up selling muffins for three months! Mark discovered he had a secret flair for it and was made head chef, and they offered us a contract to become managers of the shop along with a luxury apartment complete with swimming pool and tennis courts!'

Unfortunately, Mark had to be back in the UK to start university, so they had to turn the offer down. However they did manage to save up enough money to do the rest of the bridge-the-world trip in style. With the money they had saved up from selling muffins, they visited Fiji, Hawaii and spent two weeks in LA. Lynda says, 'It all just worked out perfectly. If that man hadn't come in the jobcentre at that moment we would probably have had to come home. It's all about being at the right place at the right time, and I think you experience that a lot when you are travelling. If you want it to happen, and you're there, and want it enough, opportunities will come along.'

USEFUL ADDRESSES

Willing Workers on Organic Farms (Australia): Buchan 3885, Victoria, Australia (Tel: 61 03 5255 0218, Fax: 61 03 5155 0342, Email wwoof@net-tech.com.au, Website: **www.wwoof.com.au**). WWOOF Australia provides jobs on over 1,200 farms and properties around Australia. Work is not paid, but food and accommodation is provided in exchange for four to six hours work per day.

Australia Work and Travel (AUSWAT) Programme: CIEE, (Council on International Educational Exchange, 52 Poland Street, London W1F 7AB, Tel: 020 7478 2022, Fax: 020 7734 7322, Email: auswat@councilexchnages.org.uk, Website: **www.councilexchanges.org**). AUSWAT helps British, Canadian, Dutch and Irish citizens resident in the UK to travel and support themselves in Australia. It assists in all stages from obtaining visas to finding work and accommodation.

Work Australia, Bunac, 16 Bowling Green Lane, London EC1R 0QH, Tel: 020 7251 3472, Email: downunder@bunac.org.uk, Website: **www.bunac.org**. Contact Bunac to find out about this work and travel scheme to Australia, organised by International Exchange Programme, for up to a year for eighteen- to thirty-year-olds (inclusive). The package includes a round trip flight, working holiday visa, two nights' accommodation in Sydney, and guidance on jobs, accommodation, health, and so forth. The programme is open to British, Irish, Canadian, Dutch, Swedish, Norwegian and Danish passport holders.

NEW ZEALAND

Like its neighbouring country, New Zealand manages to pull working travellers like a magnet, and it's not hard to see why. The country has much to recommend it – a relatively low cost of living, friendly locals and the ease of casual short-term work, mainly in agriculture and tourism. It also has budget accommodation and people can usually camp on beaches and in woodland. Despite the fact that working in New Zealand should only be allowed if you have a work visa, there is ample opportunity for casual work for tourists issued on a cash-in-hand basis.

VISAS AND REGULATIONS

Although citizens of the UK, Ireland, US and most European countries do not need a visa for tourist and business trips of up to three months (six months for UK citizens: on arrival they must have valid passports, return tickets and evidence of sufficient funds – about £300 per month of stay), all nationals except Australians must have a work permit or visa in order to work. This applies to any form of paid employment – including internships, voluntary work and jobs which are paid in board and lodging such as working on a farm – and must normally be obtained before entering the country. You must also have a job offer at the time of application. You will usually be offered a New Zealand work visa if you have a written offer of employment for which you are qualified.

You can apply for a work visa or permit by completing the application to work in New Zealand and downloading the application form for work visas and permits from the New Zealand Immigration Service (NZIS) website. Processing time normally takes three weeks if you have provided all the relevant documentation. People on working holidays can now apply to extend their stay or even residence without leaving the country. Applicants with skills in demand – such as doctors – may apply for a new work permit option that will be valid for up to six months at one of the seven Immigration Services offices in New Zealand.

The New Zealand – United Kingdom Working Holiday Scheme This enables young people (aged between eighteen and thirty) from New Zealand and the United Kingdom to undertake working holidays in each others' countries. There is an annual quota of 8,000 visas available for British applications, starting on 1 September.

To apply you need the right application for work visa form, your UK passport, the fee of £30 and evidence of a return ticket and proof of NZ$4,200 (about £1,200). This scheme doesn't require proof of a job offer and allows you to pick up work as you travel around. However work permits obtained under this scheme have a few limitations. Holders of working holiday permits may not reapply for subsequent permits and may not undertake permanent employment. Working holiday permits are supposed to be restricted to temporary, casual and part time work.

To apply call the NZIS UK call centre: within the UK, telephone 09069 100 100 (calls charged at £1 per minute); from outside the UK, telephone 44 1344 71 61 99. Or download an application form from the New Zealand Immigration website **www.immigration.govt.nz**. Alternatively, you can turn up in person along with your current passport and £30 application fee, and have your visa issued on the spot.

Other working holiday schemes There are also a number of working holiday schemes open to citizens of Netherlands, Canada, Malaysia and Singapore who since April 2001, do not need to be resident in their home country in order to apply. A similar working holiday scheme is open to the Irish but application must be made to the London branch of the NZIS in New Zealand House. For more information visit the Immigration Service website: **www.immigration.govt.nz**.

TAX

Like Australia, workers must register with the tax office and obtain a tax or IRD (Inland Revenue Department) number before starting work. Ring the toll-free number 0800 227774 for a form or visit the tax office in Takapuna or Manukau City. The number will be sent to an address you give and should be received within ten working days.

WORK OPPORTUNITIES

FRUIT PICKING

Fruit picking is a popular backpackers' job in New Zealand. Most of the fruit-picking work is centred around the Hawkes Bay region although there is plenty of work elsewhere around the country. The main fruit-picking season is between November and May. Farmers often advertise in local hostels and have links with hostel owners who may put you in touch with work. During the season, you can normally turn up and find work.

TOURISM

Unsurprisingly there are lots of opportunities for tourism work – from working in bars to tour operators. Head for Queenstown and its huge Mecca of bars and restaurants. Its economy thrives on tourism although it is worth remembering that it also draws immigration officials who may ask to see your passport. Wellington is another popular place for casual work in hotels and restaurants.

There are also numerous ski resorts and tourism work is widely available in the resorts of Ohakune and Whakapapa during the ski season (July to October). If you are a qualified ski instructor or ski patroller, for example, then apply in advance to the resorts or book a place at one of the hiring clinics usually held at the beginning of July. Snowboard instructors are in heavy demand.

BUSINESS

Your best option for work is to register at temporary employment agencies. This fits within the scope of your working holiday permit and also lines you up for reasonably well-paying work. You could try contacting the following agencies on the net: Adecco, Advanced Personnel, Andrews Partners/Sapphire Technologies, Clayton Ford, Eden Brown, Education Personnel, Executive Taskforce, Job Net NZ, Manpower Services, Morgan Banks, Maxim Recruitment Group and Wheeler Campbell.

TEACHERS

There is still a slight shortage of teachers in New Zealand, especially pre-school and primary teachers, although this is steadily improving, and the New Zealand government offer a relocation grant of NZ$3000 for two-year visas. For more information, check out **www.teachnz.govt.nz/overseas.html**.

USEFUL ADDRESSES

Call Tourism New Zealand's General Information Line on 09069 101010 (calls cost £1 per minute) for a brochure. You can also get a wide range of free brochures from the Information Point on the Ground Floor of New Zealand House, 80 Haymarket, London SW1Y 4TE (open 9 a.m.–5.30 p.m. Mon to Fri), Tel: 020 7930 1662, Fax: 020 7839 8929.

The website **www.purenz.com** carries comprehensive visitor information plus links to other useful sites.

Bunac (16 Bowling Green Lane, London EC1R OQH, UK, Tel: 020 7251 3472, Email: downunder@bunac.org.uk, Website: **www.bunac.org**) runs a Work New Zealand programme which allows British passport-holders aged between eighteen and thirty (inclusive) to spend up to one year working and travelling there. The package includes a round-trip flight, stop-over in Bangkok, first night's accommodation and a three-month tourist visa for Australia.

American students can apply for a six-month work permit from Council Exchanges or Bunac USA to work between 1 April and 21 October.

CCUSA at 2330 Marinship Way, Suite 250, Sausalito, CA 94965 USA (Email: outbound@campcounselors.com, Website: **www.campcounselors.com/australia.html**) runs a three-month work experience programme (June to September).

WWOOF. PO Box 1172, Nelson, New Zealand, (Tel/ fax: 03 5449890, Email: wwoof-nz@xtra.co.nz, Website: **www.wwoof.co.nz**) have 550 farms around New Zealand where volunteer farm labourers can work for free food and accommodation only.

The website **www.workingin.com** lists job vacancies and produces a recruitment magazine *Working In*, PO Box 3394, Shortland Streeet, Auckland, Tel: 09 425 9540.

USEFUL ADDRESSES

Australian High Commission, The Strand, London WC2B 4LA, UK, Tel: 020 7379 4334, Fax: 020 7240 5333.

Australian Honorary Consul, Scotland, 37 George Street, Edinburgh EH2 3HN, UK, Tel: 0131 624 3333, Fax: 0131 624 3701.

Australia Honorary Consul, Manchester, First Floor, Century House, 11 St Peter's Square, Manchester M2 3DN, UK, Tel: 0161 237 9440, Fax: 0161 237 9135.

Australian government websites in different countries:

UK – **www.australia.org.uk**
Ireland – **www.australianembassy.ie**
Canada – **www.ahc-ottawa.org**
Japan – **www.australia.or.jp**
Germany – **www.australian-embassy.de**
Hong Kong (HKSAR) – **www.australia.org.hk**
Netherlands – Email: dima-the.hague@dfat.gov.au
Malta – Email: dima-malta@dfat.gov.au
Korea – Email: dima-seoul@dfat.gov.au

New Zealand Immigration Service, Mezzanine Floor, New Zealand House, 80 Haymarket, London SW1Y 4TE, UK.

New Zealand applicants for the UK Working Holiday Programmes should contact: The British High Commission, 44 Hill Street, PO Box 1812, Thorndon, Wellington, NZ, Tel: 64 4 495 0889, Fax: 64 4 473 4982, Website: **www.brithighcomm.org.nz**.

Got hold of the booklet *Australia and New Zealand Guide* published by London-based travel magazine *TNT* (14–15 Child's Place, London SW5 9RX, Tel: 020 7373 3377). Send a sae with 70p. Look out for their free pocket-sized regional guides at airports, stations and backpackers' hostels.

27 LATIN AMERICA AND THE CARIBBEAN

LATIN AMERICA

Vast deserts, lush rainforests, breathtaking mountain ranges ... it's no wonder Latin America is one of the most popular destinations for travellers. It is also one of the poorest and most dangerous continents in the world, which is one reason paid work is hard to find. Quite frankly, what employer in their right mind would employ a spoilt westerner when he could find a local to work much harder and for less money. No surprise then that paid jobs are in short supply. Latin America tends to lean closely to America so Americans may find it easier to find work than their British counterparts. That said, native speaking is prized highly from anywhere, as conversational skills are in great demand.

For those in search of the authentic working Latin American experience, there are basically two choices for you: the first is teaching English, and the second is voluntary work. Apart from this, there are some openings for experienced mountain and expedition leaders, while the Caribbean throws up some opportunities on the big, glamorous charter yachts and cruise liners. Another option is computer work. Several of the big IT companies such as Ericsson, IBM, Compaq and Apple have offices in the larger cities, and the hundreds of Internet cafes, even in the most remote places of Ecuador, Peru and Bolivia, require programmers, mechanics and hardware and software specialists.

VISAS AND REGULATIONS

One of the biggest barriers to finding work in Latin America is the difficulty in obtaining work visas. However, most people work illegally on tourist visas, which are renewable every ninety days. Most people leave the country and then re-enter at the border. However, teachers are warned that the three-month tourist visas can take a long time to come through and you may also be required to show your original degree certificate. Make sure you check with the country's embassy before you leave, as the red tape is usually far from straightforward.

The best way to get a work permit, of course, is to get a contract first, before entering the country. While this is extremely difficult for teaching posts (few schools recruit from abroad), IT workers may have a head start. One way in, particularly for American and Canadians, may be to fix up work in one of the international IT companies at home.

TEACHING ENGLISH

Latin America is a popular haunt for prospective English teachers and with the growing popularity of English as *the* international language, demand for teachers is high. As such, there are plenty of teaching posts around throughout the continent, with demand particularly focused in Ecuador, Peru, Brazil, Venezuela, Chile, Argentina, Columbia and Mexico. Traditionally, Latin America has been the place to head for if you haven't got a Tefl. In many places this is still the case, although for the more reputable schools, particularly the big language chains in cities such as Buenos Aires, a Tefl certificate may be required. Some countries, such as Columbia, which have a reputation for crime, have problems recruiting teachers. Pay and conditions vary across the continent, ranging from good in Mexico to poor in troubled countries such as Chile.

Saxoncourt Recruitment and English Worldwide (124 New Bond Street, London W1S 1DX, Tel: 020 7491 1911, Fax: 020 7493 3657) places teachers in schools in many Latin American countries including Peru, Mexico and Brazil.

Many of the big language chains such as Berlitz, International House and Wall Street Institute have a big presence in Latin America, while The Education and Training Group, (British Council, 10 Spring Gardens, London SW1A 2BN, Tel: 020 7389 4764, Website: **www.britishcouncil.org**) places language assistants for schools in Latin American countries.

The International Student Exchange Centre (Isec) sends volunteer teachers to Latin America. Contact International Student Exchange Centre, 35 Ivor Place, London NW1 6EA, Tel: 020 7724 4493, Website: **www.isecworld.co.uk**.

Many other gap-year and voluntary organisations such as Teaching Abroad and World Teach also offer volunteer teaching programmes in South and Central America. For details see the Voluntary Work chapter.

TEACHING ENGLISH IN MEXICO

Learning the English language is still seen as a ticket to better things in Mexico, conferring upon Mexicans higher salaries and better jobs. Mexico has close links to America, both geographically and culturally and, as there are many American offices throughout the country, being able to communicate well with their American counterparts is prized highly indeed.

Conversation skills are very important, as most Mexicans learn English grammar and vocabulary at school but lack the opportunity to practise conversation. Native speaking teachers, then, are in great demand, especially those who can check pronunciation and fluency skills. As with most English teaching, it is not necessary to speak Spanish: the more the students have to communicate in English, the quicker they improve.

It's no surprise then that jobs are so plentiful. Generally it's easy to find a short-term teaching job in Mexico – many schools offer work for three-month periods. Generally, the view is that it's easier to find teaching work in Mexico after you have arrived, than fixing it up before. Jobs exist in private language schools, universities and state schools. Many companies – particularly those with close American ties – hire English teachers to run group classes and private tuition, although much of this work will be farmed out to agencies and schools who provide teachers. There are many agencies and schools which supply language instruction to business.

It's normal for teachers to work for a variety of schools and agencies, spending some evenings a week teaching in a private language school, and combining it with private tuition or freelance one-to-one business English classes which they are sent to by schools.

In most cases, you have to be at least 21. It is a good idea to have some college education and preferably a BA since it may be necessary for a work permit in some destinations.

According to the website **www.employernow.com**, the demand for English teachers in Mexico is currently at an all-time high. 'Salaries are the highest they have ever been and are continuing to rise. You can live comfortably working less than thirty hours per week.'

Generally, the feedback coming from Mexico is that it's easier to find work once you've arrived. Why? One reason is that employers like to meet teachers before hiring them – perhaps because conversational skills are valued so highly, they like to make sure they are getting the right kind of person who can give the students what they most need to learn. Another reason could be the fact that some schools get 'burned': teachers say they are coming over and then don't arrive. However, if you really want the security of having something once you get there, you can look for jobs in the usual sources: the *Guardian's* Tuesday Education section, *The Times Education Supplement*, as well as the vast number of websites. Here you should find plenty of advertisements for posts, or you can contact the recruitment agencies direct. Saxoncourt Recruitment and English Worldwide recruits teachers for Latin American countries including Mexico. Call 020 7491 1911.

For those who turn up to find work, approach the job hunt in the same manner as you would in all countries – check out the Yellow Pages and visit each language school in turn, or if your Spanish is up to it, phone around and ask if they have vacancies. Take with you a CV (in Spanish is possible) and a copy of your Tefl certificate if you have one. Some employers may also wish to see proof of permission to work here. Head for Mexico City, Guadalajara and the resorts Puerta Vallarta, Cancun, Acapulco and Mazatlan. However, if you are travelling around, keep your eyes peeled and you could find work anywhere.

The English newspaper *The News* and the Spanish-language paper *El Universal* carry vacancies. You can also try the British Council in Mexico City for a list of language schools.

The one complication you will have working in Mexico is clarifying permission for legal work. Canadians and Americans are subject to the Free Trade Agreement, which makes the work situation easier – check your consulate for more details. For UK and most other nationals, however, visitors are not allowed to work on a tourist visa, which specifically bans people from engaging in any 'remunerative' work. Many teachers in private institutions work illegally on tourist visas, renewable every ninety days, usually by crossing the border and re-entering the country. Teachers with longer-term contracts may be able to get a visitors' card with the help of their school (see **www.mexicanconsulate.org**).

TEACHING ENGLISH IN ARGENTINA
Buenos Aires has a reputation for being one of the most European cities in Latin America – not surprising when eighty per cent of Argentinians are of mixed European descent after mass immigration from Europe throughout the nineteenth century. In recent years, it has also been reputed to be one of the most lucrative places to find teaching jobs in Latin America, with rates ranging from anything between US$8 and $30 an hour. However, the economic recession appears to be taking its toll. Salaries in jobs across the board have been frozen and with the economic situation as desperate as it is, it is difficult to imagine who can actually afford the luxury of English lessons. Prospective teachers are advised to check the situation thoroughly before arriving, or they may well be in for a shock. Even in better days, competition has been fierce, and many schools in Buenos Aires demand at the very least a Tefl certificate.

The best way to find work is by turning up and finding it, preferably in February before the schools have filled up with teachers. Argentina has been so well served with backpackers and foreigners eager to fill its posts, that there has never been much need to recruit teachers from abroad. Approach the language schools by looking up addresses in the Yellow Pages or look in the jobs section of the English language newspaper, the *Buenos Aires Herald*. Most people will find work, but it may take time and you should bring plenty of money to tide you over. Buenos Aires isn't cheap to live in, despite its troubled economy.

Like Mexico City, much of Buenos Aires' teaching market is made up of institutions that provide teachers for the big multinational or American companies. Again, many teachers work freelance for different institutions and combine it with classes in schools or private tuition. The British Council may supply you with details of Culturas Inglesas language schools. You can find it at M. T. de Alvear 590 4th Floor, 1058 Buenos Aires, Argentina, Tel: 54 11 4311 9814; 54 11 4311 7519, Fax: 54 11 4311 7747.

Despite the high number of them, most English teachers in Argentina report that they are highly respected and usually well paid. Learning English is considered a serious and expensive business, so you will be expected to approach it in a professional and committed manner. In 1996, English was made compulsory in all Argentine schools, while in many private language institutions, students sit for British exams. Times are difficult in Argentina at the moment, and as in many countries, learning English is seen as a ticket to better and brighter things, such as improved job status and economic security.

Red tape Work visas for Argentina are difficult to obtain, and are really only an option for teachers on a long-term contract (at least a year). Like most Latin American countries, they can only be obtained outside Argentina and require proof of employment, as well as a raft of other complicated paperwork. Most teachers work instead on a tourist visa, which must be renewed every ninety days, again by crossing the border and re-entering the country.

Expatvillage.com is an excellent resource if you are living or contemplating living in Argentina.

TEACHING ENGLISH IN BRAZIL

In order to teach, you must have a work permit legally. However, obtaining one isn't easy and in order to get one, you must have a sponsor, usually through fixing up work first. Unfortunately, most schools rely on teachers who are already in the country (either travellers or Brazilian English teachers) and don't tend to recruit teachers from abroad. Like in Argentina, employers have no guarantee that teachers will show up and because of the difficulties in obtaining work permits, it is difficult to offer teachers legal work. According to English teacher Michael Hardiman on the website **esl-lounge.com**, in June 2002, 'In the last couple of years it has become extremely hard to get a visa . . . so be prepared to work illegally if you go there and your school does not have "connections".' Many teachers get round the complicated red tape by working on a tourist visa which you should get from your Brazilian consulate before entering the country. This isn't exactly legal, but seems to be the way most teachers work. A tourist visa is valid for three months and is renewable for three more months at any federal police office in Brazil. A foreigner may visit Brazil for the maximum of six months out of every calendar year.

Like most South American countries, the best way to find work in Brazil is by turning up. Demand for English teachers is high, and despite reports that there are many Brazilian English teachers around, the general consensus is that work is easy to find. The large cities such as Rio and Sao Paulo boast many private language centres, many of which will hire native speakers without Tefl certification. Once you arrive buy a copy of *O Globo* on

Sunday, which has many advertisements for *professores de Inglês*. Private tuition is also easy to fix up – advertise in a local paper or on community notice boards. Generally, the pay is not so good compared to North America and Europe (between R$15 and R$20 per hour working for a school), although this is balanced out by the lower living costs. You must have a teaching degree to teach in regular schools (K-12).

Eddy Cantor taught in Rio, Brazil, for one and a half years. Armed with a Tefl certificate, he found work by asking around institutes, and worked his way up from the dubiously run, low-paying schools to the highly reputed Brittannia, the 'best British language school in Rio'. Private students were easy to find, and soon Eddy was working privately full-time, teaching a steady string of students from his comfortable apartment. One of his selling points, he says, was the fact he taught British English. 'There are so many Americans in Brazil, it can be difficult for people to find British English classes if they want to. I'd advise any British teacher to start advertising for private lessons as soon as they arrive. Many students just want to practise their conversation. I had one who I taught twice a week – all he did was ask me a series of yes and no questions, and then afterwards, take me out for lunch.' In fact, such is the demand for English conversation, it's not unknown for Brazilian people to befriend you simply for free English lessons.

With the value of the real so low compared to the pound and the US$, Eddy says it's a good time to go to Brazil as you can take plenty of money to act as a buffer. 'Rio can be a difficult, humid, macho city and it's best to have found your bearings before you take work, so you need plenty of money to tide you over.'

Although he enjoyed his time in Rio, his advice to prospective teachers is to head for the more remote areas, where they stand a better chance of learning Portuguese: 'Rio's not a cosmopolitan city but it is full of foreigners, and in some ways you get the worst of both worlds: you're surrounded by expats but you can't get a decent cappuccino. Another problem is that, being a teacher, you tend to mix with British and American teachers all the time and it's easy to be dragged into the expat scene. Sao Paolo is a good place to go – the people are nice and you can earn good money. I know private tutors there who charge US$70 per hour.'

TRAVELLERS' STORIES

Nick Rogerson went out to Venezuela on a one-way ticket last year because he was 'sick of England – I had to get out': he landed in Maracaibo in Venezuela on a tourist visa, although he says even this wasn't necessary, and immediately set about finding work. Unfortunately he arrived in November, just before the schools shut down for Christmas. 'That was a very bad move because I ended up spending most of my money. By January, however, it was a different story. There was a massive demand for teachers, there were jobs everywhere. It was a doddle finding work.'

Although Nick had a Tefl certificate, he says that this wasn't necessary. 'Most private language schools will expect you to do their in-house training and observe lessons. They're not interested in any qualifications you might have.'

The best time to head out for work is in late August/ September and January. 'There's no point trying to fix up work before you come over. I phoned up schools from England, but they told me to come to Venezuela – they couldn't offer me work unless I was there.'

Be prepared for heavy questioning at immigration about what your plans are. Nick was quizzed about his intentions, and asked to show his return flight (which he didn't have) as well as contact details for accommodation and his route. He had neither, but somehow managed to bluff his way through.

CRUISING IN THE CARIBBEAN

For all you glamour pusses out there, how about seeing the Caribbean in style? Like, from the deck of a plush, 1,000-passenger super-liner, complete with all-night casinos, top-notch restaurants and glossy boutiques housing designer clothes? The Caribbean is where the world's most illustrious big cruise liners and private yachts head for in the winter, so if you're suitably equipped (see Working a Passage chapter) you may be able to find work.

The website How to get a job on a Cruise Ship **www.geocities.com/The Tropics/Cabana/1590/index** has plenty of information about working on cruise ships and links to cruise liners.

Talented performers could earn their keep singing their way around the Caribbean. Most cruise ships employ singers, entertainers and dancers to keep the masses amused. Openwide International is one entertainment consultancy recruiting 'talented' performers, singers and dance couples for entertainment programmes on cruise ships and in hotels throughout the Caribbean. Go to **www.openwideinternational.com** for more details.

VOLUNTARY WORK

With all the breadth and depth of environments, culture and social difficulties Latin America affords, it's not surprising there is such an extreme range of voluntary work on offer. Many of the voluntary and gap-year organisations listed in the Voluntary Work chapter, including Concordia, Gap Activity Projects, Gap Adventures, Greenforce, i-to-i, Concordia, Coral Cay Conservation, Cross-Cultural Solutions, UNA Exchange, Peace Brigades International and Earthwatch, run volunteer programmes in South and Central America, and the Caribbean. Projects can range from conservation work in the Amazonian rainforest to working with HIV patients, helping Brazilian street kids, to running an English language magazine.

Otec International arranges volunteer and work internships, and work and travel programmes, in Costa Rica. Contact Otec International, Paseo Colón & Avenida 2, Calle 34 Edificio Elizabeth 2do Piso, Tel: 506 255 4233, Fax: 506 255 5605, Email: product@otec.co.cr, Website. **www.otecinternational.com**.

There are also more locally based programmes. The jungles of Bolivia, Peru, Ecuador, Venezuela and even Colombia can also offer many opportunities in the way of eco voluntary work – particularly for biology, pharmacy, medical and anthropology students or graduates. The South American Explorers (**www.samexplo.org**) has a list of many organisations where you can find work from trekking with elephants to studying freshwater dolphins to working with and protecting indigenous tribes. Of course, jungle life is not for everyone – conditions can be difficult, humid and downright dangerous at times, so think carefully before rushing into a commitment.

TRAVELLERS' STORIES

Iain Hook taught maths, biology and sports in a secondary school outside Kingston, in Jamaica, for three years. His first year was fixed up through a voluntary organisation Global Action which cost £1,200 (excluding flights) and included travel insurance, an orientation programme and assistance in obtaining a visa. Iain had no teaching qualification but after the first year, decided to stay for another two years in a teaching post the school had specially created for him.

His arrival proved to be a bit of a fiasco. 'The voluntary placement was set up by a local priest who helped run the school. The only thing was that the school principals and staff had no idea I was coming. So I arrived on my first day never having taught before, with no materials, and I sat in the principal's office and he said, we've got no work for you. It was a total shock – I'd come all that way and thought I may as well go home. In the end, the principal decided to make the most of me and gave me a full timetable.'

Despite the culture shock of living in Jamaica (which, he says, is a long way from the idyll perpetuated by Bob Marley songs and the Jamaican music scene and Bob Marley), his work proved very rewarding. 'All of my students were from very deprived backgrounds. It wasn't unusual to find candlewax on their homework because they had no lighting, but they had an amazing attitude to school. They knew the importance of education and despite everything that was stacked against them, they were well behaved, disciplined and very committed to learning.'

For three years he lived in very basic conditions, staying in a communal block on the school's campus for £20 a month. There was no running water and only intermittent electricity. Instead, he had a nearby stream and two big oil drums, which filled up with rainwater when it was raining. 'It was amazing how quickly I got used to it. There was only one time when I had no water for two to three days, although washing clothes was particularly difficult as I was very conscious of using all the water.'

He says, 'Jamaica itself was a demanding place to live. Kingston was very intimidating and you had to be aware at all times. I couldn't smile in the street for example, because people would easily take me for a fool or assume I was a tourist. I tried to blend in as a white Jamaican but even Jamaican white people are generally frowned on. I took racial abuse every day, from students, teachers and people on the street. Walking down the road, people would often start shouting 'white boy' at me and hurling abuse, although they never got violent.'

Jamaica, he insists, is not for the faint-hearted. Kingston itself is known as one of the murder capitals of the world, but Iain says most of these crimes are either reprisal killings or drug-related. Hijackings on rural roads were also quite common and Iain advises 'never travel alone in Jamaica'.

Physical attacks are very unusual but there's an awful lot of verbal intimidation and robbery. I was robbed three times. Pickpockets on the town buses were commonplace and they would usually target the white person. We were packed in so tight, there was nothing we could do – I'd feel these hands sneaking into my pockets but I couldn't move or fight them off. I never carried a large amount of cash in my pockets, and kept valuables in my money belt under my clothes, so they didn't steal much but it still left a feeling of being violated. I was also mugged at knifepoint in the resort of Ocho Rios where the thieves made off with £30. Luckily I was so drunk I was oblivious to what was happening.

VOLUNTARY ORGANISATIONS

The following other voluntary organisations run programmes in Latin America:

AmeriSpan, PO Box 58129, Philadelphia, PA 19102-8129, USA, Tel: USA & Canada: 800 879 6640; Worldwide: 215 751 1100; Fax. 215 751 1986; E-mail: info@amerispan.com, Website: www.amerispan.com.

Association of American Schools in South America (AASSA), 14750 NW 77th Court, Suite 210, Miami Lakes, FL 33016, Tel: 305 821 0345, Fax: 305 821 4244; Email: info@aassa.com, Website: www.aassa.com.

Australian Volunteers International Office National office: 71 Argyle Street (PO Box 350), Fitzroy VIC 3065, Tel: 03 9279 1788, Fax: 03 9419 4280, Email: avaenq@ozvol.org.au, Website: www.ozvol.org.au.

Inter-Cultural Youth Exchange (ICYE UK), Latin America House, Kingsgate Place, London NW6 4TA, Tel/Fax: 020 7681 0983, Website: www.icye.org.

Latin Link Britain & Ireland, 175 Tower Bridge Road, London SE1 2AB, Tel: 020 7939 9000, Fax: 020 7939 9015, Website: www.latinlink.org.

EXPEDITION, MOUNTAIN AND TOUR GUIDES

The sheer breathtaking beauty of Latin America, with its rugged mountain terrain and vast stretches of Ecuadorian jungle, draws tourists by the lorry load. And where there are tourists, there are always jobs – or in this case, expedition leaders and tour guides.

The first thing to say about expedition leaders, is that most work is only open to those with special skills. Many leaders will be working in dangerous terrain such as the jungles of Ecuador and mountains of Bolivia, and Peru, and will be expected, at the very least, to know the region in depth and to be a qualified mountain expedition leader, white-water rafter, kayaker (canoeist) or climber, depending on what the expedition involves. If you think you've got what it takes to lead a group of tourists in challenging conditions, are suitably fit and thrive off outdoor pursuits, you could look into training. (See Working a Passage chapter.)

There are also openings for the more culturally inclined. Some travellers with good spoken Spanish and a good knowledge of the area have found work as tour guides in historical sites such as Macchu Picchu, whether it's exploring the ancient art of the Incas or following the trail of the indigenous Indian cultures.

To enquire about opportunities, you can contact tour companies such as Journey Latin America or Tucan who operate throughout Latin America including Peru, Bolivia, Ecuador, Argentina and Brazil. Himalayan Kingdom and Jagged Globe are two large companies who offer expensive moutaineering trips to the Himalayas and South America, including Peru, Venezuela and Tibet. You can find vacancies in the mountaineering magazines *On The Edge*, *High Magazine* and *Climber and Trail Magazine*. Mountain and expedition leaders will usually be expected to have at least a Mountain Leaders Certificate.

USEFUL ADDRESSES

Argentinian Embassy, 65 Brook Street, London W1M 5LD, UK, Tel: 020 7486 7073; 1600 New Hampshire Avenue, NW, Washington DC 20009, USA, Tel: 202 939 6400, Website: **www.embajadarrgentina-usa.org**.

Brazilian Embassy, 32 Green Street, London W1Y 4AT, UK, Tel: 020 7499 0877, Website: **www.brazil.org.uk**; 3006 Massachusetts Avenue, NW, Washington DC 20008, USA, Tel: 202 238 2700; Website: **www.brasil.emb.nw.dc.us**.

Chilean Embassy, 12 Devonshire Street, London W1N 2DS, UK, Tel: 020 7580 6392; 1732 Massachusetts Avenue, NW, Washington DC 20036, USA, Tel: 202 785 1746.

Mexican Embassy, 42 Hertford Street, Mayfair, London W1Y 7TF, UK, Tel: 020 7499 8586; 1911 Pennsylvania Avenue, NW, Washington DC 20006, USA, Tel: 202 728 1600, Website: **www.embassyofmexico.org**.

Venezuelan Embassy, 1 Cromwell Road, London SW7 2HW, UK, Tel: 020 7584 4206; 1099 30th Street, Washington DC 20007, USA, Tel: 202 342 2214, Website: **www.embavenez-us.org**.

28 UNITED STATES AND CANADA

UNITED STATES

The dream of working in America is a pervasive one. Whether it's serving cocktails in LA to living in a hippy commune in California, or mixing with the metropolitan elite of New York, the American dream is fed to us every day through our TVs, cinemas and magazines. According to a recent survey from the UK's newspaper the *Daily Telegraph*, the USA was the most popular country Brits would like to emigrate to.

However, for many of us, the dream stops here. The fact is that working in America isn't easy – immigration rules are strict and the Americans viewed non-nationals entering their homeland with suspicion even before September 11. 'Unofficial' casual work is also a risky (but popular) option, no matter how clever you think you are.

The good news is that there are many travel and work programmes that can arrange a special work visa for you. There are also plenty of summer camps around, many of which have been experiencing problems filling temporary and seasonal vacancies. Therefore your best bets of finding work are to:

- **fix up work before you leave (work permits are difficult to get hold of and although there is plenty of work around, working without the necessary permission carries some harsh penalties)**

- **apply for a work and travel programme which can arrange a special working visa for you**

VISA AND REGULATIONS

The visa-waiver scheme allows British citizens and citizens of 28 other countries to enter the US visa-free, but they must obtain a visa-waiver when they arrive. This is valid for one-entry and lasts for up to ninety days. If you plan to stay any longer, you must obtain a tourist visa in advance from the embassy. In both cases, you are strictly prohibited from engaging in paid or unpaid work.

Therefore working legally is a much more tricky affair. There are several visas around including the Q visa (the International Cultural Exchange Visa), which allows you to work for up to fifteen months if you can argue that you will be providing practical training or sharing the culture, history and traditions of your country to the Americans (if you do a mean Yorkshire pudding, for example). Another one is the B-1 'Voluntary Service' visa which you can get if you are to do charitable voluntary work, for no payment, and have been sponsored by a charitable and religious organisation. The H-1B visa allows professionals with a degree to find prearranged highly skilled work for which there are no suitably qualified Americans. And there are many others – all similarly difficult to obtain.

However, by far the most relevant visa to working travellers is the J-1 visa. This can only be obtained if you are taking part in an Exchange Visitor Programme such as the Work and Travel Programmes and Summer Camp schemes listed below. This allows you to undertake any paid work.

WORK AND TRAVEL PROGRAMMES AND INTERNSHIPS

There are many work and travel programmes which operate in America and enable participants, usually students, to work virtually anywhere in the country by fixing them up with a J-1 visa. Whether you fancy working on a ranch in Texas, or a Californian national park, you could pick the working holiday of your dreams. Remember, with a population of 285 million, and covering fifty states, America is a very big place – the land of opportunity indeed!

Work America is a work and travel programme for students run by Bunac. The programme enables students to take virtually any work in the US. The programme is only open to British university or college students studying for a degree (or equivalent), and gap-year students who have already received an unconditional offer at a university. To help applicants find work, Bunac publishes a directory listing jobs you can apply for before you leave.

For other ideas for jobs you can check out the website **www.coolworks.com**. This has listings of plenty of jobs in summer camps, national parks, amusement parks, ranches, state parks, resorts, ski resorts and voluntary work with links to relevant companies and websites. It's primarily for US citizens, and international applicants must have arranged a work visa before writing to the employers. However, the listings can be a good starting point to research what opportunities are out there, and you can contact the companies *after* you have registered on a Work and Travel Programme.

The Work and Travel USA programme administered by CIEE allows you to work 'for just about any employer in the US'. The programme enables full-time students aged over eighteen to work and travel in the USA from early June to mid October. Check out its website **www.councilexchanges.org.uk** to search out over 18,000 jobs and download documents. Contact CIEE, Council on International Educational Exchange, 52 Poland Street, London W1F 7AB (Tel: 020 7478 2020).

CIEE also runs an Internship USA programme. This enables students and recent graduates (within twelve months of graduating) to work in the US for up to eighteen months. Work experience placements or training must be course-related and arranged by the students themselves. The Council arranges the J-1 visa and provides orientation on such aspects as housing, tax and so on, but applicants finance the trip themselves. There is an administrative fee of £270 plus £30 for each additional month. Contact the above address (see Work and Travel USA).

Alliances Abroad (702 West Avenue, Austin, Texas 78701, Tel: 512 457 8062/1 888 622 7623, Website: **www.alliancesabroad.com**) runs internships with practical training experience in Denver, San Francisco and Washington DC.

The Work Experience USA programme enables students between 20–28 years old to work in the USA between June and September. Visit their website, **www.ccusa.com** for more details or see the address for camp counsellors in the summer camp section.

InterExchange (161 Sixth Avenue, New York, NY 10013, Tel: 212 924 0446, Fax: 212 924 0575, Website: **www.interexchange.org**) runs a Work and Travel Program which offers foreign university students the opportunity to live and work in America, filling positions in hotels, inns, amusement parks, country fairs, national parks, campgrounds and restaurants and resorts for up to four months during their summer break.

Here are some other agencies that can help you fix up a J-1 visa for work and travel in the USA:

Apex USA (**www.apexusa.org**)

Association for International Practical Training (**www.aipt.org**)

For Canadian citizens: Student Work Abroad Program (**www.swap.ca/english/html/home**)

AU PAIRING

In order to work legally as an au pair in America, you should have a J-1 visa, which only a US-approved agency will be able to obtain. The basic requirements are that participants are between 18 and 26 years old, speak English to an acceptable standard, have a full driving licence, be a non-smoker and have a criminal record check and two hundred hours of recent childcare experience. Many UK agencies organise au pair placements in the States, or you can try these official programmes:

Worldnetuk organises a Nanny and Childcare Programme USA. Applicants must be 18–26 years old with childcare training. It also runs an Au Pair Programme USA for 18–26-year-olds and Ski/Summer Resort Nannies (no age limit but must have childcare training). Contact Worldnetuk, Southern Office, Avondale House, Sydney Road, Haywards Heath, West Sussex (Tel: 0845 458 1551, Website: **www.worldnetuk.com**).

The Au Pair in America Programme sponsored by the Interex Change places au pairs in posts throughout America. Contact The Childcare

Solution, Emberton House, 26 Shakespeare Road, Bedford NK40 2ED, Tel: 07002 287247, Website: **www.childcaresolution.com**.

Irish citizens should contact UsitNow, the Irish student travel service (19–21 Aston Quay, Dublin 2), for details on its work and travel schemes.

The American Institute for Foreign Study organises an Au Pair in America programme. Contact AIFS, 37 Queen's Gate, London SW7 5HR, Tel: 020 7581 7300; Website: **www.aupairamerica.co.uk**.

InterExchange runs an Au Pair programme. Contact 161 Sixth Avenue, New York, NY 10013, Tel: 212 924 0446, Fax: 212 924 0575, Website: **www.interexchange.org**.

Au PairCare Cultural Exchange: 2226 Bush Street, San Francisco CA 94115, Tel: 414 434 8788 or contact their UK office at Solihull Au Pair & Nanny Agency, 1565 Stratford Road, Hall Green, Birmingham B28 9JA, Tel: 0121 733 6444, Fax: 0121 733 6555, Website: **www.aupairs4u.com**.

go Au Pair Programme, 6965 Union Park Center, Suite 100, Midvale, UT 84047 9723, Tel: 801 255 7722, Website: **www.goAUPAIR.com**.

SUMMER CAMPS

Despite the difficult visa requirements to enter the States, there is plenty of tourist work around, particularly in summer. Summer camps are a very popular way of fixing up work, particularly as most schemes include free return flights, pre-arranged visa and afford you the luxury of independent travel for up to two months after the camp is over. Participants can find themselves posts teaching American kids skills such as archery, windsurfing, dancing or crafts, depending on what they have to offer. Hours are long and the children can be demanding, but the camps can give you an illuminating take on American culture.

TRAVELLERS' STORIES

Andrew Whittaker taught windsurfing in Waziyatah Camp in a forest in Maine. For nine weeks he and another camp counsellor slept in the same dormitory as twelve seven- to eight-year-old American boys, taking it in turns to look after them.

The day started at 7 a.m. when we had to wake the children and take them to breakfast. Then we went off to teach our activities until lunchtime where we had to supervise the kids and try to stop them from throwing food at each other. The afternoon was spent teaching windsurfing again until dinner time at 6 p.m. Then in the evening we had to amuse the kids by playing games and organising competitions, until 9 p.m. when we had to make sure they went to bed. Sometimes I even had to read stories to them.

The children were mostly spoilt rich kids and we sometimes had problems with fighting and bullying. One boy used to wet his bed all the time. It was hard work and with only one day off a week, I didn't have much privacy. But our days off were good and we had organised trips to national parks, Mount Washington and the beach.

It was a bit of a culture shock being an eighteen-year-old lad from Manchester in America for the first time. It opened my eyes, because I thought I was cool being into all these Manchester bands but no one else knew what I was talking about. I met people from all over the world and went travelling for two months with friends from the camp afterwards. We went to Canada and then travelled down the east coast via New York, Washington, Boston, Florida and then into the Deep South, stopping at New Orleans, Memphis, Philadelphia, St Louis, then back to the east coast via Detroit and Chicago. It was an unforgettable experience but there were some hairy moments – in downtown Detroit we nearly got mugged trying to score some dope. I ended up coming back to Manchester wearing a paisley bandanna, a goatee beard, a Mexican shawl and speaking with a Deep Southern accent!

SUMMER CAMP ORGANISATIONS

The following organisations run summer camp schemes:

Bunac (16 Bowling Green Lane, London EC1R 0QH, Tel: 020 7251 3472, Website: **www.bunac.org**) runs two summer camp programmes.

KAMP is a low-cost programme that places staff in kitchen and maintenance positions in American summer camps for two months.

Summer Camp USA places camp counsellors (aged 18–35) in US and Canadian summer camps. Camps last nine weeks and applicants receive free flights, salary, board and lodging and independent travel for a flexible period after the camp.

Camp America places people aged eighteen plus in summer camps throughout America to work as specialist counsellors or youth leaders. Camps last nine weeks and positions available include childcare and specialist activities such as sports, watersports, music, drama and arts. Participants receive free board and lodging, pocket money, free London–New York return flight and up to two months' independent travel after the camp is over. For details contact Camp America, Dept. SJA, 37A Queen's Gate, London SW7 5HR.

The Campower scheme, run by the same organisation and operating from the same address as Camp America, places students in kitchen and general maintenance work for the nine-week camp period. Perks are the same as for Camp America.

Camp Counsellors USA run a similar scheme, recruiting people aged between 19 and 28 years old to work in selected American summer camps. Applicants receive a free round-trip open return flight to the USA, pocket money and after camp travel.

Contact UK Offices: Green Dragon House, 64–70 High Street, Croydon CR0 9XN (Tel: 020 8688 9051, Website: **www.ccusa.com**) and 27 Woodside Gardens, Musselburgh, nr Edinburgh EH21 7LJ (Tel: 0131 665 5843, Website: **www.ccusa.com**). US Office: 2330 Marinship Way, Suite 250, Sausalito CA 94965, USA.

Worldnetuk organises Camp USA. Contact Worldnetuk, Southern Office, Avondale House, Sydney Road, Haywards Heath, West Sussex RH16 2AN (Tel: 0845 458 1551, Website: **www.worldnetuk.com**) for more details.

VOLUNTARY WORK

There are many voluntary organisations that operate workcamps in America. Typical areas could be conservation and environmental work in national parks and forests, urban renovation or working with disabled children. Try the usual organisations such as Concordia, Youth Action for Peace, International Voluntary Service, the Quakers and so forth.

SOCCER COACHING

If you have a love of football (or soccer as it is called in the States) and can match your passion with aptitude, it might be worthwhile to train as a soccer coach. Many companies recruit British soccer coaches to work on summer coaching schemes, based at children's summer camps all through America.

The company Goal-line sends over expert soccer coaches to teach children in America and Europe. For more information, contact Goal-line Personnel Director, Goal-Line Soccer Clinics, PO Box 1642, Corvallis, OR 97339, USA, Tel: 541 753 5833, Fax: 541 753 0811, Email: infoa@goal-line.com, Website: **www.goal-line.com**.

The UK football magazine *FourFourTwo* carries adverts for soccer coach vacancies, and is a good first port of call.

TRAVELLERS' STORIES

Maria Hardy worked as a soccer coach in Oregon, USA in the summer 2001. She says, 'I'd been working for ten years straight from university and felt the need to do something different. Luckily, I was in the kind of situation where work would let me have some time out. I'd already been working towards a football coaching qualification so it was the ideal opportunity to have an adventure, a holiday and gain some experience all at the same time.'

Maria found an advert in football magazine *FourFourTwo* for listings of American coaching companies. Then she sat down and systematically wrote to each one. 'Eventually I received a reply from a soccer camp in Portland, Oregon offering me a month's work coaching seven- to sixteen-year-olds and I took it like a shot. It was hard work, but worth it. I only had one day off a week and I could be coaching kids in the pouring rain or 110 degrees heat who had never played football before. But it was wonderful. I made loads of great friends and the families I stayed with made me feel really welcome. Altogether, it was a fantastic experience.'

CASUAL WORK

If you're an adventurous soul and long to experience life 'On the Road' (vis-à-vis Jack Kerouac's novel or *Zen and the Art of Motorcycle Maintenance*), you can always try your hand at picking up casual work as you travel around. There's plenty out there, and despite the strict rules, many travellers do manage to find work on a tourist visa. However, it's best not to make such a decision lightly. According to US law, all employers are obliged to examine the documents of anyone they employ, and employing an illegal 'alien' carries a heavy fine. Being discovered working without the necessary documentation also carries a similar risk and you could find yourself deported and even banned from entering the States for another five years.

If you do decide to risk it, there are some steps you can take to safeguard against any problems. Having plenty of friends and even family around is certainly a bonus, as is having the funds to tide you over in an emergency. Bear in mind that casual work is often hard to find, and the last thing you want is to end up homeless on the streets in downtown America. Other good advice is to buy yourself a car and a mobile phone.

THE JOB SEARCH

Hostels will sometimes exchange free board and lodgings for work such as cleaning or running the reception, and you can check out their notice boards for advertisements for work. It is also the perfect place to meet fellow travellers who can often pass on rumours of other work opportunities.

Check out the local press for job vacancies – telesales staff are often in demand. You might also be able to find work in the summer and ski resorts, particularly at high season.

Again check out the website **www.coolworks.com** for current vacancies, or **www.seasonalemployment.com**.

HARVEST WORK AND AGRICULTURE

Another option is to head for the fields and do some fruit picking. Farmers frequently employ illegal workers to help them with their harvests. Head for the wine-producing regions in California, Oregon, Washington, Idaho and New York where you might be able to pick up work in the grape harvest.

Kansas is a big wheat area (May to August) while the southern and eastern states are known for their soft fruits (May and June). Florida is the place to head for citrus fruit (October to May) while you may be able to find work picking apples in the north-east in September.

DRIVE-AWAY

How about enjoying the freedom of the open road, seeing America and saving yourself hundreds of dollars in travel costs? Sounds too good to be true? Well, in fact no. Many US and Canadian drive-away companies use independent travellers to deliver cars to a destination for them. How does it work? You, the driver, agree to deliver one of the company's cars to an arranged location by a set date. For a small processing fee of around $10, you get free use of the car for a certain number of days and miles. Oh, and you have to pay for your own petrol.

The deal comes with certain provisos: for one thing, the company may set down certain requirements on the route you have to take. You will usually also have to provide a cash deposit of around $200 to $350, which is fully refunded after the vehicle is delivered as agreed. All companies require a current driver's licence, and you will probably be asked to show additional identification, as well as references and telephone numbers. You may be asked about your driving record and you may even be fingerprinted.

You can find details of drive-away companies in the Yellow Pages under 'Drive-away Companies' or under 'Automobile Transporters'. Not all car-transportation companies use independent travellers but many do, and if you just bang out a few calls, you should strike lucky sooner or later. Alternatively, you can check out the website of Auto Driveaway Company **www.autodriveaway.com** which contains a list of available cars from each city the company services. You can also search the drive-away directory on **www.movecars.com/toc/find/index.htm**.

CANADA

Canada . . . the majestic Rockies, vibrant cosmopolitan cities, acres and acres of forestland and stunning mountain scenery. Who wouldn't want to work here? Add to this Canada's high standard of living and you can see why the country continues to pull foreign workers every year. And yet, despite all this, it is notoriously hard to find work in Canada, due to a strict immigration policy.

Canada has always had a strict attitude towards immigration but since September 11, security has become even tighter. Canada and the US have largely agreed to harmonise their entry arrangements and both countries can be equally vigilant in preventing and tracking down illegal workers. There is also a great deal of attention placed on language skills, so make sure you speak good English and, if you're in the French-speaking Quebec, polish up your French, of course.

VISAS AND REGULATIONS

In order to enter Canada for tourist purposes only (and not to work) most foreign visitors must have a passport, proof of intent to leave, and proof you have sufficient funds to support yourself during your stay. Citizens of Australia, Ireland, Mexico, New Zealand, the UK, and the US, do not need a visa, as long as they plan to stay for no more than ninety days.

In order to work legally in Canada, you must obtain an employment authorisation from a Canadian high commission or embassy before you leave your country of residence. In most cases this involves finding work before entering the country, which your future employer must prove cannot be filled by a Canadian citizen. Once you have been offered a job, the department of Human Resources Development Canada must normally provide a labour market opinion or 'confirmation' of your job offer. Once they have confirmed that a foreign national may fill the job, you apply to the Citizenship and Immigration Canada (CIC) for your work permit. Americans can apply for an employment authorisation at the port of entry to Canada.

Although it is usually difficult to obtain an employment authorisation (work visa) in Canada, some people with special skills are given priority, such as some software professionals. Canada is facing a severe skills shortage at the moment, particularly in technologically skilled workers, highly trained doctors, nurses, and teachers, and in other sectors, such as construction workers. For more information on skill shortages, contact the Canadian high commission in your country.

Commonwealth teachers may be able to arrange exchange placements – write to The League for the Exchange of Commonwealth Teachers, Commonwealth House, 7 Lion Yard, Tremadoc Road, London SW4 7NQ, Tel: 020 7498 1101, Fax: 020 7720 5403.

Before working in Canada, you have to obtain a SIN or social insurance number. SIN means you can work in Canada legally. You can apply for it at the Canada Employment Centre where you live and it usually takes about one month to arrive.

HOW YOU CAN DO IT

The rest of, us, however, needn't be too discouraged. If you are young and a student, there are plenty of work exchange programmes which will enable you to find work usually before you arrive – except the Bunac scheme which allows you to find work once you are there.

WORK EXCHANGES AND PROGRAMMES

The Canadian government runs official work exchanges for eighteen- to thirty-year-old full-time tertiary-level students wanting to work in Canada. The scheme requires that you fix up work before you arrive. Interested British and Irish students should check the website **www.canada.org.uk/visa-info** or send a sae with a £1 stamp and marked SGWHP to the Canadian High Commission, Immigration Visa Information, 38 Grosvenor Street, London W1K 4AA, Tel: 09068 616644. (Calls cost 60p a minute.)

Swedish and Finnish students should contact the Canadian high commission or embassies in their countries to find out more. Other participating countries tend to vary from year to year, so check with your Canadian embassy first to find out if you are eligible.

Bunac run a Work Canada Programme which enables students to go to Canada and fix up work once they are there. The scheme is open to gap-year students, providing they have an unconditional offer of a place at a university. Contact Bunac for more details (see Chapter Three on finding work).

Swap Travel run a Work Canada Programme in Ireland. For details contact UseitNow, 19–21 Aston Quay, O'Connell Bridge, Dublin 2 (Tel: 353 1 602 1667).

CIEE run an Internship Canada Programme (see the address in Voluntary Work and Gap Year chapter). This enables British and Irish full-time students and recent graduates (within a year) aged 18+ to do course-related work experience for up to one year in Canada. The programme costs £270 for two months, which includes assistance with obtaining visa and so on, support in Canada and advice on housing, tax and other such problems. The programme is also open to gap-year students with an unconditional offer of a university place. Applicants must secure a work placement before arriving in Canada.

WORK OPPORTUNITIES

Assuming you have found a way of securing the necessary permission to work here, once you are in Canada it shouldn't be too tricky to find work, particularly in the resorts and big cities. Competition can be tough, so take plenty of money to keep you going in case it takes a few weeks. Take with you a copy of your CV (on disc and on paper) and certificates of any qualifications. Look out for vacancies in the newspapers or on the Internet, and ask around – or, alternatively, bite the bullet and turn up on the doorstep with your CV in hand. You never know, you might land somewhere at exactly the right time.

TOURISM AND SKI RESORTS

Seasonal work in ski and other resorts, particularly in the Rockies, should be easy to find, especially bar and waitress work. Tips can be good and remember that in Canada there is also a minimum wage, which varies from province to province but works out as roughly $6 an hour. You should usually be paid more than this, but make sure you are being paid at least the minimum wage.

Alternatively, you can try and fix up work before you arrive. Many ski companies and tour-guide companies operate in Canada. Try First Choice, Crystal Holidays, Ski World and Inghams or the catered chalet specialist Ski Total (**www.skitotal.com**).

Gap Challenge recruit ski instructors to Canadian resorts. For more information check out **www.gap-challenge.co.uk**.

You can also try the riding centre and residential children's camp in Ontario, The Horse People (**www.thehorsepeople.com**).

Bear Creek Outdoor Centre (**www.bearcreekoutdoor.com**) offers a ten-week summer programme in outdoor adventure leadership.

Moraine Lake Lodge (**www.morainelake.com**) employs seasonal workers in Alberta in summer (June to October) and winter (October to end of May).

USEFUL JOB WEBSITES

www.seasonalemployment.com
www.summerjobs.com/do/where/jobtree/Canada

VOLUNTARY WORK

The other option is voluntary work. UNA Exchange organises programmes in French-speaking Quebec (see Voluntary Work chapter for address).

You can also try Frontiers Foundation/Operation Beaver (2615 Danforth Avenue, Suite 203, Toronto, Ontario, Canada M4C 1L6, **www.frontiersfoundation.org**) which recruits volunteers from across the world to work on community and recreation projects. If you are taking part in a voluntary scheme through a religious or charitable organisation, you may be able to qualify for a special visa. This takes about a month to process, so make sure you allow plenty of time before you leave.

AgriVenture (**www.agriventure.com**), run by the International Agricultural Exchange Association, arranges working exchanges to Canada on farming and horticultural enterprises. Applicants must be aged between eighteen and thirty, have no dependants, be British citizens, have a full driving licence and have good practical experience within agriculture or horticulture or around the home. Programmes depart all the year around (applications required approximately two months minimum before departure). Programme costs start at around £1,700 and include: return flights (and transfer to host family), full travel and work insurance, work permits, job placement, departure information meeting, seminar in host country and full emergency back-up through offices in hosting country. Programmes are also available to Americans, Canadians, some Europeans, Australians and New Zealanders through offices in their own country. See Voluntary Work chapter for address.

CASUAL WORK

Working without the proper documentation is a serious offence in Canada and carries the real risk of deportation, should you be discovered. Not having an employment authorisation also makes finding work and getting paid (never mind, decently) fairly problematic. Bear in mind there will be plenty of immigration officials around who are vigilant on clamping down on illegal aliens. That said, for you hardy souls who will carry on regardless, here is some advice. Remember that you are more likely to 'blend in' if you try to find work in the more cosmopolitan big cities. It is also helpful to have a good network of friends and, even better, relatives who can pull some strings for you, help you in a crisis, put you in touch with work and provide a roof over your head.

Good 'unofficial' work may be in catering, telesales and door-to-door selling, fruit picking and tree planting.

Tree planting Tree planting is a form of casual work that is unique to Canada and can give you a kind of reversed lumberjack experience, helping to reforest areas that have been burnt or logged. The payment is piecework and tends to be around 10–12 cents per tree. Rumour has it to steer away from Ontario for tree-planting work, where the price per tree is dropping, and instead head for British Columbia. For more information check out The Tree Planting Website, which gives all the insider information: **www.web.radiant.net/harihari**. According to this, 'rookies should expect to average about $120/day per two-month season' which accommodates a 'learning curve time' and can be brought up to $200 per day once you are experienced. Money can be made tree planting, but bear in mind that out of this come other costs, such as camping and planting gear (boots, raincoat, shovel and bag).

Agriculture Fruit picking, particularly in British Columbia, can be another great way to make some unofficial dosh. As usual, hostels can be a good way to track down work – both on noticeboards and through conversation with other travellers. The Agriculture Labour Pool (**www.agri-labourpool.com/jobseekers/postings/home**) lists rural jobs in British Columbia, although you will have to be legally entitled to work to use it. If you're not, you could always get a legal friend to check it out for you (the benefits of having contacts!). Another useful site is **www.ruraljobs.com** which has regularly updated job listings.

Au pair Although there is no official au pair programme in Canada, the Live-in Caregiver Program more or less amounts to the same thing. This, however, requires more extensive education and training than an au pair usually has. On the plus side, the programme allows the caregiver to work in Canada longer than the usual twelve-month au pair stay and after two years of employment, grants them the right to apply for permanent residency. A live-in caregiver is defined as someone who provides care to children, the elderly or the disabled in a private household. For more info contact the Canadian high commission or embassy.

Generally, the same rules apply as for finding other work in Canada. The job must be approved by the HRDC (this should have been arranged by the families before being offered to you) and the work must be secured before arriving in Canada. Applicants must have the equivalent of grade twelve education (A levels), six months relevant training or at least one year of relevant experience. You must also speak French and English.

Here are some useful agencies:

ABC Nannies Agency, Vancouver, BC, (**www.abcnannies.org**)

Anderson Au Pairs & Nannies (**www.childcare-europe.com**) arrange au pair placements to Canada as well as other countries.

TEACHING ENGLISH
Thanks to a recent argument about immigration and language skills, the Canadian government has introduced a bill where all permanent residents receive free English classes if it is their second language. The demand for English teachers, therefore, is high. However this could soon be set to decline, as immigration policy is now placing a high emphasis on allowing only English speakers to enter. For addresses of Canadian language schools, visit the Language Schools in Canada website: **www.dfait-maeci.gc.ca/-bonn/studywork/x_lslist.htm**. You can also try

Inlingua Teacher Service which recruits Tefl teachers: 1901 North Moore Street, Arlington, VA 22209, Tel: 703 527 8666.

THE JOB SEARCH

As in most countries, the Internet can be the most vital tool you use in gathering information and furthering your job search. There are some great websites covering everything to do with Canada, from travelling in the Rockies to getting work as a firefighter. So put on your lumberjacket shirt and get surfing!

Action Jobs at **www.actionjobs.com** is a great website to fire your imagination and gear you up to the authentic Canadian experience. It covers some very physically demanding jobs such as those in forestry and firefighting, as well as providing good solid information on jobs in summer, winter resorts and cruise ships.

CoolJobsCanada (**www.cooljobscanada.com**) is another great website. You can post your CV or just read and marvel at all the fantastic ways you can experience Canada and earn a bit of dosh in the process.

The following websites have regularly updated job listings:

Canada Jobs: **www.canadajobs.com**
Canada Job Bank: **www.jb-ge.hrdc-drhc.gc.ca**
Net Jobs: **www.netjobs.com/index**
Canadian Employment Weekly: **www.mediacorp2.com**
For students, Campus Canada Online: **www.campus.org/jobexchange**

It's also worth checking the newspapers, many of which carry job listings every day. Try the *Calgary Herald*, The *Globe and Mail* (Toronto paper), the *Montreal Gazette*, the *Ottawa Sun*, the *Toronto Sun*, the *Vancouver Sun* and the *Vancouver Province*. As usual, staying in hostels and checking their noticeboards may find you work.

Those of you with admin experience and secretarial skills may find it worthwhile targeting the temp agencies. Pay can be good but be aware that many agencies will take a cut from your wage, and some may require testing your computer or typing skills, or even your personality. You can look up employment agencies in the Yellow Pages or try Kirkpatrick Personnnel Ltd (**www.kirkpatrick.ca**) or Staff Plus (**www.staffplus.com**). Manpower and Adecco also have branches in Canada.

SWAP offices (**www.swap.ca**) can be found in most major cities in Canada. They have a number of resources that are available to students, including job listings and helpful information.

SWAP, Toronto Office, 45 Clarks Street East, Suite 100, Toronto, Ontario, M4Y 1S2, Tel: 416 966 2887.

SWAP, Vancouver Office, 60 rue West Hastings Street, Suite 710, Vancouver, British Columbia, V6B 1P2, Tel: 604 689 2887, Fax: 604 689 8611.

USEFUL ADDRESSES

United States of America Embassy (and Information Service), 24 Grosvenor Square, London W1AE 1AE, UK, Tel: 020 7499 9000; United States of America Embassy, Visa Branch, 5 Upper Grosvenor Street, London W1A 2JB, UK, Tel: 020 7499 3443.

Canadian High Commission, Macdonald House, 1 Grosvenor Square, London W1X 0AB, UK, Tel: 020 7258 6600, Website: **www.canada.org.uk**; 501 Pennslyvania Avenue, NW, Washington DC 20001, USA, Tel: 202 682 1740, Website: **www.cdnemb-washdc.org**.

Live and Work in the USA and Canada by Adam Lechmere, Susan Catto and Joshua White (published by Vacation Work Publications) is full of comprehensive information about living and working in the US and Canada and details many useful organisations.

FURTHER READING

Ausenda, Fabio and McCloskey, Erin, *World Volunteers: The World Guide to Humanitarian and Development Volunteering*, Green Volunteers Publications, 2002

Collier, Ian and Woodworth, David, *Summer Jobs Abroad 2002*, Vacation Work Publications, 2002

Dawood, Richard, *Travellers' Health: How to stay healthy abroad (Fourth edition)*, Oxford University Press, 2002

Golzen, Godfrey and Reuvid, Jonathan, *Working Abroad: The Complete Guide to Overseas Employment (23rd edition)*, Kogan Page, 2002

Griffith, Susan, *Teaching English Abroad (Fifth edition)*, Vacation Work Publications, 2001

Griffiths, Susan and Legg, Sharon, *The Au Pair and Nanny's Guide to Working Abroad (Fourth edition)*, Vacation Work Publications, 2002

Griffiths, Tom, *The Virgin Travellers' Handbook (Second edition)*, Virgin Books, 2002

Hampshire, David, *Living and Working Abroad: A Survival Handbook*, Survival Books, 2001

Hempshell, Mark, *Getting a Job in Europe (Fourth edition)*, How To Books, 2000

Jones, Nick, *The Rough Guide to Travel Health*, Rough Guides, 2001

Lechmere, Adam, Catto, Susan and White, Joshua, *Live and Work in the USA and Canada (Third edition)*, Vacation Work Publications, 2002

Lessell, Colin, *The World Travellers' Manual of Homeopathy*, C.W. Daniel Company Ltd., 1999

Lorie, Jonathan and Sohanpaul, Amy, *The Traveller's Internet Guide*, WEXAS International, 2001

Markes, Guy, *Travel Writing and Photography: All You Need to Know to Make It Pay*, Traveller's Press, 1997

Pybus, Victoria, *Working in Ski Resorts, Europe and North America (Fourth edition)*, Vacation Work Publications, 1997

Various, *EL Gazette Guide to English Language Teaching Around the World (Eleventh edition)*, Short Books, 2002

Wright, Martin, *The Virgin Travel Health Handbook*, Virgin Books, 2003

NEWSPAPERS AND MAGAZINES

EL Gazette is a monthly newspaper covering all aspects of the ELT industry. Dilke House, 1 Malet Street, Bloomsbury, London, WC1E 7JN, UK Tel: 020 7255 1969 Fax: 020 7255 1972

Overseas Jobs Express is a fortnightly newspaper with advice, reports and advertised vacancies and is available by subscription or in newsagents. PO Box 22, Brighton, BN1 6HT Tel: 01273 699 777

Home and Away is a monthly expat magazine that runs job vacancies. Expats House, 29 Lacon Road, London SE22 9HE Tel: 020 8299 4987

The Lady is a weekly magazine that carries articles on foreign travel and vacancies for overseas work particularly in the au pair and nanny industry. 39–40 Bedford Street, London WC2E 9ER Tel: 020 7379 4717

The *Guardian* Education section is available on Tuesdays with the *Guardian* newspaper and carries vacancies for Tefl teachers

The Times Higher Educational Supplement is published on Fridays but available from newsagents all week and carries job vacancies for teachers.

Also look out for the excellent travel supplements of the *Guardian* (Saturday) and *Observer* (Sunday).

WEBSITES

Embassy World (**www.embassyworld.com**) has a database of worldwide embassy contacts.

The World Travel Guide (**www.travel-guides.com**) carries country-by-country information including visa requirements.

The website for the UK's Foreign Office (**www.fco.gov.uk/travel**) lists visa requirements for many countries.

The European Employment Services (EURES) (**www.europa.eu.int/jobs/eures**) has details of vacancies throughout the EU and available to all EU/EEA members. It also provides information on living and working conditions, social security and taxation etc. in all EEA member countries.

Gapwork.com (**www.gapwork.com**) allows you to register for a newsletter which lists casual work opportunities in Australia, New Zealand and Europe.

Payaway.com (**www.payaway.com**) is great website with information on every country including red tape, embassies and list of addresses and useful organisations to find work.

Overseas Jobs (**www.overseasjobs.com**) is an American online recruitment network that provides career resources to American college and high school students, resort and hospitality staff, expats and international job seekers.

OFFICIAL ADVICE ON INTERNATIONAL TROUBLE SPOTS

FCO Travel Unit, Consular Division, 1 Palace Street, London, SW1E 5HE, Tel: 020 7238 4503, **www.fco.gov.uk**

US State Department Travel Advisory Service, 2201 C St NW, Room 4811, Washington, DC 20520, Tel: 202/647-5225, **www.travel.state.gov**

Canadian Department of Foreign Affairs and International Trade, 125 Sussexx Drive, Ottawa, Ontario K1A OG2, Tel: 1-800/387-3124, **www.dfait-maeci.gc.ca**

Australian Department of Foreign Affairs and Travel, The RG Casey Building, John McEwan Crescent, Barton, Canberra, ACT 2600, Tel: 02/6261-9111, **www.dfat.gov.au**

New Zealand Department of Foreign Affairs, Stafford House, 40 The Terrace, Wellington, Private Bag 18 901, Tel: 04/494 8500

OTHER RESOURCES

The British Council Information Centre (Bridgewater House, 58 Whitworth Street, Manchester M1 6BB, Tel: 0161 957 7755) publishes a free information leaflet *How to Become a Teacher of English as a Foreign Language*.

You can get the free booklets on *Working in . . .* from Employment Service, Overseas Placing Unit, Rockingham House, 123 West Street, Sheffield, S1 4ER.

The Department of Health publishes a free booklet called *Health Advice for Travellers* which also contains an E111 Form. Call 0800 555 777 or look on **www.doh.gov.uk**.

ACKNOWLEDGEMENTS

During the course of writing this book I have been surprised and touched by the willingness of people to go the extra mile to help me. As a result, I have a long list of people I would like to thank. Firstly I'd like to thank the following people for providing me with up-to-date information. Acknowledgements to Dr Richard Dawood at the Fleet Street Travel Clinic for his section on food and hygiene as well as his up-to-the-minute advice on vaccinations and diseases; The Nomad Travel Clinic, particularly Jason Gibbs, for the most up to date advice and details of the latest disease outbreaks throughout the world; the Nomad Travellers' Store for advice on the best backpack and travel gear to take; the website anyworkanywhere.com for permission to use their harvest tables for different destinations around the globe; the International Labour Office for employment figures and advice; Lyn Russell at the *Observer* travel supplement for permission to use the *Observer* travel awards; and David Creffield, editor of *Overseas Jobs Express* and Iain Martin at Natives.

The following organisations were also extremely helpful: Reliance Yachts, Concordia, International Student Exchange Centre, Cross-Cultural Solutions, Teaching and Projects Abroad, AgriVenture, Exodus, Saxoncourt Recruitment and English Worldwide, International House and the British Council.

In addition to this I'd like to thank all the lovely people who took the time and trouble to talk to me about their trips, as well as digging out friends and contacts for me to speak to: Simon Amos, Frank Baker, Kate Barlow, Alessandra Calabrese, Julie Calvert, Eddy Cantor, Lucia Cockcroft, Jilly Coombes, Darren Cooper, Richard Cox, Andrew Dobbie, Georgie Dow, Stella Eleftheriades, Karl Evans, Liz Evans, Sarah Fisher, Stuart Gilman, Angela Haddow, Maria Hardy, Tracey Hesom, Iain Hook, Pat Horton, Mair Hughes, Lindsey Hulme, Suze Ingle, Maria Jacovides, Richard Jones, Sara Lofthouse, Ian Maidens, Robert Maidens, Mary Martala, Eddy Martin, Patrick McGuire, Cathy Merry, Cath Mortimer, Olesja Okatjeva, Nick Parker, Dean Pateman, Kevin Pritchard, Ben Ralston, Alex Rayner, Joanna Rea, Shastra Reay, Nick Rogerson, Iain Rudgyard, John Starkie, Lara Silverstone, Sarah Veness, Rupert Wainwright, Rachel Walton, Anita Westmorland, Jason Whiting, Andrew Whittaker, Mark and Lynda Whittaker, Karen Widdowson, Laura Wilson and Kathryn Woolford.

Thanks to Mark Wallace, my editor, and all the team at Virgin Books, for putting the book together and for coming up with the idea in the first place!

Finally, I'd like to thank my family and friends for listening to my endless (and probably deeply boring) conversations about the state of employment markets around the world, and most of all, my partner Andrew, for putting up with such a messy, chaotic flat, and all his love, kindness and unfailing support. Thank you!

INDEX